Academia

and the

Luster of Capital

Academia
and the
Luster of Capital

Sande Cohen

 University of Minnesota Press
Minneapolis
London

Published by the University of Minnesota Press
2037 University Avenue Southeast, Minneapolis, MN 55455-3092
Printed in the United States of America on acid-free paper

Library of Congress Cataloging-in-Publication Data

Cohen, Sande.
    Academia and the luster of capital / Sande Cohen.
      p.   cm.
    Includes bibliographical references (p.) and index.
    ISBN 0-8166-2230-2 (alk. paper). — ISBN 0-8166-2231-0
(pbk. : alk. paper)
    1. Criticism (Philosophy) 2. Critical theory. I. Title.
B809.3.C54 1993
001 — dc20   92-35102
                                             CIP

Contents

Acknowledgments

I am grateful to the people who helped make this text. The initial publication reports by Brian Massumi and John Tagg suggested changes that made the outlines of other, unconsidered, affirmative thoughts apparent, even if I was unable to give them the requisite articulation. The line-by-line edit by an anonymous third reader was more than generous, as were discussions with Sylvère Lotringer. Mario Biagioli, Jeremy Gilbert-Rolfe, and Martin van Buren read chapters 1 and 2 and made important criticisms. Biagioli and Wulf Kansteiner read chapter 3 and it is now (all too) clear, perhaps. Hayden White asked me to take up the matters in chapter 4 and I was glad to be able to attempt to refute some of his suggestions. Chapter 5 exists only because of the students at Cal-Arts and Art Center College of Design, Pasadena, and it is dedicated to them. I thank all the people who gave me a chance to try out these ideas, in particular Perry Curtis and Roger Henkle, Howard Singerman, Michael Ann Holly, Janet Smarr, and the UC San Diego School of Music. I want to recognize former teachers from San Francisco State College, 1967–70: Vartan Gregorian, Elizabeth Gleason, John Diggins, and Donald Lowe.

My editor, Biodun Iginla, was resolute and noble in what must have been trying circumstances. David Thorstad's copyediting was a gift. Thanks to everyone at Minnesota.

Finally, I cannot say enough to Marge Lasky, Bella Y. H. Hui, and Max C. other than to say just that.

Introduction

> This loss of its fancied possessions, to which speculative reason must submit . . . falls, in its whole extent, on the monopoly of the schools, but does not in the slightest degree touch the interests of mankind. . . . The change, therefore, affects only the arrogant pretensions of the schools, which would gladly retain, in their own exclusive possession, the key to the truths which they impart to the public.
>
> Kant, *Critique of Pure Reason*

Memories of an Ex-Historian

Even a critic as skeptical as Edward Said succumbs to the temptation of university, academic, employment: the university's self-legitimations stand unchallenged. Said has it that in establishing connections between knowledge and politics, "each humanistic investigation must formulate the nature of [its] connection in the specific context of the study," and that such studies are intended to aid in "promoting human community."[1] This synthesis of internal and external factors is such that university-based intellectuals are guaranteed autonomy ("specific context") in the name of the intellectual reduced to a social agent who agrees with Enlightenment — "investigation" becomes social improvement ("promoting human community"). Autonomy is made possible in the name of an end, the latter an indefinite or undefinable *process*; the concept of the latter ("promoting") is, one can suppose, the rationalization of the circuit displayed by Said's microtext. That university intellectuals are anchored in rationalistic processes is the sine qua non of academic employability — and perhaps also of its intellectuality. That such processes are mythic as well is less felicitous.

The chapters that follow express doubt that our university-based legitimations of criticism, in particular its unexamined reflex of a use value belonging to criticism itself, can withstand a sustained reading of their presuppositions and premises. In effect, I propose to withdraw the automatic "cognitive advantage" of university critical writing, on the grounds that no such advantage is warranted: our writings are outfitted for the grooves of "reason," "society," "need" — each of which is a cosmos of mythology unto itself. In making this withdrawal, I am more or less expressing "no confidence" in the essential activities of the modern university.

How, indeed, do our assigned roles of translator, close reader, political polemicist, demythographer, promoter get established? Is it self-censorship, which cannot but conform with installations of identities, prescriptions on actions, idealizations of time codings (e.g., utopia, nostalgia)? Why does so much academic criticism read as a *relative* of the systems (cultural, political, social-economic) so critiqued? Jean Baudrillard, an author whose critical notions I take up in chapter 5, writes that the cultural construct entitled "silent majority," whatever else it signifies, already anticipates "the simplifying terror which is behind the ideal hegemony of meaning"; he means by this that "mass society" has its own strange mechanism(s) of filtration such that our academic will to domination finds itself frustrated. If this "public" is aggressively hostile to academic interpretations, then precisely how are we academics to proceed? Or, as Ernst Gellner emphasized in *Legitimation of Belief*, the academic disenchanting of myth (tradition, identity) provides merely *ideational* justifications for our substitutions of our interests and desires, roles and purposes for that which we dissolve; in this sorting of claimants, the aggressions of assertion and exclusion, it is exactly the problematic status of proposing any cultural and intellectual identity that is one of my themes. In this I suppose that *postcritical theory* has to now generate everything: as Vattimo suggests, the "accomplished nihilism" of the real (Western) world gives us nothing substantial for our rhetorics except an insubstantial rhetoric.[2] Drawing upon Nietzsche, Deleuze, Lyotard, Baudrillard, and others, I criticize intellectual practices that are too close to the narcissism of insiders, whose propositions and theories, despite their critical appearance, recode forms of stabilization; I seek instead to affirm the possibility of something like a nonrationalizing (counternarcissistic) intellectual endeavor.

Mindful of linguistic reflexivity, of not anchoring these remarks in the consensus of a powerful omission, I would now like to enumerate what has changed, rendering the most progressive and enlightened of criticisms (such as Said's) problematic. Bluntly: for Western intellectuals, the figurations of change do not refer to a "context" and "history" as forms that render intellectual schemes persuasive; as there are no "unknown goals" (Kant), which it is the intellectual's job to make known, the figure of *intellectual goals* (like collective enlightenment) itself is suspended. It is impossible to persuade anyone today that the future is sustainable as a stable intellectual environment. Shining in its specific opacity, the present is not attached to "history lines" but to what Kant called oppositional conflict on all sides, where each individual finds, at best, "all his powers" awakened in the "unsocial sociability" that passes for society.[3] In this, the cultural and philosophical "clarity" offered by models of "history" and "social context" are nonetheless seductions of a *reductive order*; can one learn to "reflect according to opacity" (Lyotard), to acknowledge the nonnecessity of *any* "historical model" and by that disconnect from any equation between "history and being"? Thus, the concept of context, like that of being, is something which has to be put forward but is also something which may not "fit" with discourse. Although Lyotard calls this affirmation of nondetermination (which is also not a negation of determination), "postmodernism," I think this already gives too much sense to "afterness": Cubism, Final Solution, Decolonization are all "after," but is the sense of each difference the same? I think a Deleuzian term preferable to evoke a writing and thinking that do not accept university foundations and that are open to the most varied audiences and effects; this is work that is "untimely," even to the point of not trying to "be modern at any price, nor yet to be timeless, but to extricate from modernity something that Nietzsche called the *untimely*, which belongs to modernity, but which must also be turned against it — in favor, I hope, of a future time."[4]

Now in the first place (but does an "ex-historian" still have to "count"?), the explanatory models of modern thought are arguably inapplicable, in many cases, to the very cultural phenomenon they set out to decode. Indeed, Marxian psychoanalysis, for example, has said much by way of making interrogations of modern painting (notably the argument that the avant-garde, whether European or not, was a social force), but others argue that (the theories of) Marx and Freud are not much more than ideas by which to politically moralize and in that way control subjects or turn others into illicit causal models. A painting like Cézanne's *Vase de fleurs* (1873–75), with its oscillating space in which flow makes line appear as a cultural restraint, might be said to be at least as "critical" as any verbal model that insists on thinking that the painting has already inserted itself in the regime of interpretation.[5] Linguistic reflexivity might maintain alienation between the discourses of interpretation and model building and their objects; in Lecercle's phrase, it is not settled how far writing can go in suspending one's own mastered form, that of proper language, in the face of objects and events, so that momentarily language is not that "restriction of *délire*" that, "deep down, language always is."[6] Or, in a world that has Final Solutions, one-party states masquerading in the politics of two, that allows for nuclear destruction to be considered a narrative "warning" (e.g., Hiroshima), or that provides for global eviction as so many *normal processes of restabilizing destabilization* (ecstatic are governments whose populations are reactive!), how can such occurrences be mediated in "normal language," which it is the business of intellectuals to provide? How do we, say, explain dialectically the archaic/present (e.g., the success of collecting ancient Greek writing fragments into a cultural "whole") and the present/repressed (e.g., the vast "dumbing-down" of American students over several generations)? In imagining a present conceived of as (perhaps) satirical in and of itself, ever out of sync with all the things we do to capture it for cultural determination (a theme developed in chapters 4 and 5), how can one still assume a historian whose job is to bring "important but obscure news to the eyes of the public" (Allan Megill), without first pressing inquiry as far as possible as to how the "important" and "obscure" got together (even in being separated) at the outset?

To return to the concept of "historical context": it becomes herein a tortured symbol, the name of which promises an iconic and indexical satisfaction (answers, resolution, clarity concerning what is thought to have occurred), but which is not realizable other than by the repression of meanings. All "returns of history" are so many wish-projections and, like the critical model of an intellectual discourse that conforms to linguistically constructed objectivities — a confusion of thinking and desire — oppose a desubjectifying organization of language that does not lend sense for the presumptive demand for homogeneity through the control of the heterogeneous to which it is a response. As Gayatri Spivak notes, the narrative of Capital as a socializing process, whose outcomes are structured as positive and negative, is a polarity outlining the realm of the thinkable; but Capital is also understandable as a machine of extraction, dynamic but unchanging, and thus a nonnarrative slavery, and this conceptualization is precisely what is occluded by a narrative interpretation that rationalizes.[7]

So the chapters that follow favor the discursive: argumentation, a provisional name, appears as a territory of proposals, descriptive and otherwise, and is here shorthand for acknowledging the plurality of forms and meanings, political, logical, aesthetic, and others. In addition, these anti-idealist arguments insist on not shutting down that "unstable state and instant of language wherein something which must be able to be put into phrases cannot yet be" (Lyotard). Arguing is a way of extending "it does not follow" into the domains of cultural authority and legitimation.[8] To put it in the strongest terms, one wants to be immediately critical at the level of semantic form — and escape ideations that are "correctly theoretical" at the level of desire and wish. One can argue — reason, figure forth — that just because the political code of Leninism is morally dubious on account of its narrative pretension (those who deserve the future, those who do not), it does not follow that Marxist economic theory is uninteresting; what is arguable is precisely that which is always getting reduced as prologue to its cultural and intellectual elimination.

In these terms, nihilism is not the consequence of being careful about giving historians the last word, but a self-destructive acceptance that form is final. I should say that in my "worldview" nihilism is a failure to respond to the challenges thrown in one's face by uncontrollable "others," of which there are so many kinds; but it is also the moral pretentiousness that demands reduction of not-me to what it, precisely, is not. To stress nonhistory is actually to begin to treat actual nihilisms in a nonreductive manner, as I shall shortly have occasion to emphasize in connection with what I have to say about the usefulness of Nietzsche. Nihilism, at minimum, raises the question of what Paul de Man called *priorities*, a concept that bypasses the historian's granting of "priority" to a preselected subject of narration (e.g., the decline of the people, the triumph of technology). Priorities and arguments, and not priority and history, are a provisional wedge where an engulfing absorption by one's own cultural grouping does not become the subjective form of a delusional Objectivism, in which one demands meanings that "follow as in a chain."[9] Priorities that are nonacademic but critical, ahistorical, and argumentative help one to forget narrative persuasion in an active manner — such that one draws more distinctions, erects even more elaborately complex differentiations, and activates singularities, all the while aware of the tremendous attractive energy of narrations to come, already sent from somewhere else.

Society without History

These chapters are attached to what I call an *oxymoronic social arationalism*, an inelegant construct that nonetheless pertains to a structural factor of contemporary American society: to say that society as such is "arational" means that it is not open to claims of speculative rationalism. Intellectual values stemming from university-based schemes and interests, what

Emmanuel Lévinas calls a "superfluous doubling," "bounce off," as it were, so many embedded interests that what is rational is a moot question. Capitalist practices are immediately, irreversibly, oxymoronic — human labor is, for most, subsistence only, and it is often undecidable when its rigid employer, Capital, is flexible so as to be a trap (debt) or rigid (division of labor). Fleshed out in the text as a whole, the term oxymoronic does not reduce the social to the aesthetically figural, but investigates how the social is blasting itself apart in the here and now. In any case, terms such as "arational" and oxymoronic are used to conjure the nondialectical realities of actual systems of control; Michael Phillipson gives a fine depiction of the social and human "sciences" now having to "catch up" with the artists of the nineteenth century who acknowledged that intellectuals "face the present as something alien because we no longer know how to speak/write. The modern experience . . . cannot be comprehended in the languages of the past, of Tradition, and yet we do not find ourselves except in this present — hence the need for . . . a language without history, without memory . . . a language against repetition."[10] A present overcoded by institutions (schools, banks, political parties) involved in contradictions so immediate and direct that they make the present strange and bizarre speaks to already-achieved reductions, notably politicians who define power by its abuse, teaching that dogmatizes while it denies doing so, an economy that is not an economy (e.g., the proliferation of debt), or other modes of actual strangeness that cannot be judged. A society without history experiences results that may not be able to be used: experiences destroy the use values of possible futures.

If what is oxymoronic pertains to overcoded contradictions, where practices and pressures of reproduction engender distortions throughout the cultural and educational systems, then what remains of what Charles Levin calls the "sociological ego" and its monitoring of the "projections and objectifications" of social life?[11] Consider what Fredric Jameson does in his *Postmodernism* (1990), where he narrates from absolute omniscience, and insists that cultural possibilities are circumscribed within a left version of cultural business as usual: "The point is that we are *within* the culture of postmodernism to the point where its facile repudiation is as impossible as any equally facile celebration of it is complacent and corrupt."[12]

The important alliterative instance here is surely one of repetition: "The point . . . to the point," "facile . . . facile," "complacent and corrupt." Is this the rhetorical figuration, in itself, of demand? In cognitive terms, the alliteration alone instances "no choice." "Within" commands there to appear a slew of images with ready-made interpretations (e.g., "inside," "container"), such that "within" withdraws from thought, and "postmodernism" precisely settles in the groove of a precut category, an object of academic study. What Jameson offers as linguistic certainty I read as systematic omission of meanings and thus a piece of cultural imperialism by its "let's make postmodernism something we determine." This reductive domestication of thought is "the point" that directly commands, and can be contrasted with Deleuze's remark concerning a use of language "such that a body or a word does not end at a precise point."[13] Where the former amounts to a conjunction of morality, aesthetics, history, and so on in the service of a bureaucratic fear of nonpolitical energies that cannot be fitted and reduced to concepts, the latter sustains "pass-words beneath order-words. Words that pass, words that are components of passage."

Passwords do not descend from the traditional loyalties enjoyed by going-players. In what follows I do not offer the audiences of Modernity — the Proletariat, the Political Parties, the Institutions, and so on — as an alibi for criticism. Instead of claiming to speak in the name of embattled audiences, I seek to examine the transformed circumstances of academic work, invoked here not as something external, but intrinsic to thinking.

Capitalism after Nietzsche

Many writers on the left continue to read Nietzsche as a theorist of hedonism, of radical subjectivism. Even when it is granted that there are passages of writing with real effectivity, Nietzschean texts are semantically downgraded for their cultural excess. David Harvey, in his *Condition of Postmodernity*, gives us a Nietzschean "intervention" that places "aesthetics above science."[14] Stanley Aronowitz gives us a Nietzsche screened through the Lacanian code, a producer of a "forgetting machine" that cannot render "significations from history."[15] This is always a Nietzsche who is thus, one way or another, in collaboration with Capital, an ultimately petit-bourgeois thinker who denies the primacy of political consciousness. But the chapters that follow are also Nietzschean, yet entirely critical of Capital. How to account for this?

Following some remarks of Karl Lowith's, it can be said that the Hegelian-Marxian tradition of criticism is based on "philosophical historicism," which is to theorize, or totalize in a conceptual way, contradictions and which, paradoxically, results in an "idolization of the actual." To apply Roman Jakobson, the axis of metaphoric equivalence — class-conflict or Oedipus — has been canonized and projected onto the axis of substitution, the struggle of dialectics. It is irrelevant whether class

conflict or ideological distortion (or the phallus, or the repressed mascu-
line, or the morcellated feminine ad infinitum) composes the metaphorical paradigm or not; the temporal is entirely underwritten by a dialectic
that specifies the ends and means, politics and morality, of "the social
drama." With Marx this became, as Baudrillard has argued, the acceptance of the very category of labor as defining of the human condition.
Within the Euro-American left, this failure to contest the lines of temporal integration (career, accumulation, result, but also randomness,
chaos, and unpredictability) parallels the banalization of an opposition
that is reduced to psychological wailing and moaning before a trium-
phant Capital. The Hegelian-Marxian fold is continued in many intellectual and political strands, including Sartrean and Lacanian formations. It
always presents itself as the only true rival to capitalism because it con-
ceives itself as the only claimant worthy of the "whole of history" (or
psyche) and the latter's "journey." An altogether speculative "knowledge
of history" is transposed or displaced onto the political-cultural realm as
"critical theory" or "unity of theory and practice" or "historical awareness," phrases devoted to judging claims (to represent, to mean).

What makes Nietzsche a more interesting writer about the cultural
relations that help to define capitalism as nonhistorical and nondialectical
is that Nietzsche is able to argue that Capital is nihilistic, not "historical."
Capital drains, yet exposes, energy for continued waste: it is, after all,
literally a waste of time to spend time in a securing of unnecessary means
of subsistence or whose subsistence is entirely arbitrary. *Beyond Good and
Evil* was unsparing — the language is near-impersonal — in its portrayal
of modern Europe as becoming reactive: "The production of a type prepared for *slavery* in the most subtle sense of the term . . . numerous,
talkative, weak-willed, and very handy workmen who require a master,
a commander as they require their daily bread . . . the democratising of
Europe is at the same time an involuntary arrangement for the rearing of
tyrants."[16] The money form of early and middle and late Capital — Eternal Capital — recapitulates the largely uninteresting waste of oneself in
the antispectacle (television?) of ignoble feelings. The protestating of
what one lacks postpones the self-transformative difficulty of a labor
without, perhaps, a "return." By standing for the acceptance of the cultural and intellectual division of labor, the academy actively controls the
dangers and opportunities of the world's nihilism, and in this it helps
define the social sciences and humanities as memory, monument, nostalgia, hope, despair — becoming "worldly" as becoming deadened.

Which is to say that normative intellectual categories such as class
conflict and Oedipus provide "regions" of being that render theory as
something constant, as being about something constant. Class, some-

thing to be contested and resisted, is nonetheless *defining* of one's definitions of the social — the idea of the social as something perhaps nonsocial
is thereby expunged; Oedipus, the unequivocal equivocation of split-up
eros and autonomous death, defines perception, and so the traces pursued
by critical knowledge are thought to be both intellectually adventurous
and politically important. These are but some of the reductions through
which the type called intellectual is spared the all but impossible task of
affirming potentially unsayable interests, for example, that we are more
interested in how things are carried out than in what they might "mean."

A Nietzschean perspective links up with formalism and deconstruction precisely where Nietzsche doubted the authority of phraseological
commands like the injunction to accept "to infer from," the latter stabilized only on an assumption of the type that held logic to be a deproblematized form of identity. The misunderstanding of Hegelian Marxism
concerning capitalism was to theorize Capital as a narrative subject and
not directly a challenge to values. (Obviously, a "right-wing" strategy is
available here — but then what is to be made of certain "right-wing"
truths, that Capital despises children?) The opposition to Capital mobi-
lized by the left as such was really an identification with a form of the
slave mentality recoded as the images and thoughts of a decisive, positive, reversal or as endless attempts to postpone the final orgy of nothingness attendant on a fully capitalized world. In this, Marxism shifted
(through Lukács in the German-reading academy) to considerations of
culture; the more the category of labor proved intractable — or, in the
Soviet Union, was simultaneously idealized and despised — and employment in mass society a quasi horror, the more came the incessant demands that cultural analysis "liberate" the repressed subjective desires for
the Good and Right and True. The American left now has no strong idea
of life, of existence, without its attendant ressentiment toward what it is
dependent upon, Capital.

Nietzsche's writings, on the other hand, suggest a definition of Capital
as a challenge to one's existence that is both perpetual and immediate. In
this version, Capital is not one with the category of labor, or even of
assigned values (division of labor), but is instead associated with the success of nihilism. Wage slavery and the difficulty of securing stimulating
and interesting work are horrifyingly familiar as a Capital that can twist
itself into a bewildering "conformity with the irresistible 'progress' of
each vanishing moment."[17] Mass society stands in the blazing light of
lemmings chasing each other into one straight line after another. Culturally considered, it is the historians who legitimize the collective denial
that "Nihilism is the origin of modernity" and not the fairy tales of progress, growth, development, result, end. Tellingly, that is, nonnarratively,

one of Nietzsche's more uncanny images for the success of Capital was the "noose" that puts "an end to all culture."[18] Hannah Arendt and Matei Calinescu reinforce this in their respective discussions of cultural models, Arendt emphasizing the distortion brought by the demands of specialization, philistinism, Calinescu demonstrating that kitsch, the "aesthetics" of the middle classes, is a response to the "terrors of change" that ebb and flow with the accelerations and displacements of Capital.[19] Thus the Final Solution, as I will argue, is an example of an event whose modernity thwarts our sense of "historical understanding" because it raises the nihilism of modernity to the surface; there are relations of Capital that may not be understandable as "historical" or "normal criticism."

I am aware that some of these ideations are quite unpleasant to university-based criticism — a system that stresses social promise. Capital is treated as profoundly anticultural, since it promotes that "trainability of man" that has "grown to monstrous proportions because they [individuals] have nothing to say to each other."[20] Is there a cultural will-to-power sustained by those university ideations such as neo-asceticism, inflated accusations, and impossible memories? Isn't this also about overcoming instead of reacting?[21]

To conclude these still prefatory remarks on the Nietzschean version of cultural issues, it is the oxymoronic setup of Capital — the terror that one give one's labor to it in exchange for payments that do not themselves, for billions of people, translate into *pleasure* — which indexes conflicts that are not going to be resolved by (to keep to the examples given) class or Oedipal models. The exchange of human labor power (time) for money (exchange) reduces the time available for nonexchange. The cultural and political controls, left, right, and center, on how people are able to *spend time* are more acute than the resolutions promised by these groups. Capital produces the worst prison of all: it locks time up.[22] The form of exchange becomes the immovable metaphysic capable of operating at the speed of instantaneity (a credit decision which ricochets, generating immanent chaos), and a question here is why such rapidity and viciousness is matched by "critical demands" and calls for more politics as usual?

If Capital can effect an increase in the capacity for desocialization, in which negatives are misidentified as affirmations — one has recourse to the law to solve a problem but the solving makes one poor, so that in protecting one's rights one is impersonally coerced — then what are options of difference? The Nietzschean critique of that much-discussed term, modernity, emphasizes that the elaboration of one's consciousness as self-protective work and labor rather than a spending and an excess of oneself, perpetuates the grounds of critique and opposition, the latter supporting polarization, binarism, and thus reducing meanings to values of identity. All of this results from the misidentification of Capital as something to negotiate with, the reduction of "have no choice but to" to the consequential order "it's for the better." If the cultural expansion of Capital is subject to erratic fits; if the surplus value of the code gives way to the surplus value of flux, a transformation that Deleuze denotes as the rule that "things work well only providing they break down";[23] if, as Deleuze writes, "capitalism's supreme goal" is the "production of lack," for only by increasing production can production be the screen of what we don't have, then a critical intellectual *perspective* cannot be attached to the virtues of intellectual translation and mediation, opposition, negation, synthesis, hope, restoration, melancholy.

Intellectual Work, High Universities

The high university is a complex of institutions and processes; it has more than one purpose and end. Here, as introductory material, I would like to say that university employment often prevents professors (among others) from speaking their minds, which is not the only worthy intellectual activity but is certainly a part of any interesting cultural life. What is said here and below is entirely framed by the desire for open universities, universities that are not closed societies, riddled with the override judgments of political affiliation (no outsiders allowed — the insiders' prerogative) and their attendant socializations (e.g., no close readings of *our work* is allowed). The "star" syndrome is only the most visible distortion of a system with some highly arguable purposes. If "writing has never been capitalism's thing" (Deleuze), if the roles for education have remained within exceedingly narrow confines (the personal, the political, the instrumental, the philistine), then universities must be institutions of some ambiguity vis-à-vis their own ideals; or is this nostalgic? Lowith reminds us that Bruno Bauer, in the 1840s, already described professorial life as dependent upon "this transcendence of the theory of self-surrender."[24]

Indeed, so sensitive are these topics that one suspects something hysterical is happening when the president of the University of California says that criticism of universities is now attached to "the inordinate pleasure with which that criticism is being leveled." If I desemanticize that line for its political-cultural fusion, I think that he is accusing critics of being sadists and so is claiming that criticism of universities has already gone too far. He calls for an "injection of mutual respect and civility," but fails to acknowledge that thinking has implications for "mutual respect" and "civility," both of which already connote conditions of agreement. But such conditions do not exist; as I argue in chapter 2, what cuts across race, class, and gender (and age, style, fashion, club politics) in the academic system is the controls placed on the number of positions funded in the humanities and social sciences in particular. Of course with Capital all of "higher education" manifests only the minimum of interesting "posts"; the number of university courses, for example, in which people are shown various ways of critically reading a text, is highly restricted. Reading is an effect of pyramidical management (or some similar social designation). What is feared by opening up the high university to a system tripled and quadrupled in the number of positions offered, with open arguments over every contested relation, is precisely the loss of control over what the future looks like.

How strange some academic and social mixtures, where microanalyses and macromodels coincide with the unpleasant fact that records are "destroyed by academics rather than risk exposure of unpleasant realities."[25] Exactly what does constitute the proper "context" for criticism of the high university?

In the chapters that follow, I will propose that the high university as a producer of culturally shared values is a shaky rationalization; the high university recruits very few for its own expansion, and generates many reductions, including a notorious general education (see chapter 2).[26] At present there is no rational *test* of the myriad of tests by means of which *most students fail* (every statistical index in the U.S. shows a pyramidical hierarchy, e.g., 100 nine-year-olds in the second grade = 65 seniors = 13 B.A. degrees = 2 M.A. degrees = 0.05 Ph.D.'s by age thirty-five). There is, curiously, no agreed-upon metalanguage by which to have rational arguments about the meanings of education. The shift of the university to managerial, more directly integrative, practices has benefited the new academic elites in ways that are more distorted than in the recent past. In addition, my discussion of the controls effecting competition for academic "posts" recognizes that there are very many models and stories to circulate, to add to a series of ongoing disputes about academic culture; in this regard, I embrace what Lyotard, in the essay "Pagan Instructions," calls the "forgetting of the first name," a telling of stories such that narrator, listener, and actor deform the autonomy of each other, this to build up a repertoire of images and senses that no group controls, thereby disengaging from the cultural privilege of narration.

Is there not something disturbing about intellectual work today? So many people are dissatisfied and repressed, one way or another, by the capitalist organization of knowledge. On every cognitive, theoretical, and critical side, so many doubts arise as to the value of criticism, while each new group of anti-intellectualism appears to stoke the "need" for criticism. Isn't the "culture industry" an alibi for the "criticism thing"? And isn't something like this an "epidemic of visibility" announced by Baudrillard, a kind of cultural saturation of perception a priori (or an a priori perception, another figure of the oxymoronic?). In fact, isn't it criticism that today sends intellectuals a challenge at the level of thinking itself? Baudrillard suggests a contemporary scene set up as a *symmetry* between "productive criticism" and a world that absorbs and even benefits from negativity: ". . . hypertrophy, a world that cannot manage to give birth. All these memories, all these archives, all this documentation that do not give birth to a single idea, all these plans, programs and decisions that do not lead to a single event . . ."[27] Intellectuals, break off?

I will argue throughout that *to historicize is to academicize*: the referent that we call "society" has itself disappeared and become a floating "target" of signification for political and cultural formations of the most diverse sorts. "Historical thought" is a way of establishing the power of what is believed to be irreducibly social: that is why to "suspend 'history' " is really to undermine the various theologies of the social which academics *must* circulate as part of their "right to work." We have to say that past "victims" nonetheless "resisted"; we have to say that a better future is possible; we have to say that we are not socially extraneous, but necessary agents of larger processes.

Concluding Remarks

The "struggling" social sciences? Perversely funny, perhaps even an oxymoron that is constitutive![28] Our privileges as professors are bound up with the criticisms of society that we institutionalize. From a profession that in some important ways is closed, we nonetheless lay claim to every meaning, to the assignment of significance. Of course, ever-appropriating interests will demand that intellectuals prepare "pasts" for image-exploitation, value-use, and this should be contested; but shouldn't one be suspicious of the way these practices have become codified?

Chapter 1 challenges a number of existing rationales for the "production" (or performance) of criticism. I focus in particular on the "impossible ideals" of academic criticism, drawing out their reactive aspects. By "reactive" I mean the use of concepts to make distinctions, differentiations, discriminations, and the like, which are presubjected to some identitarian Idol, meanings that purport to, say, resolve the noncongruity between concepts and experiences on the side of a meaning, a theory, an interpretation; I am interested in how language tilts the precise "machine" that is played in academicizing. Expression is "reactive" when it employs a syntax that excludes uncomfortable and potentially uncontrollable senses. Reactive is here used differently from other usages, such as Richard Rorty's, for whom the notion is connected to a pragmatic acceptance of contingency, the latter a springboard for "novel experiences and novel language" (and who is blunt about its reductive aspects). To be "reactive" is to actively will that change, mutation, and emergence are "grounded" in representations: there is a "behind which is ahead" (e.g., the revolutionary sacrifices of the past must be made 'good' in the future; the "founding fathers" have to be "heard"; there are rules to be followed). Jameson's exhortation to "always historicize" critical endeavors demands order and is a plea for the constancy of what will not change (one will not abandon "history"). To react is to limit the number of concepts in contention, as well as to take the easy way out and insist or assert that our language incorporate and absorb the nonlinguistic forces and matters of various experiences.

In addition, this first chapter works toward a theory of Capital congruent with recent attempts such as Gayatri Spivak's, which emphasizes the inadequation of a classically modern labor theory of value; the actual development of the money-form without any traces of sociality, and the enormous worldwide refusal of every socioeconomic system to make available what it coerces one to have (interesting work — it is an amazing correlation that almost everyone needs money but may or may not have work, which is the normal way of obtaining the money). A system in which one "has to have" money, but not the system's own ideal means of obtaining it — work — presents the system's moment where its own ecstatic unnecessariness smears everything, where the money-form is even beginning to jettison the alibi of work.

The "pluralized apocalypse" (Spivak) of exchange devours other categories of existence: "dumbing-down" demands someone cut machines that can anticipate the mistakes of their users. But this "apocalypse" (of the intellectual, of criticism, of theory) is itself incorporated into the "criticism industry." This "condition," this sense of anticontext, is as difficult to raise as is the reality. The first essay argues that there are no intellectually "correct" resolutions for professors concerning this capitalism and the various discourses of command systems: there are quandaries and dilemmas to come.

Chapter 2 suggests some ways in which high-university bureaucratization of knowledge operates; this essay can be thought of as an attempt to find terms to describe the "improper" forms of academic bureaucratization, in particular the control-forms by which people are employed or not. Tenure, the "superstar" formation, and affirmative action are presented as effects of the power of law and the selection/exclusion processes that sanctify the division of labor, including "progressive" forms.

Chapter 3 confronts Jurgen Habermas's contribution to the recent "historian's debate" in Germany. I argue that Habermas provides a cultural analogue or equivalent to "politically correct bureaucratization" (which is not necessarily tied to or exhausted by political names!): he renders "whole images" of the Final Solution in a way that the latter is *reduced* to academic modes of writing. The language of cultural synthesis provided by Habermas's arguments is critiqued as a form of intellectual control. The analysis of institutional and intellectual bureaucratization practices is distressing.

Together, chapters 1 to 3 imply that the contemporary academic stress on "historical" criticism places value on "being other" instead of "becoming different."

Chapter 4, the "Disappearance of History," takes up some of the reasons why a culturally dominant "historical consciousness" is redundant today and connects with a general critique of academia insofar as university-based critics relentlessly call for such consciousness. Historicisms of all sorts are well entrenched within the American scene, whether as a "progressive" form of elitism or as a conservative demand for a canon. I argue that "historical consciousness" is mostly one with academic valuations and hierarchies. Geoff Bennington's reminder that the term "history" can occupy the position of sender, referent, subject aptly suggests that "historical" is always a *political* entanglement, of joining the existing "sides." The question of "history" is really about capacities of *alienating* the terms, of separating "history" from the semantic systems of its occurrence so as to grasp "history" as political culture.

Finally, Chapter 5 takes up these issues in a consideration of contemporary art-theory. Drawing upon Karl Bohrer's idea of Romanticism as a critique of "falsely objectified traditions" (an idea all Western Romanticisms have invented for tactical purposes, hence a critical concept of any potential counterhistory), I analyze theorizations and descriptions of modernity. Attempts by critics to "rehistoricize" art and criticism are juxtaposed to the (differing) conceptual endeavors of Lyotard and Baudrillard, for whom art now occupies a much more extreme relation to society, language, consciousness. This chapter is an exercise in situating critical thinking "beyond politics," perhaps even "beyond control." Lyotard's idea of systematic "dispossession" and Baudrillard's notion of "fatal strategies" are presented as interesting thought-experiments, probing connections between nihilism, modernity, alienation, and critique.

1

What Is Criticism For?

Initial Skepticisms

The reactive aspect of academic writing is sometimes transmitted as officiality: ideas reduced to linguistic subsidizations of rank and authority.
The apparatus that ensures that ideas are safe—appropriate, correct,
transposable—is one and the same with expressions which Roland
Barthes said offered themselves as closing "gaps" between naming and
judging.[1] This signifying form is so pervasive that it can become pure
denial (e.g., hordes of legal authorities serving university aggressions
against farm workers in California, 1965–88) or be twisted into the shape
of an academic formation that relies on significations turned into cultural
weapons: "under patriarchy," for example, is thought by Laura Mulvey
to settle once and for all questions of critical theory in discussions of
sexuality, "under" saying it all, including the omission of heterosexual
desire not prereduced to the all-inclusive "induction" of patriarchy.[2] Are
the new women managers of academic culture, then, imitative of mas-
culinism? What are the closures surrounding and attending to the name
"academic"? Our "calling" is to read others intimately, as texts; but the
"job" carried out is mostly to politicize in the name of the reigning
construction of the standard of living (including the symmetry of
opposition).

The linguistic utterances of the American professoriat as such have
consistently "judged" that racism is more intolerable than stupidism
(what a choice!), the latter a disreputable name, and that Warholian
"fame" is more worthwhile than disorienting experimentation. The
American professoriat, as a whole, has never neglected the opportunity

to support judgments or distinctions that reduce naming to judging; one sees it reaffirmed that progress/terror are the only roles of subjective interest; this transpolitical attitude is well expressed in Perry Anderson's certainty that university-based Marxian criticism "has no reason to abandon its Archimedean vantage-point: the search for subjective agencies capable of effective strategies for the dislodgement of objective structures."[3] "Search for" is an irreducibly idealist tag Professor Anderson has managed to obliterate in restating the one effective rule that dominates high-university activity — the expansion of our textual "menus," including support for the maximization of meaning, power plays endemic to institutional language and which are set against mass society as something to be studied.[4]

Skepticism differs from the academic demand that one become "master" of (often) nostalgic experience, that one share in a cultural economy of use value before being allowed to engage in "mature" cultural activities like criticism. Academic historians, for example, are notorious in promoting reduction of (present) conception to the "long telescopes" of narrative models; before one thinks to a "scene" one must "see" through "thoughts" guaranteed to ensure the success of generalization, so that the present is always controlled in thought. Philosophically put, the complexes that make up "events of thinking" must struggle for the differences of those thoughts as compared to the initial reductions carried out by going discourse. Permanent skepticism is called for in relation to the demand to respect the myth of cultural use values, a demand that relies upon sign-forms — the intersection of sense and grammar — in the projection of, say, a "need to remember" (and a "will to confess," which psychoanalysts favor, and a "need for work," which the left champions, and a "need for community," which the right uses). Actions accomplished by the solidarity of memory (the people, the nation, the working class, the family, the self one used to be) are supposed paths to Real Experience: the core of Platonic recollection made culturally ever-present. Through the ministrations of the good academic, then, one is given a model by which to sustain anti-skepticism. Cynicism: the impossible future made impossible to publicly discuss?

Consider the distinction between Lyotard's suggestion of an art event, which, in its active perversion of form, in its "dispossession" of anyone's mastery, is "no longer a message, threat, beseechment, defense, exorcism, lesson, or allusion in a symbolic relation, but rather an absolute object," that is, a force, and Adorno's suggestion that critical events represent "martyred witnesses" to tragedy.[5] The latter encourages, even if unwittingly, the feeling of the sadness of life, a value that is perhaps necessary, but dangerously limiting, where the reactive comes to affirm the negative.

Undoing Academic Benevolence

Psychoanalysis revealed that "desire" was subject to the integrative destructiveness of industrialization and is everywhere today the official descriptive language of the "self," the signifier "desire" becoming deployed by *all* of the critics who want to use it, arm it, strategize it; Marxism showed that labor had been already devastated by acts of capital formation and is today dominant (in the United States) in its rigid political moralism and repression of every "outbreak" of pleasure. Today the conjunction of "critical" and "knowledge" is existentially ambivalent from the start. Criticism of inertial continuities (there is a subindustry that will challenge titles such as American Studies) or of mythic conjunctions (e.g., America as an "open" society) does not prevent criticism from becoming another link in the labyrinth of chains. Indeed, not only does criticism not transfer to inventing existences independent of the system of Capital, but it is increasingly another commodity, whose book form signifies a nonbreak with forms (this one included). As Barthes reminded us, in the West, books are irreducible icons of a supposed "victory" by knowledge and sense over barbarity, crudity, and so on, and are also more frighteningly connected to the insistent figures of a pseudophysis. Criticism has widened its territory, but it is also then attached by dependence upon the cultural markets that capitalize upon it (I am in no way suggesting, however, that nonbook criticisms are thereby legitimized).

The convenience of books is mistaken for their benevolence. Each comes forward as a "resolution" or an "answer" or model or norm, furthering the passive acceptance of the book itself as having passed various testings. This normalization indicates that under the spell of criticism there is perhaps a tightening of "archaisms with a current function," as Deleuze puts it, in discussing what is constant about an object–complex or what is generalizable from a method as issued by the Book. The academic form of the book is "a means by which we avoid going to a particular place, or by which we maintain the option of escaping from it (the thread of the labyrinth)."[6] With criticism making its own appropriation of the book form, there is the conjunction of a new *contract* between writing and state appropriation (by academia as such), in which writing is reduced to speaking as "well as possible."[7] How could criticism not become attached to the aestheticization of opposition? In his admirable *Hiding in the Light*, Dick Hebdige scrupulously outfits Gramscist notions of "conjunctural analysis and strategic intervention" with those of Rorty in calling for "sensitivity" in which every term mutually reduces to a Foucaultian concern with who "has" and "gets" power. Why isn't this critical fascination with power treated as a ruse of power?

The linguistic relay constitutes a powerful and active index of academic mythologies. There is generally a substitution of rigid interpretive recodings instead of the construction of blurred identities that are difficult to synthesize or that require one to "reshuffle" the available predicates. For example, Rosalind Krauss, a leader in the formation of "cutting-edge" critical knowledge, has recently argued that

> the Minimalist resistance to traditional composition which meant the adoption of a repetitive, additive aggregation of form — D. Judd's "one thing after another" — partakes very deeply of that formal condition that can be seen to structure consumer capitalism: the condition, that is, of seriality.[8]

Minimalism is recoded from the position of resistance (to Capital) to that of a "fall" ("partakes"), a Platonizing strategy since "fall" is itself a representative good copy of the negative form "seriality," made equal to "consumer capitalism." It is entirely enlightened today to say that "consumer capitalism" is evil (as Krauss does, and which displaces a critique of capitalism as such), and therefore we can demystify the art forms that had deluded themselves as having taken up resistance to that economy (Ingres's paintings of bathers represent the negative unconsciousness of consuming modes which reduces to the negative totality of the artistic repetitions). The problem, however, is that in setting out this formulation, Krauss confounds seriality and capitalism. One passes from the mention of *a* condition to *the* structure; to say that the former is the condition of the latter is to actually collect capitalism and seriality and Minimalism in the Hegelian code — Minimalism is both resistance and collusion, the very form of a Good Object that has been created to conform to the model of the Good Academic. The Good Object is that which demonstrates our interpretive cleverness (where nothing of the object remains outside of language), and the Good Academic is legitimized by the saturation of the object in our interpretive language. To say that seriality, this aesthetic form, conditions capitalism is to be convinced that Minimalism is never outside Hegelian discourse. Indeed, Krauss asserts that the seriality of things is identical with the creation of "multiples," which reduces the latter to nothingness.[9]

Criticism, Superhistoricality

There are devastations wreaked on language by construction of the standards of criticism. Being correct is mostly a disaster insofar as it resurrects and even expands the elimination of objects. Everyone is armed with the rhetoric of negating binaries all the better to over- and under-value one term or another. Most devastating are the political formations connected to promoting what, in another context, Julia Kristeva has called "the sadistic protection of the One." "One" is any social subject (or theory) who identifies with becoming a big or small power, who (or which, since it is unclear which pronoun is more appropriate) desires dependency, security, and satisfaction. Normal "historical criticism," for example, often produces the "one" that Deleuze has called a "narrative of foundation," the myth of a continuous development of a subject purified of simulation. In what amounts to a conceptual shock directed at the concept of a "context," Deleuze manages to suggest that all such "well-founded" scenes (= linguistic reductions) are little more than neurotic disputes over reterritorialization, claimants in becoming reactionary, since the invocation of a "proper history" ensures temporal progression.

The argument is that criticism that claims continuous legitimation — which raises the "in the name of" — is aggressively connected to the political practices of state-building; when, for instance, Jameson tells us that "only Marxism can give us an adequate account of the essential mystery of the cultural past" and "This mystery can be reenacted only if the human adventure is one," what is at issue is that the narrative of Freedom and Necessity (Hegel again) is deployed to discount, summarize, rank, clarify, exclude actual appearances, simulacra (in Deleuze's sense — as claimants without standing, not Baudrillard's as the overcoding by forms). If normal criticism, then, stands for more state-building (interpretation as control), Deleuze also suggests that we consider simulacra as attached to "superhistorical" actions, which in the sphere of language register as syntactic inversion, semantic defamiliarization, delegitimation, deterritorialization. Here, instead of reinventing a "government" by automatically engaging in the symmetry of opposition, it is more interesting and compelling to seize an opportunity to become indifferent to "one" as model, answer, method, approach, good form. If criticism is shadowed by its inability to break from categories such as resemblance (what else does Jameson, in the statements just cited, offer but a conception of the image of unity to be copied?), then a subversion of normal criticism would emphasize "the constituting disparity . . . in and of itself, not prejudged on the basis of any previous identity . . . [where] it swallows up all foundations, it assures a universal collapse, but as a positive and joyous event, as de-founding. . . ."[10]

Standard of Living and Academic Ideals

John Tagg has subtly described a situation where theoretical discourses — Marxism, psychoanalysis, Althusserian Structuralism, Lacanianism, and so on — pursue their own hegemony in "the insistence on the purging of language in the name of 'actual relations' and a teleology of scientific concepts" such that language constructs operate exactly like Capital: they reduce the number of things one can say in *this location*.[11] The conjunction of linguistic and economic standards, their unhappy mutual attraction, is part of a voyage of wastefulness, whose products create hypertedium; the ceaseless recoding (remythification) we carry out for the "public" seems tied to solidarity with collective groups who do not revive themselves by pleasure-inducing waste, which Nietzsche was able to call a kind of "intoxication," but waste that mo(u)lds us. In this, reading and writing about Western waste has itself become a wasting away.

The standard of living as it affects the high university in the United States amounts to, as it were, the maintenance of what would be considered in some places bizarre couplings. The standard of living is attached to there being no Other of money, no other time or other place once money is (t)here. The category of money and that of Other as the name of the totality of Research Subjects, belong together by virtue of the same devolution: as money excludes other exchanges, where it is irrational not to have as much as is possible "given other" constraints and choices, the category of Other is projected in an acceleration of writings that stay at least one step (or move) in pursuit of money = others. Academic writings follow from markets, a distressed political formation. Thus, in another return of the displaced, Marx comes back to us: money is confirmed as the true absolute, which crosses borders and enables worlds to multiply, except that now it is not as Marx's "galvanochemical" processes but as Baudrillardian cultural viruses. Money, cash, credit, equity, reserves — and then symbolic capital comes to the surface as a workable academic category; unable to discuss multiple reductionisms stemming from the economic or discourse — who can be said to be learning from whom once they are the same? Think of the academic résumé become a collage of nonevents as well as a badge of conformity.[12] Strange inventions, our products.[13]

What is continuous across the ebb and flow of academic "improvement" is the reigning social-scientific ideal of research science, presented as an unchallengeable category.

The idealized operational mode of language within the academic profession rests on the supposition that authoritative interpretation has established itself in research — persons challenged as to their right to speak, to give reliable evidence, must show that they previously have been readers of documents. Research as a turning over, a "finding" of what is significant, that which stands out and illumines, where something valuable is released from confinement, is calibrated with reading unfamiliar documents from unfamiliar times and places, whose social actant is the attentive scholar. This requires a cut within the division of thinking, between interpretation (what is oversaid) and formalization (objects as pieces of structures) (the poles, then, being tradition and constitutive model building, as A. J. Greimas proposed).[14] The academic research ideal has as its telos or finality that of resolve — the more negatives to dissolve, the better — predicated on the myth that research connects with the revelation of meaning, that presentation forms like narrative provide research with satisfaction and completion of form, sustaining an accumulation of infinity, which then resides in books. The latter, appropriating the signs of science, signs of a "good faith" between things and meaning, *desemanticizes* thought into automatisms: "now we know that," "it is certain that," and other syntagmas ensure an uninteresting alienation from what are then self-protective writings. Criticism, again in the mode of "in general" and "as such," comes to stand for the real pyramidical structure of this writing, for example, its *discrediting* of "outsiders" by recourse to signifiers that justify the expenditure of investments in "research." "The redundancy of the order-word is . . . primary," argue Deleuze and Guattari in *A Thousand Plateaus*. The order-word of *correction* as it commands looks something like this: Jon Weiner, writing in the *Nation*, asserts that the American Communist Party in the 1930s defined "blacks as an oppressed nation," and in so doing (ordering it so) "had endowed the black struggle with dignity and significance." Socially correct racism: did black conflict not have "dignity and significance" when it was not under the orders of a party?[15]

We academics sabotage a transforming language with our machinations: conjunction(s) between what Nietzsche termed "action, need and terror" — what an old-fashioned existentialist would have called "lived experience" — are suppressed so that knowledge "grows" as part of a larger indifference. We keep to the delusion that others are somehow "understood" or "interpreted" *through* our squelching of excessive interpretative affects, by the idealization of a euphoric, demented, objectivity.[16] One is told that research must continue protected by the "name of heterogeneity," but it is overlooked that this name is used as an order, a demand, a command, a *summons* of law. Told that the choice between "new" and "traditional" history is between "new histories" and "anarchy," that historians are "modern" when they are "scientific" and "scientific" when they are "precise" and precise when their writings enact "thick descriptions," one's suspicions increase when such designations are attached to "progressive knowledge," that is, supposedly irrefutable, *irreversible* knowledge. Always the fluidity of myth.[17] Must one suppose that "research" can never unhinge a reader, that something "in common" (e.g., narrative form) always mitigates and softens a priori? When it is said that a "history" of the ocular — conceptually preshrunk to "acts of looking at" others — with its plunge or fall into "fetish" and "blindness" must lead to a better socialization of "this [modern] vision," the ideal of "antiocularity" *governs* the politics of a "proper" academic opposition.[18]

Instead of undoing "research," instead of taking degeneralization to the point of suspending the language of "research," we insist upon pretense: when told that Lacanian descriptions of the "doomed subject" are "modern" despite their repetition of a Rousseauian and far older sensibility,[19] we stick to the rationales of "study" (the absent, the missing, the lack, and other synonyms for a collective *bad conscience*).[20] Andreas Huyssens, a writer from an ecumenical, university-based left, writes that criticism should take up and align itself with the "recuperation of buried and mutilated traditions," that thinking should examine "forms of gender and race-based subjectivity in aesthetic productions and experiences, and their refusal to be limited to standard canonizations."[21] The contemporary films of Yvonne Rainer are put forward in a straight line with the novels of Virginia Woolf in terms of their respective critical use values. It is accepted that the point of opposition is to put forward repressed subjectivity; feminism may well be contrary to "male notions of perception and subjectivity," but why not take a further step and deconstruct all the terms of race and gender and class by showing the implicit orders and commands of all such positioning? Contemporary women and others "critical" must present their own realities. But every analysis of oppression has its own norms, its attending liberation of feeling and desire, which may only serve to *expand* identity of the "real opposition."[22] Repeated as acts of self-institutionalization, an identitarian ethos, one can perceive yet another form in the desire for power.

Academic Mythification

The relentless association of criticism with improvement appears in what Edward Said calls the "fusion" of "moral will" and a "grasping of evidence" — readers should be able to "see" the writer's moral seriousness of fact and principles as something known, as legitimations for writing. Said's enormously influential *The World, the Text, and the Critic* asserted the critic as someone who creates values; responsible criticism is modeled on the identity of an acceptable role of contrariety, that of the "enlightened lawyer" whose knowledge (of case, fact, instance) is mostly negative. Said asserts that the opposition of text and world is "untenable," and indeed it is, but Said says it is untenable because "circumstances implicate the text." He does not allow that analyses of "text" "implicate the world," hence coming down *on the side* of the opposition supposedly negated, on the side of a (reduced) "world."[23] Severed from figures of ambiguous language, which cannot be made to converge with improvement, criticism is exorcised from "often comical . . . breathless mishaps that the mind slowly gets itself out of," which Bataille refers to in considering a "learning process" that is something else than a "disputation to the death on the possibilities."[24] In *S/Z*, Roland Barthes said that the "writerly" is ourselves writing before the infinite play of the world (the world as function) is traversed, intersected, stopped, plasticized by some singular system (Ideology, Genus, Criticism).[25] Barthes was also reminding readers that Euro-American Romanticism had been discredited because of its guilt by association with "originality" and "excess," of too much passion, which the social and political junkies dread; that Existentialism has been excommunicated for its cultivation of alienation (too much intensity); that Impersonalism (materialism without consciousness as the sole agency) has been suppressed as just too difficult, too unideologically malleable; that Marxism has been integrated insofar as it expands "research" into the vicissitudes of "contradictions" (the "need" for "scientized consciousness"), enacting a series of integrative devices (e.g., appropriation of the demand for permanent recoding); and that psychoanalysis has been successfully deployed to convince us of an "internal existence" presided over by cultural imperialists, in particular newer projections such that the dissolution of the ego enables the "true subject" to emerge, the "truth of the subject's desire."[26] Such models are powerful: separately and together they offer the irreversibility of the continuum, and hence acceptable answers to a thinking that wants to die.[27]

The integration of discursivity also isolates academic language-moves in terms of oxymoronic forms. The social is entirely dangerous, especially since its forms are more and more capitalized. In what is arguably his masterpiece, *Simulations*, Baudrillard terms the global form of production (here at odds with the more affirmative, even ecstatic, senses of production at the hands of Deleuze and Guattari) a "satellization of the real," one of those phrases that pulverizes the binary of elite and popular while it points to that "indefinable reality without common measure," a k a "the cool universe of digitality," where precisely that *indifference* of everything reigns.[28] On this analysis, modern production, considered as a gigantic mesh of constraints, was always in itself an enormous act of *decipherment*, for which "there is properly neither finality . . . nor value," where everyone "can think of himself only as something to produce . . . this remarkable phantasm . . . whose form escapes him."[29] Critical discourses smooth the deformations of modernizing production (= displacement of seduction, the latter what allows life to have charm and is irreducible to exchange "relations" and which gets exterminated, one way or another). Multiple and institutionally driven submission to a "destructive hyperconformity" is glimpsed where cultural production becomes a pure form, not requiring any end outside itself, *alternately realized* in such disparate cultural phenomena as Warholian repetition, or incessant "repositioning" around cultlike terms such as "modern" and "postmodern," which a fascinated public no doubt interprets as "intellectual energy" instead of the intellectual "duopoly" it is ("couples of simultaneous opposition," as Baudrillard calls it, or the "mirror stage" of culture as a whole), or crises of the "canon," in-house disputes over representation, where sign-value predominates (the "canon" debate never changes). This oxymoronic ecstasy, this relentless culturizing or concoction of identities connected to demands (for reappropriation), is unable to process the concept of events based on "a luxurious squandering of energy in every form."[30] That is, there is what can be called a quasi-permanent *shifting* of criticism, this construal of discussions that cannot keep the "public's attention" and reducing those that are disruptive to the going functions of the going players.

It is (sadly) true that extensive rereadings in Nietzsche's critique of modernity and other topics (essays on Nietzsche's sense of Eternal Return being among the most stimulating) have generated hostility and accusations of nihilism. What the "majority" political factions have against Nietzschean critique is its version of deconstruction, in particular of terms like "hope" where its cultural variety, as in "hope for greater social understanding," is argued as another reductive equation. In his *All Consuming Images* (1988), Stuart Ewen demands that "there must be a reconciliation of image and meaning," an infinite demand that could only be carried out by a violence at least as otiose as the violence of State Culture (here, the manipulating image); surely the writer knows that the form of demand is itself an aggressive move? Illusionist violence, Nietzsche said and Joe Riddel reminds us, is intrinsically woven with the "illusions of self-reflexivity," here the obliteration wrought by "must."[31] While Marx and Freud taught us to model the negative as the precondition for the emergence of the positive (acceptance of suffering — of labor for Marx, of limits for Freud), Nietzsche was interested in "differential" events — how to disconnect with the enculturation that absorbs the displacements stemming from economic activity, psychologized and deployed in the politics of culture. The Mapplethorpe issue (1990) is a case in point. The curated show was immediately overcoded by reactionary hysteria (the violation of law attendant upon the images of children without clothing) and by a progressive "defense" of its integrity (the photographs were defended as culturally necessary); everyone ignored the fact that Mapplethorpe was also Mapplethorpe *Inc.*: the latter institution was playing for its own stakes, in which every trace of attention added to the value of the part called "Inc." The academic formation of this "controversy" — claim/counterclaim of public representations — was already subverted by the setup of the "Inc." Nietzschean writings remind us, if we choose to listen, that criticism is not a question of taking sides, but of ambiguating a relentless infolding of knowledge, its becoming a rigid "inside" such that we come to accept that critical analysis is, for example, reducible to the ethnology of one's education.[32]

Adding positions, complicating the very notion of sides, to say more than is required are extra-academic practices, irreducible to activism or scholarship, terms largely confined to the status of territorial markers. Here one can begin to speak of a forced exile from academia, an exile of writing insofar as academic departments must exclude whatever they find unrecognizable (see chapter 2). The guardians of the solidity of writing are not going to see it turned into gaseous states.[33] One might speak to the controlled promiscuity (another oxymoron!) in the demand for meaning.[34] How does it happen that meaning so often is nonexistent until we call it into being?

In his extremely fine disentanglement of modern French philosophy, Vincent Descombes emphasizes that what has mattered in the Deleuzian assemblage is the latter's stress on conceptual difference and not "nonconceptual difference," where the former tries to think what is already different, bodies that are not instantaneously reduced to what we think.

The concept of difference is open to empirically vivid *nonconceptual differences; the question of the concept and the nonconcept turns on whether one has enough energy to allow for differences that one has not yet thought.*[35]

It is not principally whether thought can operate without assuming a transcendental pole (history, desire, need, etc.), or occupy a "distant and close" (Deleuze) articulation of mediation, or manage to slip in subjective significations among the sedentary massification of discourse. It is rather trying to make enunciations, or phrases, that put their own rules in suspension all the better if "one can't really tell if submission doesn't finally conceal the greatest sort of revolt and if combat doesn't imply the worst of acceptances."[36]

Without Hegel

The academic "post" — as in being posted to the scene — of convincing others to take seriously the contradictions and constructions of the existing players and the corresponding imaginary and symbolic levels is of a similar effect-spell of "melancholy haphazardness," which Hannah Arendt ladeled over the theory of history. Arendt argued that theories of history had been replaced — by the writings of historians, no less — by "social techniques" that made "expressions of history" irrelevant.[37] To continue to conceive of "history" (or culture, or society) after one could not rely on even perceptual trust, so deeply was the "social contract" broken by capitalizing technology, was to embrace culture as disaster. The West has created an impossible conception of "history," for if facts and relations existing now do not make available to thought the judgment that the "whole" is thinkable as meaningful now, then now cannot properly be thought "in the now." Now as actually reduced to random eventualities raised the veil on a consideration of what is dominant; the Western penchant for a boundless "acting into" nature and desire, with Capital as the experimental agent, might then be the form in which experience was surrendered (doesn't Max Weber, in *The Protestant Ethic,* describe how white male *ethnicity* surrendered to money?).

Hegel says in *Reason in History* that "to he who looks at the world rationally, the world looks rationally back." This sedative, bromidic thought — belief in the symmetry of cultural concepts and social experiences — ushers in the overvaluation of the *conceptual difference*; in Hegel's case, that Prussian statism meshed with "philosophical reconciliation," which is to say that for Hegel Prussian statism was the material expression of the philosophical Idea. States and subjects in the contest for mutual recognition. Today Hegelianism supports belief in the transcendence of historical consciousness, an elitism of the academy considered as a cultural/social identity, a repression and control placed upon material transformations subject to clarifications through "proper" consciousness (of "history"). The invocation of Hegel is to reconcile the real with utopia (or value, or symbol) by means of concepts like "freedom" or "spirit" or "history" or "liberation" or "necessity," all of which is infamously enunciated in Jameson's astonishing reduction; Marx, he writes, *urged* the self "to do the impossible" (the sense of which is an ecstasy of oxymoronic purity), which is nothing other than "to think this development [capitalism] positively and negatively all at once."[38] It is worth noting that even Adorno, often associated with such figurings, was able to acknowledge that modernization had *actually* obliterated the material basis of reconciliation — "once causality is as thoroughly disenchanted as it would be by tabooing the inner determination of objects," he wrote, it will "disintegrate in itself as well."[39] Adorno postulated that the most "intimate reactions of human beings" had been reified and that resistance had to take the form of an "obduracy of thought against the ruling power."[40] But even this version of negative Hegelianism has to suppose that someone/something is coming from the future to meet those alienated (now), the sheer linearity of it all elbowing out one's evoking "intensities beyond the intentions," that is, nonsymmetrical thinking.[41] The philosophical horizon that Adorno took for granted — where negativity resonated with the possibility of completion, of stopping — is itself finished in terms of a cultural/political program. The critical model of a "crossroads" belongs to some 1950s scene.[42] The Hegelianism that warranted it, the speculative model of negativity, which is nonetheless a "magical affirmative force," is insulting to anyone who must deal with nonspeculative realities.[43]

Speculative "passage" furthers an ignobility of thinking, since speculation is really that form of elevated passivity in which one "resolves" (if that is what it is) that the future will be like/the same as the present, even when projected as different. Hegelianism frames hope to the detriment of thinking.

Unhistorical Nonspeculation

It is incontrovertible that today "revolutionaries" must appear in conformity with signs of "revolution," signs designating the "formatting of the real," as Baudrillard has taught us. Singular signs tied to a perceiver's consciousness have given way to the mobile sign, an event analogous to the shift from index to symbol. Life as such is more and more culturized: immediately full of signals, networks, perhaps referents. The wife of one of Nicaragua's leaders appears in *Vanity Fair* (1987) costumed as a visual representative of upper-middle-class fashion, but grafted to the textual rhetoric of a "critical theory of history" displayed in statements about a better future, "children's needs," and more. The children are dressed in the international style of the rich; Benetton colors prevail. These "revolutionaries like us" who present the aura of a well-bred family, are also an appeal to elite Darwinism; this sign-form, of a "cultural selection" available to revolutionaries, opens to an audience that is "chic," that is aware of the war(s) between the competing "states" of Nicaragua as well as image wars.

The overcoding of "radical chic" shows a powerful affinity with an expansive cultural rule of identity; making signs is connected to the liquification of power, its becoming "media-ready." Identification draws upon the cultural activity of *division* in order to "support strata, segmentations, sendentarity and the State apparatus" (Deleuze). What is unhistorical and nonspeculative concerning such signs is their reaffirmation of "narratives of foundation," which confirm the practices of existing players, who have already established their cultural claims to the future by virtue of such sign-stories (stories of universal progress, necessary rules, essential codes, etc.); new players recode cultural integration by affirming the historical as it is used to speculate on the future.

Deleuze's arguments corrode these hierarchies, which are also overcodings, but especially those that "endow" academia with value, worth, prestige, and other story forms that subtend its ranking function. Arthur Danto, for example, writes that art-making can be set within an "infinite play with its own concept," which manages to affirm Hegelianism (concepts = identities) and instrumentalize deconstruction ("infinite play" a reduction thereof). The sense of "infinite play" reiterates a model of criticism that *reduces by expansion*, by the addition of self-referentialities, an academicism of form (*pace* Lévi-Strauss); "play," considered as a device of ranking, is not detached from the power-moves of truth, representation, access, and so on.[44]

My argument, then, is that what the concept of criticism "looks like" or is supposed to look like, along with many convergent relations, is contentious and opaque. The ubiquity of criticism unable to generate concepts indexes the success of domesticated critical discourse. Chapters 3 to 5 address this topic in some detail. Because no one knows what "history looks like" (though there are countless possible signs), or what "academia" should do, an ahistorical and independent criticism from both political and academic sources might operate in some ways that were usefully offensive instead of contestatory over the same old ground: there would be no question of promoting contestants "in the name of" correcting divergence, "to recenter the circles or to make order of chaos, to provide a model and make a copy."[45]

I am reading a journal entitled *Zone*, offered as an alternative to "normal" academia. In an issue devoted to the "history of the body" I read that the subhistory of dentistry is a worthy historiographic item of cultural conflict. This because the role of the dentist, the "only medical practitioner we regularly visit," is attached, as it were, to the "tooth [which] is the only part of the sentient body we fear and consider it normal to lose." The dentist "himself retains the aura of torturer." The "history" of dentistry equals normal torture (which is not the argument of the essay in question). Not "only" are these "onlys" a sign-form of *demand* in giving us a hackneyed historiographic object of study, but they *materially* inaugurate a discourse, politics, cultural model: that of a (projected) child's fears objectified, made available for that type of work entitled research. By means of such hyperbole is expunged the fact that the dentist might be epiphenomenal (precisely because so easily overcoded) and has a terrorist destination within the realm of adult visual practices, where dentists were used to sustain children's susceptibility to pain. Such qualifications make no appearance here, in a journal so "perfect" in appearing Other that it reaches for what could be called the "good unconsciousness" of "radical discourse."[46]

The Linguistic Relay

What is the academic form of linguistic constancy? Is there one or many? Can it be aligned with positive and negative as its attractive and repelling forces? Is it ahead of and yet a detour through the "real"? Pierre Bourdieu thinks that "homo academicus" is conveyed through the language-form of classification, but this seems at once too broad and too "historical," relying as it does on a sort of deferred, yet eternal, Aristotelianism. In adopting Deleuze's phraseology of the *mot d'ordre*, we might consider as academic constancy the reduction of sense to acts that are "linked to statements by a 'social obligation.' "[47] Enunciation is always public: I speak, therefore I owe. The popular bumper sticker "I owe, I owe, it's off to work I go" becomes "I say, I say, it's here I stay." So constant is the demand to make sense in the most economical manner possible — the least variation — that academic history-writing comes to be ordinary in its preservation of lines of continuity, just as scientificity ends up as the form of ultimate rationality. The "impersonal collective assemblage" we call the "high university" expects academic statements to "look like" small mortal blows to every honest doubt: at once official, authoritative, thoughtful, careful, balanced. Paul de Man wrote that there are three irreducible types of language (a k a rhetoric, logic, and grammar), by means of which one moves across figural, literal, symbolic, proper, improper modulations. If there is an academic type of statement, it may well be close to the composition of judicial/legal pronouncements, embeddings, in which complex and potentially recalcitrant materials are subjected to an *incorporeal* transformation, as when a biographical reference turns a document into an "accused" simultaneously processed as a member of the idiotic couple, "innocent/guilty." The incorporeality of much linguistic presentation, where semantic effects are virtually registered without analytic discussion, may well acquire its academic "force" by the rigid *nonrecognition* of meanings that come from elsewhere. In a rush of language that tries to bring into being the very thing the words generate, Andrew Ross *orders* into being the following cultural complex: after writing that "debates" about postmodernism had started out as "dissenting" to the "universal claims of modernism," it has come about that

> suddenly, postmodernism has become an epic production almost in spite of itself. . . . Suddenly we are faced again with the big questions. . . . postmodernism, after all, holds the promise of a cultural politics . . . that would fight over, if not infiltrate, every last inch of a new historical terrain.[48]

The obliteration of materiality is on a rampage here: "suddenly" brings about the absolute of a code-switch, from the mention of an idea ("big questions") to the certainty that fulfillment of this idea is occurring all the time (= linguistic constancy). This piece of academic word-magic tries to govern, as it were, the transportation of its readers to cultural alignment with their roles as subjects of sociopolitical-economic capture.

Of course, the academic text that elegantly presents antiquarianized materials, like lists of symptoms of a disease specific to a past era,[49] is not the same academic text that narrativizes its readers with the argument that the North was "more correct" in its goals than the South; yet both reduce writing to providing readers with blocks in the construction of homogenized spaces.[50] Such variations on a textual *promise to pay*, which academic language performs while closing its productions to outsiders, may suggest an archaic exorcistic desire.[51] After all, what is actually required for the sound of the term "people" to evoke a motricity that could become an event of acting alongside, feeling with, or deciding "in the name of the people"? "These people," "my people," "those people," and similar expressions foster ideas that sustain the myths of existing players.

In sum, the constancy of academic writing is calibrated with processes in which extremes, the highs and lows of experience, are edited into a domesticated, tamed thought. One does not have to quote Nietzsche or Derrida to make this point; the Pink Floyd song (1975) "Wish You Were Here," with its refrain about one's ability to tell heaven from hell, mocks one's ability to tell (separate) "telling" and "told" once the linguistically constructed "self" is within, contained, and rhetoricized to the social. (See chapter 5, on Baudrillard's evaluation of linguistic constancy treated as a social *physis*, where society is subject to "a priori perception," preformed — but anonymously generated — relations of displacement and self-deception.) When "reality" is defined as the *impossibility of definite reversal* — linguistic presentations where definition is incontestable — then it would seem that a critical issue is the introduction of sememic discontinuity, one that moves out of the range of positive and/or negative critique, since negation (e.g., ranting against the inhumanity of Western modes of representation) still precipitates the promotion of the thing judged (e.g., larger and larger art exhibits, which reduce the Third World to our interests).

So an energetic criticism might take account of how we professors appropriate the linguistic relay and give it the appearance of being "on our side." We are overinvested in extinguishing semes and connotations where uncomfortable ideas might materialize in unexpected ways. Example: Professor Jameson wants to promote, put forward, and "necessarily begin" a politics of the "public sphere" on the foundation of a "historical consciousness" free from the severe inadequacies of the class-consciousness of Capital. Writing that there are "learning processes that have deadly outcomes" (e.g., Positivism, Romanticism, Scientism), he asserts that "new learning processes" must be imagined (e.g., an updated "dialectical materialism") so as to compete for the future. This imagination of otherness, of a future, can take place because "public life" has "already been accumulated" in enough *safe terms*, a reservoir of proper meanings that show us how things might turn out better, and hence serve to enable us to raise "the original Aristotelian virtues," for a "rethinking of the individualist traditions of conventional moral philosophy." Jameson's suppression of linguistic ambivalence here equals reduction of the entire past to the linguistic controls of the present; we possess the forms of constancy, which allows us to set aside a present economy which is superirrational. Once more, present culture is projected as *only speakable* as the "original Aristotelian virtues," which are thus not actually past. No mention is made that Aristotle's "wrestling" with general terms was criticized by, among others, the Stoics, who had the sense to challenge the manipulation of *lekta*.[52] Instead of embarrassing questions, we are to reread Aristotle in our seminars. How about "Aristotle against television"?

Realism or . . . ?

As described by Baudrillard, the concept of simulation sets forth the hypothesis that the semes by means of which thinking imputes object-ness — attributes, predicates, relations — carry out the activity of *precession, a withdrawal of differences* from language whereby errant or wayward interpretants are consigned to the oblivion of nonbeing.[53] This process, a perverse "superhistoricality," cuts across existence as a whole such that, from phonetics to clothing, distinctive arrangements of art, politics, and social relations are drained of their raison d'être. More disastrous than the Marxian notion of commodity fetishism, simulation has it that "real-ity" is more than "real" now — (the real demanded a relation with the imaginary; it was defined by its being in opposition) — there is a veritable riot of conformity in all spheres whose form is that of "exchange in itself, in an uninterrupted circuit without reference or circumference."[54] Once delimited forms like tautology and redundancy are at the center of what is supposed to be rationality as such. Interpretations determined by, for example, academic requirements (e.g., a refereed article in a prestigious journal) may or may not signify a contribution to knowledge; but it is out of the question that they do not *simulate* the interpretants of "seri-ousness," "thoughtfulness," and so on. The body of Salman Rushdie is certainly in some ongoing difficulty, even crisis, but the media's presen-tation of the affair reduces to the simulation that there is some contest taking place where Muslim fundamentalism is the Devil. The emergence of a "right to borrow" makes, does it not, a simulacrum of the realist economic code of saving and accumulation. As I read Baudrillard, he is daring to say all over again that every attempt to resuscitate descriptive realism equals a reduction to archaic interpretations.

Criticism is "washed out" in the general laundry of effacement, where effects "go off" in ways that make Hegel's "unintended consequences" seem naive. Baudrillard's sense of simulacra, which parallels, to an ex-tent, Rousseau's critique of the identity between social desire and cultural integration, implies success of redundancy in the sphere of semiotics and the triumph of the death instinct in the spheres of pleasure and subjectiv-ity. Critical agitation is threaded, for the most part, to an expanding in-difference of "reality" to realisms of every sort (Marx, Freud, Structur-alism, Logical Positivism, etc.). The analogic world of, say, Freud's use of whole-part model (the Oedipal complex), or the stress that Frankfurt school-style "rejectionism" (the term is Sheldon Wolin's[55]) ladeled over the resistant ego (the last particle of Hegelian negation), belong to a realism concerned with human *legacy*, which is daily overthrown by the introduction of *haptic space*: events without landmarks, without memories built into them, the context of which is the reproducibility of new shapes of exchange power.[56]

Is Peter Sloterdijk wrong when he states that the "new, integrated cynicism thus even feels itself, understandably, both as victim and as sacrificer"?[57] And isn't this another way of suggesting that the neurotic world postulated by Freud and the idealization of a statist resolution by Marx have ceased to excite and generate interest, that talking cures and workers' strikes, expressive art and denunciatory aesthetics are felt to be archaisms? If the West is "more like" a paranoid world of controls and fears, based upon a past that is anything but past because it "goes off" in exceedingly arational ways (the great thesis of Hannah Arendt, on which see chapter 4), where the cynical is *worked into* the texture of signification, where even the "supplies of dissatisfaction have been used up," then isn't one "logic" of criticism that of pushing beyond sarcasm, of sustaining the energy to respond to the challenge that even cynicism is another form of integration? In short, is there a writing that exceeds cynicism without falling into any number of traps (e.g., psychological naiveté)? At question is not to "take over" what is dominant but rather how to leave it, how to walk away from it, to let it become without use. Can one imagine a criticism, even if university- or school-based, which set off various processes of *disinternalization?*

There is a vast difference between such conditions and normal academic criticism. Where critics like Aronowitz continue to speak of, make reference to, a "rescue [of] history from its own traditions," that is, by narrative revisions (putting forward excluded pasts, demanding recognition for the contribution of the masses), a different job would not rely on the fantasy of an "intervention [on the social] that goes beyond voluntarism" and which is carried out by an intelligentsia that arrogates to itself the role of representing the nonrepresented. For there is only voluntarism, which may or may not be much; but a voluntarism that proliferated at the threshold of concept formation: would this still be voluntarism?

Not Identity Books but More Ideas

Sheila Chandra, a Near Eastern voice recording in London, sings about an "unchanged malady," which she deploys so as to contemporize and displace the American sentimentalism of an "unchained melody." She reminds us of the cultural despair of repetition, which short-circuits the American projection of liberation through self-expression. Chandra is singing about the destructions of repetition in a way that performs a small-scale destruction on the concept, by a voicing or sounding that carries its listener into the heart of the stupidity of sentiment; Chandra would dissolve what, in *A Thousand Plateaus*, Deleuze and Guattari use to designate as academic book-machines that submit the "line to the point."[58]

Books give rise to various memory systems, which are indistinguishable from prestige-systems and from social blocks; thinking is spared much labor by the booked. Reactive memory is an extraordinarily resilient time-form with powerful chains running to, in particular, history books. The extensive use of the recent tag "age of Reagan" is a conceptual disaster because it personifies the visible and simultaneously inoculates the dominant (Reagan = social malevolence = Progressives are spared); instead of a completely shattering analysis of any such identity, phrases like "age of Reagan" are whole books in and of themselves. Such tags as the "fall of" or "the emergence of" require a departure and arrival of thought such that "molar structures"—traditions, systems, institutions—become thought of as the sole means of temporal transmission. Analysis of the functions set off by "historical discourse" can never go too far in exposing the role played by *aggressive reactivity*, whose book code is the reductive control over the future brought about by making the future identical with the present. Carlo Ginzburg, for example, insists that the book called "historical writing" is threaded to an experience of dilemma: the historian can judge or understand, and even when doing both, never argues so that thinking eludes the form of the book.[59]

Critical work is attached to memory by making it perform the operation of "mending" (de Certeau). This "mending" closes an opening (to the strange, the unknown, the inexpressed). We forget, as it were, the violence expended by the routine form of the book against the sin of forgetfulness: criticism remains connected to the passivity of expectation, that if reality and experience are not grasped by this book, they will be by another; it is not difficult to see that the figure of continuity, the line from initiation to result, is thereby built into normal criticism. But an active memory stimulated by the discontinuities of ideation would also move toward what Bataille called "the token of its death," where it ceases to define what is "living" but becomes alive in and of itself[60] and opens an "undecidable psychic space."[61] Active memory, which "forgets" in order to stimulate an idea, an affect, is irreducible to the form of the book.

Is it possible to envisage abandoning the "lineup" of ideas along the axes of contraries that are thought to define what is to be settled in criticism? Contraries are so much raw material for the making of connections that might slip the tie of number, to encourage an end to the numbering of things: who said there are four politics, three economies, or six literary genres? Why not eighty-three and three-fifths and and and . . . ? If the book is that which fixes (a map? a pet?), which stabilizes and depassionizes, which then keeps language and thought in place, Nietzschean "untimeliness" is not immediately a countertime, but what escapes feeding a system of temporal coordinates most often deployed in order to depress one (e.g., "it is too late," "not soon enough").

If we pursue William Labov's suggestion that the overcoding of memory employs "subjective reactions" and "the fixation of past experience" to create a "point of view from which the future appears as the past," then alternatives to these subjective-objective anchorings may well accomplish "advances of the imperceptible" where a "line frees itself from a point" so that it can form a connection somewhere else.[62] This would be the most difficult task of all: to deacademicize the devices and apparatus of memory.

Culture and University: Gravest Doubts

For many people, "epochal feelings" have become jammed in the onslaught of an economy more and more oxymoronic (work = the persistence of being in debt) and a national culture abusive toward thought; one watches incest survivors on TV demand that their (mutilated) memory of child abuse acquire legal recognition, that justice be granted, and despite the obviousness of the demand as displacement, the demand for redress opens another black hole of "what next?" Did the Zeitgeist appear today on American TV? Did one miss it? Here is Baudrillard's designation of the present "conjuncture" between the terms "mass" and "society":

> . . . giving way to a pure and empty, or crazy and ecstatic form. . . . The masses plunge into an ecstatic indifference, into the pornography of information, and place themselves in the heart of the system, at the blind and inert spot from which they neutralize and annul it.[63]

Baudrillard's writing may be wildly optimistic (at times) in theorizing that the masses survive by a kind of cultural migration from political formations to superculture (e.g., mass sports). But can the "masses" have epochal feelings, a living sensibility, in relation to the activities that are invasive, like the economy or a narcotized public nondiscussion? Concepts such as the "implosion" of the social suggest an excess of "ductile" signs, whose sheer physics corrodes any synthetic grasp of an epoch. Another epochal model, delivered in a softer, more traditionally humanistic vein, is that of Umberto Eco, who suggests a "new Middle Ages" in which, or better, as which, there (is) or will be the setting-up of a virtual "permanent transition," an obvious oxymoron, and evokes a culture bound by the game of zero-sum. The "exploitation of disorder" and "logic of conflictuality," a "culture of constant readjustment fed on utopia," results from Eco's choice of a "mixed historiography," determined by the projection of immobility and the bricolage of creation and destruction.[64] Lyotard's description of an accelerating increase in knowledge — codified and purified to the point of being stripped of conflict — where information is threaded to a process of "exteriorization," suggests the power of exchange as the only goal of cultural systems;[65] unlike Eco's model of an indefinite future, Lyotard posits the disastrous fusion of the categories of culture/economic, where

> capitalism . . . submits . . . all objects to . . . the annihilation of objects as
> symbolic values coincident with desire and their conversion into
> indifferent terms of a system that no longer has outside itself any instance
> to which these objects . . . can be grounded.[66]

The linking of a process of annihilation in the cultural sphere with a controlled dyad of scarcity/abundance in the material one suspends, one would think, any strong sense of an epoch; the concept comes to a halt.

Such models distill new doubts: are individuals a thing of the past? (Deleuze employs the notion of the "dividual" to evoke the tightening of a society of control.) Isn't the "ego" raised by Freud out of many psychobiologic strands lost and even rendered absurd, despite last-ditch efforts by intellectuals like Marcuse and Sartre, who adhered to the idealist fantasy of a consciousness that "leads" and "directs"? Isn't the body, too, a thing of the past (soon Olestra, empty fat calories, oxymoronic food) — as well as the mind and every constitutive concept of cultural interest and desire? And aren't these doubts themselves materials of an objective judgment, one that comes from things? Strong suspicions that the future is increasingly more arbitrary, at every level, and that it is more determined: the oxymoronic cancellation of culture?

Let us go further. The force of analogies and comparisons about the high university are also cast into doubt; semiotics suggests that at this "point" of cultural semiosis, of *areferentiality*, the arbitrariness of pairs such as knowledge/interest or analysis/solution refer to their sign-functions, which are generally mythifications of social practices. Cultural production and image have fused, although they can be pried apart for analytic as well as mythic purposes. Although the university promotes an "avant-garde science" for each distinctive era (e.g., chemistry in the 1880s, physics between the wars, fusion and microchips of today), its supervision of roles — the professor as helper, as transmitter, as speaker for the oppressed — is now stretched without the possibility of cultural or any other sort of resolution. The black hole confronting especially the high university is that its textual products generate an intensification of oxymoronics: one is to speak for reality, about and of reality, while conserving an academic "post of speaking" (as expert) that cannot be challenged except by one's identical other. In this sense, there is the background rumble of a *nonevent* — all that we produce is infinitely small by comparison to the criticisms not spoken by us, these criticisms which are not negative and oppositional, but affirmative and which would shatter the closed world of knowledge and culture production.

Although the university presents itself as having merged with mythical figures of intellectual success (Prometheus), and signals this in the language of "breakthrough," which evokes social progression, it in fact brings about the destruction of otherness: the category of the "expert" is also organized as a "finality" of interpretation supported by the acquisition of certification (e.g., Ph.D, LL.B. M.D.), pure power-forms of test taking, yet mobile or flexibile for presenting oneself as a political entity, as in "witness." The formation of an academic "expert" legitimizes the use of violence-in-reserve to exclude those who have taught themselves — by experience — or who otherwise insist upon an equality of reciprocity in anything called the production of social/cultural knowledge.

Hannah Arendt pointed out how "history" was "inconceivable" the more many "pasts" keep "going off" in the futures of such pasts, making mincemeat of the idea of historical "direction." Lévi-Strauss formalized the notion of an indeterminate narrative-model for the West when he stressed that the writing of "history" was no more or less than the code of chronology, ceaselessly grafted to memory, to noteworthy dates. All of this was aimed at voiding the famous "existential" world whose Sartrian refrain was the pathos and agony of choices, which gave every individual "their history." *That* version of "existence" is romantic and naive, yet if there is a contemporary oblique sense to Roquentin, it is not a "flight from history" but from the conjunction of "history" and university. Implied is that our intellectual constructs — Oedipus and related topics, such as Habermas's belief in consensus — are hopelessly secondary and reactive elaborations that carry very large image value but have no plausible sense when treated as thought-forms to *learn from*. Universities do not help people to build more models — to the point of an absolute surplus of them, which would still not be enough — so as to really test

Marx and Freud and Friedman and Parsons and all the rest, and because of this built-in self-perpetuation of professional production, it is hard to see how the university would generate ideas that might interfere with its own privileges.

In this scene of extroversion, cultural and social choices are shaped by codifications, the spinning of factions, the taking of sides, forming sub-alliances, betrayals, and so on; at a certain point in an increasingly random and chaotic piling up of processes (political, cultural, mythic, some dropping off, some coming into existence, some channeled into complementarity with others, while still others multiply inside of one another), we arrive at a cultural order where more selves become wards of institutions and so subjectless within an anarchic despotism of Capital. Access through culture to the economy absorbs the earlier form of cultural identity/memory, a not inconsequential transformation. Such models of experience put an end to ideology/truth; all consciousness is finally epiphenomenal in relation to Capital.[67] With such reproduction, or a kind of "hyperproduction," the replacement processes triumph, hold sway everywhere. What, then, of the high university in particular? If there is an epochal shift, to that of the dominance of cultural myth, which replaces economic integration, then how is it possible for any of the players to actually establish the primacy of high-university "normalcy"? The "something elevated, weightless, Hellenic" about academia may well signify its "almost artificial lighting, which serves to display the ruins."[68]

Wasn't it always? is the refrain. What about the paranoid Levantine or the German tribes?[69]

Consider again that the high university requires that texts be presentations of great stability. It favors sign-forms acting as air chambers that seal categories off from spills occurring somewhere else in the "vessel." Whether it turns on the "citative authority" of the footnote, on the thoroughness of "examination of the literature [shows]," or the "judicious handling of countervailing hypotheses" — the jargon of law, its security and importance as language, protects the existing cultural players. The militarized aspect of this "academic calling" works like a saturating fat cell; by absorption of meanings, it drowns the other elements. Academia gives itself foundations in the conceptual apparatus of society; it claims to provide criteria by which society can make choices or reposition itself vis-à-vis the various problems and disasters of modern life. But here is the gravest doubt: not that academia enacts such claims, but that its "desire" to replace world with itself is both irrefutable and of a futile critical difference.

Rosalind Krauss tells us that the most interesting thing we do, as "progressive" intellectuals, is to test methodologies: it is not asked if this presupposes our having emptied the world — a world reduced so that its "openness" can "expose" itself to scholars who act, as Nietzsche argued, with relentless competitive energy and fanatical "correctness," and thereby fool themselves into substituting "academic state" for "world."[70]

Concluding Remarks

Academic writings forge chains and links — the high university as a chain-link assemblage for determining the enclosurability of things spoken of and to: a procession of military forms that obey what the critic John Tagg has called an "unremitting war of position," but which configure big and small "states" and so are opposed to the war machines of anyone who threatens to go native, that is, without the protection of cultural mediations.[71]

The materialism of academia meshes with contemporary life. We are not monks. While some critics bemoan the absence of a "bohemia" (make your own), real professorial life encourages absolute normalization of degrading social functions: "histories of mall culture" are being written and there will be "interdisciplinary" academic sectors taking up its vicissitudes. The malls themselves now operate as "transformers," that is, serving as "community centers" that sponsor "health care," the latter reduced to passive walkathons, which, in turn, "mesh" with shopping. A looped design: made in university? Aren't some sectors of "reality" academicized a priori? Or for the most part? Walter Benjamin, with his interest in the aestheticization of vulgarity, projected the extension of political control onto what remained of a "mass psyche," a thickening of melancholic "richness." But aren't these topics actually connected to the ongoing success of an oxymoronic society which has already rendered "history" passé? Our textual products — lecture, book, essay, review, conference paper — overwhelmingly confirm a writing that *does not exceed* what is expected of it, and that allows for expansion insofar as "society" is predicated on the wreckages generated by Capital. The university as such is all too willing to provide "semantic fixes" of every sort.

Considered, then, as both form (of containment) and expression (of study and research), academia partially manifests itself as passivity before the "master signifier . . . a transcendent stock that distributes lack to all the elements of the chain . . . that channels all the break-flows into . . . the bar that delivers over all the depressive subjects to the great paranoiac king."[72]

The skeptical moment without reserve: we academics are buried alive in the tautologic form that professors are removable from consideration in an inventory of *problematic* social roles. The professoriat of the Nazi "period" (or that under McCarthy or the Stasi) was, after all, skilled at making its performance within the academic institution a nonevent. An "Academic Thing": the appearance of our disappearance.

I emphasize that institutionally based criticism is one where our practices and writings are too often identifications with "officiality" and set up an unsayable, socially constructed model of behavioral control. It "goes without saying" that *newcomers to the scene are enlistable* in our ongoing conflicts, meaning there are no newcomers. One is tempted to say that the feeling that language/speaking makes no difference to cultural regimes stems from the judgment that all wars and conflicts are received ones in which the professoriat acts as a depressant-narcotic. The idea of the Idea of "passing on tradition," in whatever form, is in fact a radical political model of indoctrination. This depression was isolated by Nietzsche as the "underside of culture" in his essay of 1872, *The Advantage and Disadvantage of History*, where the arbitrary substituted for the production of something necessary — the triumph of the Disembodied, Vampire Culture.

Finally, since no sector of academia is an *opposition willing to sacrifice itself on its privilege*, this standard prevails for us professors: to live well = to idealize = to displace. Bromides like Rorty's assertion that academic writing supports "only the dialogue" of "meaning in transformation" do no more than contribute to the myth of Academic Plenitude.

I remind myself that Clement Greenberg argued that modernity was also a triumph of academicism, accomplished by the latter's destruction of all but paper tigers (absence of controversy, the maintenance of cultural authority) and an empty virtuosity of appropriating experience(s), an evasion of any real clash against the powers that be. Academia was kitsch. Greenberg used this description to frame the situation of art and criticism within what he called "the midst of the decay." This notion of a "historical decline" in turn allowed him to project the "avant-garde" as that group conscious of this "decline" and malaise; modern art-consciousness is thus born with the "avant-garde." A version of the "idea of progress" was its optimistic ethos, whose ashes are still burning. The sense that *some aspect of life*, treated as culture, is inherently turned to the future is what this sense of "history," even as decline, carried over from the church (sect, cult, politic). Greenberg's pessimism concerning academia has turned out to be appropriate. I suggest that if there are bases for cultural optimism, about what to do in the face of the "systems" (global and otherwise), it is an optimism of a "nonhistorical materialism."

Such a "nonhistorical-materialist" criticism judges that cultural formations like the media or academic institutions are not themselves "historical." They are ways of becoming acceptably infantile when set against the fact that medicine, for example, will soon reach into the bloodstream and "degrease" arteries or that the oceans will be given over to the "harvesting of body parts." Indians are murdered, everywhere they are. Academia and "history" collaborate in make-believe.

One absolute rule, a rule that is truly not arbitrary: the "standard of living" matters. As this is the only constant of the dominant flows that accompany us as the new material systems quicken the pace or slow it, we live more and more in an obscure but certain future, a blurry present — instead of "history." In academia, political and cultural achievement is defined as the property of prestige, what prestige owns and loans out, prestige as the final money. Instead of giving our actions a "ground" as "history" did (to emancipate, to liberate, to penetrate, to discover, to leave behind), the rule of the "standard of living" — the matter of prestige — a priori enslaves us to a future which, after it happens, becomes itself determinate of more reactivity ("How did this come about?"). Not the triumph of the will, not the triumph of the people, not the triumph of science, not the triumph of knowledge, but the triumph of the *autopsy*.

At the close of the film *Dirty Harry*, the psychopath of "liberation" is blown up, and Harry throws his badge into the fetid waters of San Francisco Bay. He has made himself into a machine that shreds paper tigers, the legal papers, the social papers, the police papers, psychology papers. The badge hurled into the waters is neither a utopian (however reactionary) image nor one of flight — it cuts off from a resolving closure because Harry has left, deserting the senselessness of producing his kind of social use value.

2

The Academic Thing

Introductory Remarks

To summarize the main arguments so far: (1) articulations founded upon order-words sustain conceptual reintegrations; these maintain academic self-absorption as a whole; "historical criticism" or criticism "founded" upon "history" is an unnecessary recoding of one or more versions of the endemic myth that criticism equals enlightenment; (2) criticism would be better off if it were groundless *and* elicited meanings that tried to reach the limits of language rather than constantly producing the effect of *oversignification*, a concept related to what Lévi-Strauss meant by the academicism of the signifier. David Harvey closes *The Condition of Post-modernism* with the coda that since real-estate developers declare "post-modernism is over" it must mean "If this is where the developers are heading, can the philosophers and literary theorists be far behind?"; there is nothing really to say once the noose of irreversible orders (philosophers = crass ideologues) leaves no room for a countersignification. Left strategies concerning the function of critique are stalled: verbal depictions do not help "lead" or direct legitimate victims to the *means* of "righting" the wrongs that have occurred. In Deleuzian terms, critique remains stitched to the image of a "supersensible world," which is "the constitutive element of all fiction . . . a will to deny, to depreciate" so long as it continues to axiomatize what John Tagg properly, I think, calls "unlocated knowledge."[1] Academia is unable to "loosen" its grip on having the "last word" on cultural meanings.

In this chapter I argue for a materialist phrasing of the high university, and given what has been said in chapter 1, the writing of its criticism is bereft of familiar, comparative "historisemes." The high university is not treated as an effect of the scientific revolutions of the twentieth century or as a primary force of socialization, but as resonant with phrases that would disturb the self-image of its players, phrases undetermined but discussable — it is a question of presenting arguments whose genre is unclear. Here I move across philosophical, sociological, cognitive, and institutional "plateaus" in an attempt to put forth specific experiences that would make it impossible for high-university players to sustain their rigid dualist fantasy: the high university as "for" sense, value, truth (however defined) and "against" myth, ignorance, nonscience. By materialist I want to take up the issue of academia's institutionalization of *controls on one's right to work*, which are intrinsic to academic labor codes, and which are subject to the prerogatives of bureaucrats, including the development of "critical" ideas (and their relations).

One manner of beginning to speak of such topics is to acknowledge *semantic* codes of control that the professoriat has devised for protecting itself, its privileges. In his *Political Unconscious* (1981), Jameson tells his readers that there is an "impossibility of immanence" and that this is connected to a "dialectical reversal," which is "a painful 'decentering' of the consciousness of the individual subject." The construction of "dialectics" enables university work to turn outward, toward the largest of horizons, that of the totality of "history." It does not require much effort to notice that "dialectics" thereby has the function of providing an *actual* bracketing of university machinations, a point that remains repressed in Jameson's idealist rendering of the university as a neutral territory of research production. (It is unthinkable that "dialectics" is itself a phrasing of repression).[2] Jameson recodes an academic mode of displacement, for it *saves Hegelianism* as the control code of criticism, but at the very real "price" of preserving institutional formations. The actants of theory and hope and reconciliation are salvaged, while it is made unmentionable that academic production might be connected to an overall dissolution of the social field.[3]

So when Jameson exhorts his readers to "name the system" and "dramatize issues" as purposes of cultural criticism, as he does in *Postmodernism* (1990), this is also an acceptance of inactivity, the success of "dialectics" as omission of discussing high-university production. He places the university "in the trough" (between national and global Capital, whose "new international proletariat" will "reemerge"), generalizes from an interpretant of an existing player-relation ("trough" = descent of the socialist idea), and thus returns his readers to the destiny of criticism (ensuring that concepts of "postmodernism" are screened through Hegelianism). "In the trough," then, effects a hyperreduction of the university: its future as mediation is assumed. Nietzsche had the nerve to name this ethos, this "haughtiness which goes with knowledge . . . which shrouds the eyes and senses of man in a blinding fog, therefore deceives him about the value of existence by carrying in itself the most flattering evaluation of knowledge itself." Its most universal effect is deception.[4]

What follows is a critique of the *repression of immediacy*, to bring forth some determinations of the high university through which readers can think the university not as mediation but as a contested formation.

Three myths: the liberal one of an education that is personal and universal but not in contradiction to economic self-interest; the left-progressive one that the functions of "criticism" prepare the way for political resolutions of social contradictions; the conservative phantom of a "natural" stratum untouched by distorting socializations. If "happy periods" of "history" are as rare as Hegel — who claimed to know and who said they are — "periods" of successful "learning" or education must be like Bataille's description of "mites in the presence of an acetylene torch."

But where to start a contemporary presentation of academic work that enables one to describe its double binds and traps, its forceful illusions, as well as its stimulations, excesses, and entrapments, with as little "make-believe" as possible, and without comforting delusions about one's "scientific credibility"? And isn't a "starting point" itself mythical? As Mary Carpenter points out, even the most "open" model of high-university practices — Derrida's analysis of the university as divided between memorizing "tradition" and receptivity to "what is not known to any knowledge" — is insupportable in framing a model, since it recodes a dualist numbering of sides.[5]

My proposal is to engage these topics by presenting experiences (usually reduced to the personal and subjective, even if documented) as conceptualizations of a transpolitical control of academic *work*, as micromodels (but with range, one hopes) of control (which is legion, the many names of subjection). The analytic descriptions that follow are neither a diagnosis with attending prognosis nor a "cognitive tracing" (a k a resolution, in the last instance, of cultural issues to class consciousness); they are *particularizations*, not generalizations, and as this formation they invite not a program, but more phrases. The events and relations described are not distilled from memories of experiences cast into written form as the narration of settling "scores," of a political accountancy; they defy politicization insofar as they exert an energy to actively pass into what Lyotard calls the phrasing "whether this experience was a component of the situation in question." Did it happen? What matters is that other than going players are invited to *say more* about the high university. Perhaps, and in keeping with Nietzschean "meddles," one can say that what follows is "like" an "afterstrike" in one's emotions, a transformation of *ressentiment*. The contours of argumentation without foundational subjectivity or an objectified continuum are, then, not speculative or meditational, but "maximized" descriptions that open onto (again in Lyotard's words) a "free field open to the reflective judgment's capability to go beyond the boundaries of sensible experience."[6] This movement toward a "new competence," this nonteleologic gathering of speech, is not inspired by "history" and "lesson" but by a "differend," which is here worth citing in Lyotard's theorization:

> The differend is the unstable state and instant of language wherein something which must be able to be put into phrases cannot yet be . . . a feeling. . . . a lot of searching must be done to find new rules for forming and linking phrases that are able to express the differend disclosed by the feeling. . . . In the differend, something "asks" to be put into phrases, and suffers from the wrong of not being able to be put into phrases right away. . . . what remains to be phrased exceeds what they can presently phrase, and . . . they must be allowed to institute idioms which do not yet exist.[7]

Control Codes, Affirmative Action

It is widely believed that the effects of affirmative action on American academic institutions promoted a different arrangement at those institutions. It is often assumed, for example, that affirmative action "opened" various "doors" and so was (is) an instrument of enlightenment, one that initiated a setting aside of racism and sexism in a modernizing of the university. The adoption of legally mandated affirmative action programs at some colleges during and since the 1970s fit very nicely with a social myth: knowledge was not to get "ahead" of its social base. But this inoculative gesture of acknowledging an "evil" (here, sexism) enabled the university to have its ordinary selection practices elude public inquiry.

In the late 1970s public or private "research" universities *used* affirmative action in order to expand the inflow of monies; with affirmative action came new positions, which in turn required various support systems (some academic groups claim that bureaucratization of American institutions has doubled since the mid-1970s). Expansion steamrolled its detractors, since those who oppose the high university's becoming more enlightened found themselves devoid of arguments. The important point is that neither an "antiscientific" valuation (rendered impossible by its being associated with antihumanity) nor a "nonscientific" one could receive legitimation from the university's owners and managers — trustees, regents, legislatures, sometimes connected to the people/state axis, sometimes only to research or pedagogy or training. Affirmative action was, to put it as strongly as possible, a *scientifically* underwritten codification. That is, within "research" institutions, affirmative action became a force in the narrative trajectory of an open society, itself a variant on the idea of progress; this latter superconcept validated the existing players, connecting them not with their "history" but with the positive future to come.

Situation: all through the late 1970s, funding by the Mellon Foundation generated academic "posts" that served as tests or site-specific cultural "trial balloons" prior to institutions (universities) granting permanent funding for these "posts" (or "lines" in academese). Affirmative action required that such posts be advertised or "posted" (in the older sense of "posted to") in ways that would encourage applicants who had been historically excluded. At _____ University (1976), 112 candidates applied for a position (in an area of cultural and intellectual "history") and each of them was subject to the provisions of a Consent Decree that the university had recently concluded with the State of _____. Here are the intentions of the decree, whose encoding is presented as a series of order-words, in the sense discussed in chapter 1:

> (1) The Consent Decree entered into by _____ University is designed to move toward full utilization of women. . . .
> (2) While the Decree enables departments to maintain autonomy, it requires affirmative action to be exercised on behalf of women faculty.
> (3) This affirmative action gives preference to women of equal qualification over men in the areas of hiring, contract renewal, promotion and tenure.[8]

The "full utilization" of lexia 1 announces the reconfirmation of the universality of labor, that women are a "reserve" of labor; as not-used, they have not been able to labor, and this raises the sense of a prior blockage, which is here being removed. Lexia 1 is surgical. This seme of industrial efficiency encodes the idea that women who have not been used have been exploited; this exploitation is set aside by, first, an affirmation that the legal decree is not negative (as affirmed, "autonomy" is thereby not placed in opposition to the decree); the force of "exercised" and "gives preference to" is then linked to the affirmation of women threaded to a law that is itself not negative (no one will be harmed; past suppression will be made "good"). Order is proclaimed.

Hence affirmative action expresses a "shock" of enlightenment, which happens all at once, but "gives preference to" what is "equal" is an immediate contradiction, which is overriden by the rush of violence that must at once suppress the illegality of discrimination. Lexia 2 anticipates objections from what would be a conservative academic faction, but suspends them: the sense of "while" in the first part, its temporality of inclusiveness, absorbs autonomy, replacing it by this law. Autonomy — of selection, of ranking, of promotion, of responsibility, and of evasion — is something that can go on "while" affirmative action requires a bureaucracy and so indexes enforcement and responsibility (in fact the consent decree called for an extensive apparatus, which it sanctified as an "overseeing" of the court's legal provisions).

This full and exuberant positivity is brought to a halt, however, by the second contradiction, that of lexia 3; here is a joint or place where, as Lyotard has suggested in *The Differend*, the incommensurable rules of phrase-genres make their power felt: for to "give preference to women of equal qualification" over men jams one's capacity to affirm "equality," so that the very firing of the verb is already the outline of a result (a legal fait accompli), that of injustice. This power of bringing about results is shattering because to "give preference" to what is of "equal qualification" produces the not-equal. Ranking what is equal makes them not-equal: what carries the marking of this differentiation has thus already been judged superior to the equals. What is this superiority? The law? It is violent, whatever its name.

"Preference" instantiates a particular future, but it affirms the claims of women by separating women from "minority" and all other suppressed groups (e.g., women of color, men of color). So while it is directed against men regardless of their color, the consent decree is also illuminating insofar as it does not establish a legal relation between the previously excluded white female and persons of color. This consent decree, from 1976, was to cover "any complaints of discrimination raised by current or prospective women faculty members." Interestingly, its only reference to another group occurs in phrasing that shifts the "burden of proof" as to one's qualification to work onto white males:

> (4) If the department recommends a man in preference to a woman . . .
> the selected candidate must be demonstrated to be better qualified than
> any woman or other protected group member.

I shall come back to this complement to lexia 2's de-equalizing, but lexia 4 overcodes: the de-equalization of "preference" between those who are equal here gives way to a demand that men — of any ethnic group — must be "better than" women, and so the positive is really negative (another figure of the nondialectic of negativity — or the casting of experience into the abyss of not-possible). The being of men is doubly articulated: once as "not preferred" and again, in the last instance, as having to be better.

Now let me add some further qualifications of this situation. The consent decree affected me inasmuch as I was the standing academic. The "post" I occupied was irregular; my contract ran for two years, and it was to become a permanent "line" on the university's budget (that is, a permanent "post"). The Mellon Foundation's initial funding for the position enabled the university to update its curricula, which occurred simultaneously with the extension of "media" knowledges, apparent in the popularity of Structuralism, the dominant intellectual discourse of the period. It was widely projected by academics that one form or another of Structuralist "medicine" would prevent "higher" education in America from succumbing to the larger processes of the "dumbing-down" that had already taken place through the media and other channels.

Affirmative action coincided with this episodic intensification of academic expansion, the latter legitimized by scientific narratives. Academic officers formed a national "phalanx" in demanding support from the federal government and state legislatures for this "rescientization" projected onto Structuralism. Such an increase in positions within the humanities and social-science faculties was one with their "scienticization," whether it took the form of, say, statistical work in urbanism or E. P. Thompson's description of the processes of "class conflict" which academicized English Marxism in the United States (how workers had resisted Capital despite themselves). Such "scientization" stopped at language itself. The notion that language in and of itself was the object of extreme skepticism, that neither the poetic nor the referential "poles" were conceptually "stable," did not dislodge the rhetorical model that justified the "new humanities" application of Structuralism; in the area of critical theory, Marx and Freud were presented as the negation of intuitive models of the self, ideological notions of the social, and so on. The tenured or regular faculty censored the critique of language via distribution and allocation of academic "posts," not by blocking every representation of its critique. At _____ University it was not uncommon for historians to retreat to terrorism when confronted with an "aberrant" reading of, say, Dostoyevsky: one could hear anger directed at Deleuze and Guattari (it is often forgotten that Lacanism was rejected for a long time, that is, until feminist critiques revived psychoanalysis) for suggesting that Dostoyevsky's writings were not a reaction to the insanity of Russia (psychotic literature reflects). In short, the academic protocol of sustaining an image of openness undercut explicit reactionary formations; the demon of theory was tamed as soon as it was "scientized," since one of its essential predicates was the narrowness of its audience.

_____ University's faculty was some eighty percent tenured, but performed fifty percent or less of the teaching — the difference made up by hiring a part-time faculty. The mythology of research permeated the university, giving the lie to its advertising of a "quality undergraduate education," since the least "scientized" instructors carried such a disproportionate burden of classroom instruction. This is undoubtedly a global fact of Mandarin education.

The irresistible coding whose advantage made the lawsuit that produced the consent decree in the first place was that of *tenure*, a premodern, cultural-economic overlaying of ownership and obligation-to-perform, which has been translated, as it were, into a property right; the legal status of tenure protects its holder from loss of post. Tenure is the *legal form* of knowledge production; it is granted, first, as an economic position when the funds for a "post" are made a permanent budget "line" and, second, when a faculty ranks and selects from a list of contenders. Being given tenure by one's superiors is to receive a *place* through which an income sustains acts such as "research" and "instruction," the number of which is regulated and controlled by the "central" administration (the Academic Officer Corps); the latter is the "inside," which controls a particular institution's *capacity* to make variations (in what is taught, which extradisciplinary "methods" are worth pursuing, etc.). This bureaucracy is hardly a social mediation of knowledge since, most frequently, the academic officers themselves first enter the university as tenured instructors. Articulated by the prerogatives of deans and provosts, who ensure the containment of rebellion from the ranks (the Teaching Corps), there is a horrific sadness about the controlled and private competition for academic posts. There isn't a faculty in the United States that offers resistance to its Officer Corps and bureaucratic "center" (e.g., legislature); academic discourse at times is where the most elementary processes of concept formation are *dependent* upon one's loyalty to an institution. As Gayatri Spivak notes in her discussion of the creation and reproduction of an academic "subject of true knowledge" (the university narrativized in the shape of a helper to society), we can say that this Officer Corps ensures that the university will not be contaminated by acts of reading that undermine its own consistency.[9] There will be no excess of critique that removes the rationalizations and mythifications responsible for our evasions. The institution called academe will not contribute to the problematizing of its own practices. As one ascends its "chain of command" (e.g., joins oversight committees in regulating other groupings), it is assumed that the combination of increased economic integrative dependency and cultural identity (one has an image to keep up) will reinforce the qualities of liberal conservatism or conservative Marxism or . . .

Affirmative action, then, was another stake raised in the war for tenure; as a constant subsidy for future work — a promissory note — a legal and economic granting of "research" time, affirmative action for tenurability thus joined with the myth of an unending social "good" of knowledge, determined in a capitalist system by a version of the Invisible Hand: academic writing has an absolutely guaranteed future, even if its audience equals itself. In this regard, it is not going too far to insist that the American research university has nearly canceled acts of intense reading, "close reading" as it is sometimes called, seen as far too threatening to various academicisms of the signifier. Indeed, many search committees are internally set up by using the criteria of one's *being collegial* having superior value to one's writings being interesting; many academics are in fact incapable of performing intellectual judgments on writings judged "too difficult." Thus the now infamous procedure of "outside review" — an Other whose "reading" of someone's tenure dossier (a k a writings) guarantees "objectivity." Collegiality and criticism are thus separated at the outset. Tenure dossiers can be assembled that are no more than a pastiche of self-interested quotations: outsiders would gasp at the audacious moves of an academe that shows this will to adapt, this "will to power" of its "disturbing ground" of reactivity, where "commentary" or "hermeneutics" or an empty "intervention" fill its task "to the brim" (*pace* Roland Barthes). What is academic determination but force denying force, driven by the reactive negativity of displacing what would be effective continuities, those not necessarily linear but at least differential? How, in short, is one to assume "the position of rationality" in the face of the academic machine, which hates anything of the vitalistic, and praises the unity of the body and identity?[10] In Deleuzian terms, tenure is one of those "reactive specializations, expressions of one or another reactive forces . . . consciousness sees the organism from its own viewpoint . . . from the petty side . . . [belief] in the false consequence of a final state."[11]

In cultural terms: the American system supposes that the faculty is first "avant-garde" in terms of "breakthroughs" of research, which includes model building (e.g., for statistical theory) as well as methodological innovations (e.g., Kuhn's redescription of "doing science"), and is a benevolent transmission of similar, past, "avant-garde" knowledges. Research and meaning, the body and desire, define a machine of synthesis, but which is riddled with exclusions: it scans for warnings of its becoming useless, superfluous. The seeming anachronism or premodernity of tenure dissolves when one considers that it gives *currency* to knowledge: what is taught now has an exchange value (history, tradition, craft, etc.) and a use value that is not only "intact" at the time of instruction, but is "good for" an indeterminate future.[12] Thus tenure sets up a moment of the suspense of Capital within itself: it is time for exchange that is taken out of exchange. Tenure should have been used by its holders to *expand* differences from and to Capital; instead, it becomes another bureaucratization of modern critical knowledges: their production and canonic transmission are co-coded. The professoriat teaches — information, models, methodologies, theories, axioms, facts, testings, and probings of the same — to an audience that is an actant of the clever; we teach within an "ambience" (the term is Baudrillard's) for socialized minds, which are already a "kind of ciphering strip, a coding and decoding tape, a tape recording magnetized with tape."[13] In other words, we talk to those who also wish to become tenured.

_____ University's history department, which had passed on offering Michel Foucault a tenurable position in the mid-1960s, had exactly twenty-one FTEs, which are that number of funded, tenured, full-time "posts," or the going translation of "knowledge" into *economic* slots that comprise the core of the tenure system. At any given moment in any given department, the FTE number signifies the *minimum of "tested" knowledge*, what de Certeau has called the plateau of the "technical practice" of a scientized social order, a minimum that governs the "ordinary" right to expand. For example, this department had six areas of American history "covered," but one in Near East, and so on. FTE is also the form of a budgetary governance. The expansion and contraction of FTEs, given changes in the larger politicocognitive relay, arrive at the classroom at the end of a series of administrative decisions that stabilize the system as a whole. Each "post" is remarkably *overterritorialized*, for players so "posted" can recode or reterritorialize (that is, are equipped with the right knowledge machines for deciding what to study, a Platonic echo from the immemoriality of control).

The history department at _____ University was ordered by this consent decree to rectify its sexism, leaving untouched (or deferring) the issue of race. A "post" in European intellectual and cultural history was designated for a regular FTE; assurances were given that an utterly "gender-blind" national search would take place. History faculty spoke of their autonomy from the administration's bind of having to satisfy the courts while they omitted discussion of conflicts of interest since a good number were themselves administrators and professors. The question of whether any existing faculty would be sacrificed to fulfill the legal obligation of the university was not raised. In essence, and in accordance with what was required by the recently ascendant Marx-Freud synthesis, which absolutized the present as a place for the enactment of the return of the repressed, the past was given a claim on the future and the question of present unfairness was washed away: the Bakke case and everything else about "counteraffirmative action" was disposed of by "progressives" in the *modern* sense of the term, that is, by those possessing the authority of history. One was not allowed to discuss the attendant codifications of affirmative action; one was bolted to the semantic universe of positive and negative in which affirmative action — for while women only — was portrayed as the negation of the negation: questions of ethnicity and color were banned. And so was any systematic critique of the *rhetorics of study* — the putting forward of academically coded "needs" as necessary for some program or other of social rationalization. The passive-aggressive confirmation of identity was made unmentionable. Questions as to transformation — how one can lose oneself in an interesting way by means of knowledge — were rendered entirely unsayable.

The legal rule of affirmative action's quotas and timetables was decried by many faculty as a violation of their power to select, but this "violation" did not affect the larger myth formation of an autonomous "learning process," which would continue independently of this legal arrangement. Dependency upon the "officers" for grants and benevolent committee assignments or reduced teaching loads is unsuitable for the staging of potentially uncontrolled arguments about selection, autonomy, what are actual "learning processes," and so on. It was a Kafkaesque victory: an exhausting and depressing familiarity immediately set in, the kind that accompanies constant and unrelenting punishment associated with "chains of tormented mankind . . . made out of red tape."

So in April 1977, with the consent decree in place, the history department at _____ University established a search committee for a "modern intellectual historian," the latter defined by memorandum to mean

(5) a preference for someone interested in the main philosophic or ideological movements of the nineteenth and twentieth centuries.

Soon after, a meeting of that committee took up some of the emerging paranoia in relation to the autonomy of selection, this most privileged "right" of academics:

(6) Various members of the department expressed alarm over the trend to reveal to candidates the names of those serving on department committees.

(7) Judging the appropriateness of promotions, reappointments or tenure.

(8) It appears that the department could be coerced into making such revelations by the actions of other departments.[14]

These lexias are expressions of paranoiac loss: they reiterate something already ("trend") picked up by thinking machines that are trained to warn, the switching on of territorial protection. "Appropriateness" opens onto a supercultural space, an assemblage whose acts ("promotions") are obviously of the law, but not identical with it. Hence lexia 8 with its quality of criminality (subconnotations: violence, perversity) is not enough: what is at stake is the past, the negative precedence of the consent decree itself. The decree might make an autonomous future impossible. The machine that here warns also suggests a "need" for repair: in its weakened condition, the "could be" of lexia 8 is empty enough to allow for various scenaric futures. The "past weighs down," said Marx from a million worlds ago: *that* specific dread — the past prevents the future from happening — is recoded here by this small group of professors within a fractal space of instruction. The most basic acts of intellectual expression were such that they were immediately reducible to concerns of loss of control; the charges brought against the university by the women who generated the consent decree dissolved into what one could call a Lacanian syndrome: a proliferation of sentences pronouncing the "lack of" or "need for," which were at once preparatory and "reflective" of this loss of "mastery" and control.

Once the national search for the position began, the department's legal dilemma was rendered by Professor R., who was an administrative/academic dean, as well as a member of the search committee. Two months into it, he said that the search was proceeding according to the legal, scientific, and ethical guidelines — affirmative action procedures were followed and had not destroyed the paramount importance of "merit," that is, that no woman hired would be less scientific and professional than a male. "But ambiguities remain," he said, of such magnitude that he feared

(10) . . . the obscurity of the wording [of the decree] . . . may lead to grave misunderstandings. . . .

Professor R., who as an American official in postwar Germany had participated in the denazification of German professionals, presented this scenario:

(11) Suppose ten members of the department vote for Mr. Y and nine (eight? seven?) vote for Mrs. X, does that mean that Mrs. X is or is not equally qualified?

(12) Let's add another variable. . . . How should we in the future weigh the views of the specialists against the views of those in a different field when we are trying to weigh equality of qualifications?[15]

The semantics of "to weigh equality" would require too extensive an analysis here, but it is worth noting that the phrase evokes an agrarian seme ("weigh") combined with an abstraction, so it's a messy concept from any inception. It of course raises again the scientific mythos — of the "expert" whose evaluation may or may not be reliable. Lexias 11 and 12 raise the myth of a struggle: the "weighing" of supposed incomparables. This formation of defensive warning had been precipitated by the hiring of a white male for a position in French history, over the written anxieties of the president of the university, who warned the department of possible court sanctions. The leadership of the university was adamant about enforcing the decree: sexism was interfering with scientistic myths. The chairman of the department protested this "intervention" of the university president in the hiring process.[16]

By mid-March 1978, the search committee condensed ninety-two applicants — seventy-three men and nineteen women had applied — to six men and six women (in 1992 numbers, fifty-four percent of the candidates would be women). In a memorandum of March 20, 1978, the search committee indicated that it had reduced those finalists to a list of five — three women and two men. The nonexistence of minority applications did not require discussion. Ominously, this same memorandum stated that

(13) The committee has made no attempt to rank-order these five candidates whose approaches to intellectual history range from the highly theoretical to the heavily contextual.[17]

This is quite untraditional and radical, although not in terms that are ultimately pleasing to the self-image of a university department. The tags "highly theoretical" and "heavily contextual" are the lazy way of repeating the equational logic where "theory" is abstract and "heavily contextual" equals archival, factual. But "no attempt to rank-order" effectuates the leap from selection processes that are "normal" to a situation that is not normal: the purpose of a search committee was to "rank-order" in the first place. The result of a failed search is presented in terms that do not present the reality. "No attempt to rank-order" thus introduces suspension of the determining order-word. "No attempt" indicates that a nullification of argumentation had occurred; the everyday bureaucratic processes of selection pass under another law.

Not ranking the finalists meant that the search committee could not render a judgment on what the candidates tried to say in their writings or public lectures. That in itself is telling in a system that demands some form of a final interpretant (Peirce) that would prevent the a- or designification of normal understanding. One of the most elementary cultural clichés about historians is their notoriety in celebrating the myth of a common language (is this not their own "final solution" of the problematics of social argumentation?). Here are some presentations about which the evaluative code was in such perplexity. One candidate's texts showed a

(14) relatively sophisticated narrative framework . . . [but] there are all kinds of sociology of knowledge possibilities that [   ] neglects. . . . [   ] should say more . . . does not have the maturity of. . . . If [   ] makes the short list, it should be toward the bottom.

To "neglect" and to not "say enough" carry the negative metaphysics of evaluation; the evaluator, Professor G., merely reduces unsayable criteria — what he would desire of himself — to mythemes. This echo of "this person has not done what I would have done" is passive-aggressive narcissism; given the academic "investment" in signs of objectivity, lexia 14 might be thought of as a weapon: "my wishes = reality." Another candidate, from the same notes, writing on Hegel, is said to have done an "enormous labor of research and conceptualization on the background to Hegel's thought," that is, has performed a "good job" in the garden of establishing a "context" (*the* most undefinable of those "common terms" so loved by historians), and so receives affirmation:

(15) . . . this is really a person of promise . . . Despite various difficulties and uncertainties, a strong candidate.

Lexias 14 and 15 are obscenely typical: writings that blocked the dreaded "takeover by theory" were taken as a positive sign of "historical consciousness," the historian naively made to represent an Ideal Sociology (i.e., thinking without thoughts). Another candidate had really sinned by invoking too much language, which did not add up to a smooth narrative:

(16) . . . not terribly convincing . . . only marginally qualified (if at all) to teach _____ University students.

In the spirit of Barthes's *Mythologies*, one would want to know who this professor "thought" those students were.

These enunciations represent various *tests* removed from *contestability* — such evaluations are a language beyond language, connected to an oxymoronic but also despotic setup: these assertive negations and affirmations are judgments impossible to reconstruct in terms of their "rationality," since their formation is ruled by unsayables. They are a defeat of language *in a system that says it is founded upon it.* I am tempted to say that one is dealing with a politicocultural state machine directed at language, a mode of self-identity whose discursive assemblage is that of a regime in the protection of the institution, and which effectively reduces judgment to tautology. "We are giving the orders." Two models are readily apparent. On the one hand, the "classical" industrial order provided the model of a test in which subjects are *products* "passed" on (or not): an evaluation committee need only recognize certain signs — letters of recommendation scanned for the current prestige value of their authors, a candidate's written work viewed as more than competent, or satisfaction of that mysterious power called "collegiality," which amounts to appearing to possess signs of future success — this Order at once a process of developing "subjects" and the systematic removal of uncontrollable "spirit." The industrial model of "quality control" holds this sphere together. Which perforce makes for strategic shifts between sign-regimes: at different times a Positivism, a Marxism is called for.

But on the other hand, the evaluations have built into them a second model, something more fundamental than such "product control," what Baudrillard has called the "precession of the model," an a priori determinism stemming from the pressure of the reduction of the future to present codes. In the context under discussion, the signs are more real than abilities, talents, and so on, so that one is deemed "hirable" only if signifiers are present that enhance the status and/or exchange value of the department or relevant academic sector. This "spiraling" of *sign-value* is now frequent — one of its forms is the "superstar" phenomenon. This mode is projected as a replacement for the Western Mandarinism that was founded on the esoterica of knowledge. What matters today are "players" whose texts enable the administrative sector to thicken its image/exchange identity, the increase of value imputed directly to the academic institution itself. In terms that are harsh but perhaps not untrue, Charles Levin has called this the "discursively positioned subject . . . the perfect material for a neodisciplinary exterminist society." What is written is thereby prepared for its resurrection as sign, the object itself exterminated by the increase or decrease in sign-value. To be avoided is the concoction of "shaky" meanings.[18] In the situation given here, the candidates only appeared and disappeared as the power of language commanded them to or not, these discursively positioned "candidates" becoming subjects of what Deleuze and Guattari call a *signifying semiotic,* where "overcoding is fully effectuated by the signifier . . . uniformity of enunciation . . . control over statements in a regime of circularity . . . redundant and perpetual referral from sign to sign." Subjective states and states of subjection that "spin toward black holes."[19]

The public lecture was the last test, after which one male (me) and one of the three women remained; at which point, the recommendation of lexia 13, the nonordering, issued forth a sort of completion in the following command. The committee reported to the history department that it had

(17) voted to eliminate all active candidates except Cohen and _____. The committee decided to recommend both for consideration without rank-ordering them.

(18) The committee has also kept in reserve one inactive candidate in circumstances which will be explained later.[20]

The extraordinary circumstances of the search had resulted in *stalemate*; this line continues the dread of loss of autonomy (lexia 8). Lexia 18 with its reference to an "untested" candidate was provocational and degrading to both of the finalists; they, after all, had risked quite a lot (e.g., to not receive the "post" becomes, for committees at other institutions, an active disqualification). The by then normalization of a highly contested situation was itself placed in an extraordinary mode — another "search" had taken place, evoked by the ominous sense of "in reserve," which suggests an "along with," "alongside," a "next to," all of which coagulate around a secret academic committee.

A vote was called and Cohen received nine of fourteen votes cast. His candidacy was forwarded to the administration for the requisite approval by the school's affirmative-action officer and provost. His candidacy was immediately contested by the provost and the university president, who forwarded a letter to the chair of the history department stating that the search had been "impeccably" conducted but that they were not persuaded of differences from which they could conclude that a suspension of the consent decree was allowable.

The phrase-regimen (Lyotard) of *drawing conclusions* always involves a kind of closure; it forces closure, and does so as a recoding of politics, where politics comes to equal, as perhaps it always must, the form of expediency. Everything occurred according to the "schedule" of an academic institution's displacement of its own rules.

The university as a safe place was maintained, even enhanced, by so much administrative concern. What is at stake is undoubtedly the fusion of some cultural and economic territorial links, particularly those of sign-value (university = rationality) and production as such (expansion of departments); for since the university must make *attractive* "alternatives" to the reigning social practices, it must, for example, promote canon formation *and* a legal "activism" *and* a "critical legal studies" and much more, but encoded (always?) in an overcoding, which I would provisionally describe as *variations of integration as changes in subjectivity.* Male/female did not — could not — dislodge the overall *strategic value of the university* itself, which, in Paul Virilio's terms, was preserved as a power "to morally and physically deny the adversary the chance to rework his hypotheses . . . to launch an enterprise . . . this kind of expansion is the model for any monopoly, seeking less the accumulation of wealth than expediency."[21] Which is to say that the hiring of the woman in this situation helped to salvage an overall Positivism, evoked in the following description by Lyotard:

> The technocrats declare that they cannot trust what society designates as its needs; they "know" that society cannot know its own since they are not variables independent of the new technologies. . . . What their arrogance means is that they identify themselves with the social system conceived as a totality in quest of its most performative unity possible.[22]

Women were integrated but, in short, the porosity of a discipline such as "history" required this becoming-insider to confirm the larger resocialization of the high university as immersion in value-production, the didactics of information, and role, *even demanding criticism and theory.* The expulsion of practices of "paradox" and experimentation with form meant that the university officers supported moving away from the very scientific rationalizations their own language required and demanded the kind of negative identity associated with theology.[23]

The difficulty of raising questions of "transformation" relates to its impossibility; we imagine another system through the cultural contours and delineations of existing contradictions, which is to say that we are dealing with a "zero-sum cultural game," or, better, we are in a genuine quagmire, a quicksand situated entirely within the cultural. The academic system should lose its privileges and normativities, but who is going to carry this out since outsiders are defined as not qualified and the oppositional players are like junkies, overcoded by their repetition of the politics of power and exclusion? Aren't some major academic practices necessarily strapped to a narcissistic oblivion, which always expresses itself as thought falling back on what it will not think? Here the "framing" or setup of learning rests on privileges that elbow out new players in the concoction of solutions.

A letter sent by the history department chair was received:

(19) The department made you its first choice.

(20) The administration therefore chose to overrule us on the grounds of affirmative action.

(21) We protested.

(22) The department majority then concluded that it could not do anything more, in the way of a regular appointment, on your behalf.[24]

There was a consensus that "quality" and "autonomy" had not been defiled. The Virgin of Learning appeared in the sky — I am not referring to the woman who received the position, who was a person of responsibility. The threading of assertion, the persistence of multiple varieties of identity, the court decree (given the statistical exclusions practiced against women), the shift to social history as a discipline in its own right, the demand that the successful candidate "relieve," as one department member put it, the "excessive" teaching load of the subfield of instruction in modern European field areas, ensured that controlled, safe, malleable men would find women of the same type — it was, as an exchange of one gender for another, the *minimum change* with the maximum sign-value. This would accommodate existing players; hence the court decree was an irresistible move for the institution.

Seven years later, I applied for a position in another department at _____, encouraged by former colleagues. During the interview I was asked by a white female, whom I will call Professor Groan, if I believed in and accepted "affirmative action." Sent into space aboard this piece of libidinal academic surplus hate, I was swept up in what Greimas has called "practical diffusion in a mythical manifestation," the meaning of which is partially found in considering acts of intellectual targeting: an event where everything is overdetermined, the revisions operative in rationalizing the "right to exclude" and control. This discursive assault achieved thereby an axiological qualification: if a male and a female are in conflict within the university, the male is antifemale by virtue of being in that conflict. Between the pseudolegalism of military/academic fusions and the ease with which antifeminism can be charged, the academic system has succeeded in passing into normal politics the *unprotected* white male as target, the suppression of conflict between white females and people of color, and ceaseless antagonism between people of color for what is left over.

Pseudolegalism and Cultural Exclusions: An Art School Context (1985–86)

In 1985, while teaching at an arts institute in the Los Angeles area, I was asked to serve on a grievance panel convoked at the request of a faculty member in another department. Involved was a contract dispute between a dean of the School of Art, Ms. C., and a faculty member, hereafter G. The latter, at a local restaurant, had received warning a year or so earlier, which now resulted in nonrenewal of his contract. The "charge" was alleged aggression and disrespect toward his colleagues.

G. was not fired, he was not renewed. The finesse of the difference lies in the consequence: the former invokes a "show cause" required of employers, whereas the latter is separated from similar legal requirements. Nonrenewal, often characterized through the term "special contract," pertains to what are called "program changes" and the like, where academic "posts" are staked out as temporary, subject to withdrawal. G.'s case fell under the category of "not renewed" because his length of service was not sufficient to require more extensive criteria of discharge. These kinds of "special-contract posts" vary from institution to institution according to various speeds: lead time demanded by legislatures before professors are made permanent; budgetary restraints; a new dean employing an old friend; someone not working out because of professional incompatibilities. Nationally, the percentage of each department's budget for nonrenewable contracts varies from roughly fifteen percent to nearly seventy-five percent; the "higher" the institution, the greater the (supposed) security of employment. Prestige and science merge in the permanency of FTEs. Even in a discipline that is merely protoscientific, as in most English departments, prestige value receives a scientized plus from exchange value. A document from a large public university (Fall 1990) shows that a history department with twenty or so European FTEs managed to offer a total of four upper-division lecture courses, that is, courses not ordinarily professional.[25] This starving of general education is a normal practice; the giving over of undergraduate education to the most overworked sector is borrowed from the practices of the laboratory sciences.

G.'s nonrenewal was unbound to most explanatory requirements; the act of severance was attached to a minimal level of explanation and so operated very closely to the structure of language/violence analyzed by Elaine Scarry in her *The Body in Pain*. At institutions where tenure is nonexistent or exceptional, nonrenewal entails nonrecourse, an instantaneous becoming *decoded*, since the affected individual literally disappears from the institution.

G. filed a grievance with the school's Academic Council, the sole recourse for faculty members. He claimed that he had been "dismissed by the Art Department for insufficient grounds and without proper notice."[26] The Dean of Art vigorously resisted discussing any such "grounds." G. stressed that such "grounds" (thus accumulates the rhetoric of burial, the rhetoric of responsibility already a death) had been described to him by the art school's program director: "whether I respected my colleagues."[27] The Academic Council convened an Appeal Commission after listening to the Dean of Art's refusal to specify. The administration, speaking through its provost, whose job is to monitor the academic performance of an institution's faculty, insisted on the legality of nonrenewal and something called a "no-cause contract" ("special contract") — this "screening" performed by institutions over a course of years (which I described earlier). Hence the law was simply affirmed: the administration intimated that G.'s nonrenewal did not generate a challenge or counterclaim to its authority. This is close to what Lyotard, in *The Differend*, terms the "sign of an incommensurability between the normative phrase and all others," where the phrasing of statements of authorization reigns.[28] Such is a modality of *precedence*, which indicates that the only "real" stakes are those of the future, in constant challenge from current players' appropriations of the past or radical destructuring of what the going players think is "at stake."

The positions and the politics of the School of Art were aligned so that an economically conservative (budget = social control) but liberal aesthetic of the administration ("thrill me," was the president's motto) and a "revolutionary" Dean of Art — who claimed to be a "tribune of history" (to speak for lesbians, socialists, and feminists, and for whom modernism was a step in the bourgeois destruction of the working classes) — were in agreement that a *radical* and "difficult" and "elitist" painter, G., was guilty of nihilism in particular because he did not affirm the discourse of market-driven social critique (i.e., did not assent to power plays masking as utopian projections). One potent context here was the contention over modern art, particularly since so many trends of it had *become discursified, become sociology*. As Charles Levin suggests, it had acquired the function of "reassurance" (identity), wherein critical languages of art were subject to a rather witless situation in which "devaluations chase after idealizations." Descriptions riddled with one myth after another made it appear that the objects themselves warranted the various languages of criticism; G. objected to what he argued was the inept production of criticism that was little more than a political overcoming of objects, and objects that tried to legitimize themselves in one or another discourse of the self-same critical discourses.[29] In particular, there was the notion that by means of citationally pure critique (quoting the "right" people "on the left") and the invocation of transcendental use value (critique = rationality), art objects could themselves possess use, give use, render themselves useful — but the way to do this was to purge such objects of everything but their political effects. G. objected to any theory that rationalized the redundant preparation or "targeting" of language and consciousness; the dean, on the other hand, had no use for language unless it was safely on the territory of denunciation of pleasure.

The context, in other words, of an arts education was vastly more *overcoded* in terms of so-called worldly politics and enormously *undercoded* in terms of professional rules of conduct. G., taking off from what are sometimes called high-modernist movements (Russian Formalism, Deconstruction, Heidegger, Derrida), challenged the category of value, its *solidity*, and this was seen by many as utterly objectionable. It is worth pausing over an example here. Imagine arguments over the circulation of this cultural seme: William Sarnoff, chairman of Warner Books, stated at a meeting of American booksellers that "books have to compete with a lot of diversions for disposable time and expenditures, and it appears that this spring [1989] the people chose not to buy many hardcover books."[30] The tropes of a "politically correct" interpretation would focus on the expansion of commodification, the reduction of "reading" to disposable time, a capitalist assault on social consciousness. Reification and worse. It then "follows" that opposition to the commodification type requires that one become conscious of what such words refer to (the "totality" of capitalist life and practices) — this to initiate a transformation to a more appropriate identity (the addition of "politically correct" as a predicate of the self who has "worked through" to the strategies and tactics of being in opposition). Note that such an argument is not founded upon making books difficult to be so reduced, but in attacking the reduction. It is a model of *political seizure* — of opposing Capital with a socialist critique — and it is inane but for the fact that it is initiated not by real proletarians but by academics with larger than smaller shares of power. An unjust state must give way to a just one. On the other hand, G. focused on the *radical* nature of such capitalist acts, their *asociality*, not their "violation" of logically symmetrical categories. Opposition to the "commodification of the book" was pointless, a hysterical response on account of its own impossible demand structure, an excuse for further suppression of an "artistic" *x* or an "aesthetic" *y* as distinctive practices, and so another reduction of something potentially "more than political" to identity. A more effective strategy, which might not produce recognizable "results" (hence the "elitist" tag), would be to make something, form and matter being irrelevant, *unappropriable*, or, in Deleuze's terms, an object that could "complicate" its "difference in the chaos without beginning or end . . . the power of affirming divergence and decentering."[31] In a recent paper entitled "A New Aesthetic Paradigm," Guattari has suggested a stronger distancing from "autonomized and transcendentalized" constructions of critical, aesthetic experiences, those which inscribe "all differential qualities and nondiscursive intensities in the exclusive category of linear, binary relations." Terms such as "resingularization and heterogenesis" involve intensifying both language and art object to the point of producing their difference to their own category and to any mirroring identifications.[32]

The Appeal Commission consisted of three faculty, one representing G., the others indexing the interests of the faculty and the art institute as a whole. The territory of law once again was overcoded: commission meetings were taped, agreements of confidentiality were signed, accusations were refuted, documents were denied. There were gag rules, privacy protections, and the social transformation of oneself in an "acquiescence in a dazed, tranquilized, functional type of behavior."[33] The provost, with whom I was never invited to speak during the entire process, wanted the commission to exclude the Academic Council's concerns that (1) a "proper" review process of faculty had been set up and followed (a standing irritation among the long-term faculty) and (2) student concerns be presented to the commission.[34] The provost's attempt to exclude faculty review would isolate G.'s case, depriving it of solidarity with the concerns of other faculty; this isolating exclusion was itself an attempt to suppress the larger question of faculty evaluation, retention, promotion: why had some faculty, whose "records" suggested violations of professional ethics, received long-term contracts while others had not? What ranking and selection criteria were intrinsic?[35]

Having assumed the position of formally *representing* G.'s "interests," and believing that he had better than a substantial grievance, there seemed little point in calling for a structure that would have conflicted with the institute's legally codified procedures. It was either proceed or capitulate to the unfairness of a faculty member being unprotected by a union (a nontenure-granting institution) and whose legal fees were plainly unaffordable (the dean was protected as an employee of the institute).

G. and I decided to focus on the *official denial* that he had been "fired." Since the dean and the provost denied that "firing" was the name of this event, this "official denial" unleashed an aggressive pressure against affirmation of faculty rights. It politicizes any inquiry that might reveal it as an indefeasible practice. As the authors of *A Thousand Plateaus* indicate, there is a bureaucratic "plateau" expressed as "suppleness of and communication between offices, a bureaucratic perversion . . . another regime, coexistent with the separation and totalization of rigid segments."[36]

Complementary to the overcoding of the law and the bureaucratic mixtures, the professional relations among the faculty of the art school were abysmal, which is not to say irregular. In the face of multiple divisions (generational, gender, race, aesthetic, and so on), faculty relations were akin to the characterization by Michel Leiris of social moderation during which the judging gaze and perception of others momentarily suspends the retargeting of others; in other words, passive aggression was the dominant code of behavioral relation.[37]

The dean's response of December 9, 1985, to the Appeal Commission concerning G.'s claim was that he had provoked a "demoralization of the faculty." This response read as if drafted by the institute's attorney.[38] Conservative lawyers and the "revolutionary" dean were thus linked in protecting each other's interests; we can call this conjunction of institutional Darwinism and progressive politics another case of supercondensed Hegelianism — a disaster inasmuch as it shows the domination of law as one with the domination of cultural negation, one of the identities between left and right, although not entirely so. Also, then, classical and comical. The feint that "not rehired" was "not fired" was enough to allow this admixture to surface. All along, the contract system was attached to what I have called language as order, and which as "easily mark[s] a tolerance as indicates an enemy to be mowed down."[39] The administration was saying "no" to the faculty ("we make the rules") by saying "yes" to the dean. The dominant power set up at the institute was to sustain the right to hire and fire as the prerogative of deans; anything would be better than an independent, potentially uncontrollable, faculty.

G. claimed, in his request for an appeal, that Dean C. had acted so "one-sidedly" that "doctrinal homogeneity" was the norm in that school; he located such one-sidedness within Freud's "theory of the narcissism of small differences," which was a reconceptualization of incest.[40] He argued that the dean was intolerant of experimentation as well as of actual transgressions and was supportive of only "correct transgression" (an oxymoron wherever one goes); his argument was that a "left" reduction was in fact generating a featherbedded network, a hoarding of "posts" destructive of public debate on the school's pedagogy and direction. The dean's response, in her December 9 letter to the Appeals Commission, was furiously legalistic: "I certainly do not tell students . . . that they 'should' not make works with certain meanings."[41] G. countered by saying that "telling" obscures the actual ways in which students are intimidated into doing certain kinds of works and that the dean was suppressing a *local mode of production*, which obtains in an arts institute: student access to funding, to mentor time, for exhibition space and so on, are all subject to administrative oversight. At this school, a student was dependent upon one of seven or so full-time art faculty for support: to analyze the student's work; to assist in progressing toward a degree; to help if a student's mentor did not adequately support efforts to obtain financial aid. If one persisted in, say, an excess of formalism, or doubted the problematics of the "dialectic in history," one could be effectively blocked from hanging on the same wall of affirmation and from filling (w)holes with meaning. (F. G. Bailey, in his study of academia, calls this the dilemma whereby "to open the box is to risk losing support" — a variation of exposure equals deposing.)[42] Students were subject, intensely so, to the American political dictum: "One is a friend of mine who is also an enemy of my enemy." In refuting the claim of "homogeneity," the dean claimed, in her December 9 letter, that "there are only two art faculty . . . this year who weren't hired before I arrived in 1983." G.'s response was to emphasize that both faculty members were "one-sided" in terms of their rejection of the "elitism" identified as a white, male, bourgeois arts education and that a host of part-time positions began to be filled with recent graduates of the art school, that current other faculty were subject to intimidating acts, and so on.

So more machinations of legality were called forth: one is committed then to self-protection, to the effective power of law, which has only one rational goal: to destroy the other in such a way that the means of destruction do not cancel the law as mediator. "Law runs the strong risk of playing no more than the role of exterior armature."[43] Is it not fair to say that a very real part of an "academic thing" (as impersonal object) is precisely this horror of what Deleuze calls, after Kafka, the "absolute practical necessity" of having to defend oneself in every manner possible?

As the administration at the school maneuvered so as to be seen as neutral, that is, successful in asserting its contractual power, so the deans wished to be perceived as "pluralist," that is, denying their power to select and control the hiring and retention of the faculty. The power of the deans in a space of such "tight" and narrow proportions (where questions of politicocultural identity are predominant) evokes the notion that

> power presents itself . . . as a paranoid law of the despot, it imposes a discontinuous distribution of individual periods, with breaks between each one, a discontinuous repartition of blocks, with spaces between each one. . . . The transcendental law can only regulate pieces . . . an astronomical construction.[44]

The legally authorized power must provide for a stabilization of names; criticism of a dean threatened change of "head" in this case, and since every change of "head" might change "face," and "desire" and "will" seriatim, there is a built-in mechanism of conservatism; as I have said, the institute's attorney counseled the dean without charge, while murderous legal fees determined that the faculty member had to rely on a nonlawyer for representation. This had extreme consequences. In requesting that she be informed of all "witnesses" who would appear before the commission, since they would be available to G. through my representation, the dean in fact brought about the power play of excluding witnesses: we did not call students because we could not agree on how to protect them from retribution by the School of Art leadership.[45] Their status reverted to that of "children" before potential abusers. In letters with their names deleted, the students volunteered that instructor X was "cryptic" in class, or Professor Q was "condescending" in office hours, that another gave "power-stares" [sic] in cutting off disagreement while "guiding" a student to an "agreement" the student felt was a call to build an "academic gulag."[46] But we could not actually talk to them. Speaking was thus reconfirmed, recognized as one of those "important occasions" Bataille describes as when the mouth is a *concentrated* interest too violent, too revealing, for the usual relay activities of speech.[47] Student letters, with their *signature/author*, could be sustained in secrecy, but verbal discourse was evidence, *telling*. Thus students were overlegalized — separated from the category of "witness" once the demand of "protecting students" was raised. In being "protected," the students were thereby reterritorialized in their "immaturity," "saved" from the "adult world" of politics. It was a hoax, of course, that compared twenty-year-old college students with, say, six-year-olds.

Many conflicts ensued: G. could not "see" (read) other documents but could "listen" to them; a commission member challenged the notion of representing "the other side" (School of Art); we interviewed G.'s colleagues. Like most teaching faculty in the United States at nonresearch institutions, some were known to the "outside" as showing artists, and some belonged to existing factions (the neo-avant-garde, Expressionism, "new historicists"). The Appeal Commission members were agreed that the outstanding issue had become, right or wrong, G.'s "relations with colleagues." During interviews, held over a period of two months, we were told by the program director that the faculty was divided concerning "ideologies," that G. was difficult to work with. The dean explained that upon her becoming dean, G. had been given a better contract, partly in hopes of getting him to "ease off on his previous behavior"; she stated that she had believed he would "change" in being given a better contract. The improved contract shortly before the nonrenewal was really a psychological palliative that had failed, and as his behavior was "worse than ever," the psychological coding naturally gave way to political and legal ones.[48] G. reiterated the existence of "homogeneity" under this regime and that the faculty was not allowed to fully participate in questions of retention and hiring. This claim of "homogeneity" was coupled by G.

with the dean's public negation of visual pleasure, and this provoked a letter from the dean to the commission in which she demanded to know to whom we spoke. She insisted that she felt "victimized" by the faculty's appeal process.

I want to reiterate here that the issue of knowledge and its divisions was not reducible just to the polarities of left and right. It was also a question of the exact practices of art's subdivision into territories, including art criticism, art theory, art philosophy, art history, attitudes toward collections of art, museums, alternative spaces, and so on, as well as a matter of the proliferation of the concept entitled "art." All of that was threaded to what Baudrillard has called the "vertigo *mise-en-abyme*" of art's possible stupefaction—there comes the time of its radical indetermination, an "ecstasy" of art experience wherein the category "art" gives way: "something redundant always settles in the place where there is no longer any-thing,"[49] incapable of provoking social wrath in any form, left, right, or otherwise. At the institute in question, the ascendant group associated with the dean bonded with the concept that "art" is determined by an economic base, but blocked consideration of the fact that such a truism is useless. The dominant group was incapable of dealing with a semiotics of implication—what has been called the theory of the surplus of the signifier—and instead favored an earlier modernist critique, especially as practiced by writers such as Lukács, for whom a consciousness that "grasps" the causal steps and links between economy and superstructure in the hopes of divesting oneself of reification was the only proper goal of thinking. The demand to demystify consciousness recoded a larger sense of linguistic inertia. Pluralizing the concept to its limits—there is art-making that concerns itself with the visualization of possibilities (cf. Barthes on Cy Twombly),[50] and there is art-making that is nostalgically political, and there is an ornamental one and a decoratively critical fusion and a naively experimental and . . . and . . . and—became what the power block feared. In other words, art, in the asocial system entitled Capital, is not defined by a synthetic differentiation—as if, in Habermas's schema, we could separate cognitive and ethical and subjective, and so on—but more so by its elision of definition; it is more interesting to ask what the potential is for a category such as "art," since it is arguable that "art effects" have "moved" from their own category (self-eviction?).[51] But all of this was too much for most art faculty, given institutional demands to regularize and homogenize art for socially acceptable reasons. The reduction of art to another routine of socialization was a significant aspect of the selection processes for hiring and firing faculty.

All such ruminations vanished at the level of complicated thinking: in order to isolate G., it was reiterated by some art faculty that his *original* appointment was merely based on his political relations with _____, a well-known "conceptual" artist. It was said that G.'s intellectual skills had appealed to _____'s political liberalism, it having been the latter's "turn" to fill a vacancy. Someone asserted that G. had "badgered" a faculty member by asking questions about the competency of the department's student review process. G.'s difficulty was taken as a sign of his having to be isolated. I would call this a *conclusionary situation*: like the form of tautology upon which it is absurdly modeled, one is "guilty" of *being in contradiction to a myth*. Because one does not display the left/right and correct/wrong signs of political alignment, one becomes unacceptable to, in this case, a left pedagogy. An artist-teacher like _____ was somewhat "insulated" from political conflict because of his status within an international reviewing system, and he did no writing that alienated anyone, but G. invited negation from all sorts of "progressives" on account of his advocacy of a difficulty, namely, that works of art should be able to invite verbal description that dissolved political categories. The only politics that mattered here was that which pushed toward the destruction of political formations; artworks that reconstituted political "states" did nothing more than announce coalition-building, whereas at least a complicated object could be associated with a (small) declaration of "war," replete with its countersocialization (e.g., intensity of making). Although perhaps utopian on its own terms, this was "radical" insofar as it granted no "long-term" mode of temporality to art-making, no stability to the image-fields. Neither in the "name of history" nor in the "name of the oppressed" meant that G. had revived what for the American left is an archaism: doubt was being cast on the plausibility of the categorical relations between politics and society. And this doubt had to be gotten rid of.

Nonetheless, in appearances before the Appeal Commission, some art faculty described a "climate of fear" concerning the new direction of institutional politics; the atmosphere was "suffocating" unless one lined up with the existing players.[52] In addition, more than one visiting artist considered the art school "impossible to understand" in terms of establishing criteria of reemployment. Many visiting faculty were afraid to speak publicly about the installation of a discourse regime that excluded more than it included — the success, as it were, of negative rules (opposition = denunciation) over flexible grammars.[53] I argued that G. was a lightning rod for this well-founded paranoia, that Dean C. had reinvented a sort of cultural version of the folkloric "plagiarism of the trickster . . . [who] has plenty of future but no becoming whatsoever" and whose sole interest was in self-serving power. To borrow from Deleuze: G. was thus a "traitor" to the role of the "trickster" insofar as his actions were antithetical to upholding a left mythology.[54] Demythologization infuriated most of his "colleagues." To insist upon utopian hopes was to be a trickster, and to betray this meant that one had to be prepared to stress the negative triumph of contemporary society as a prison of psychological processes.

I am describing, I believe, an opposition between an "art-state" (the state of art) and movements that its leaders saw as "war," provoked by a "tribal" member they could not control. The last assault from the dean of art was to call upon an "ancient" enemy of G.'s, from another institution, and, unsolicited, place his "negative history" (in letter form) before the Appeal Commission. G. was "guilty" of all sorts of monstrous crimes, the main one being the sign-value of this old enemy now acting as an agent of denunciation.[55]

The Appeal Commission dissolved: the dean of art demanded that we not "broaden" our inquiry to include individuals outside the art program or focus on "art political ideology."[56] The Appeal Commission was accused of interfering with "academic freedom." Its dissolution was precipitated by our inability to agree on how to listen to students; in Roman Jakobson's terms, the phatic relation was simply broken off on this subject. Already reduced to appearance in the form of anonymous letters, a lid silencing the students was invoked; one member of the commission asked "what the students can provide that we have not already heard."[57] G.'s response consisted of pointing out that since the dean had taken it upon herself to involve past employers, it was only fair to let students speak for themselves — "simply talk to all the graduate students [approximately thirty students] in the school of art." He added that if this was not acceptable, then volunteers from the students could be spoken with about his "demoralization" of them.[58] He further emphasized that in the course of the Appeal Commission, his opponents had in fact performed the very actions with which they had charged him — a "polarized" and "difficult environment" were certainly effects of the dean's and the program director's responses to the existence of the commission! I pointed out that the initial statements of "charges" against G. had been supported by only three of the members of the art school faculty, and these were noncoincidentally also its "officials" (dean, program head, assistant dean). I also argued the irregularity of the job critique (the only "warning" as to G.'s behavior had taken place at a restaurant); the extreme irregularity of there being nothing in G.'s file concerning either warning or documentation of said "problems"; and that G. had been given a two-year contract not because matters had gone "from bad to worse," as one "colleague" put it, but on account of a substantial record of writerly and painterly production.

So strong is the repression of conflict that might transform a horrific context into something discussable, so strong is the *transpolitical* bureaucratization of existing players, that reterritorialization operates as an effective force of axiomatization: one commission member made her "final interpretation" based on the personal belief that a former dean of the School of Art and G. had had disputes and that this "negative continuity" was surely a mark that "proved" the current dean's contention. My colleagues on the commission called for the writing of reports, one majority and one minority.

The majority report affirmed the legality of the appeal process and argued against reinstatement, while noting, among other things, that the decision not to renew probably should have "required formal procedures for evaluation." In G.'s case these were not required, since "it was a decision supported by a majority of the Art Program faculty."[59] In my counteropinion, I stressed that the majority report had unnecessarily degraded further the (very small) rights of a difficult instructor by invoking a mythical scene where actual "colleagues" would never have let things go so far as this had; I argued that the actual aggressions of the authorities were obliterated and that the majority report merely reaffirmed an academic gentry: "No faculty should be forced to accept a colleague they have determined to be operating to the detriment of their Program." But "determined" and "detriment" were precisely not analyzed by the commission.[60]

The president of the institute accepted the majority report and asked for the documents to be placed in the school vault. Out of the black hole of control, the monstrosity of legality was invoked so as to reenact a law of confinement. The pedagogical processes were once more "saved" from chaos.

Dean C. resigned four years later, after conflicts with numerous members of the administration and other faculty, and was promoted to officer status at a high university. G. continues to teach, paint, and write.

Superstars: Myth and Science

The expansion of national, academic competition for "superstar" scholars in the domains of knowledge attached to interpretive or hermeneutical territories frames this section. It is a question — again borrowing some terms from Gayatri Spivak — of suggesting the effects of an institutional setup where actual material events like intense reading (professorial expertise) is surrendered to the "complicated organizational assumptions underlying," in this case, academe.[61]

It will also be a question of considering conjunctions really horrifying, the become-ordinary of an academic oxymoronics. Here we can allow to be compared such incomparables as "scientificity" and "honor," the former transformed into something unfamiliar, while perhaps the latter merely disappears and cannot return as an event of academe.

This "case" occurred in 1987–88 at a large public university in Los Angeles. The context is that of critical "superstardom," which is a semantic caricature (whose potential truth-value is quite high) of the fusion of economic and culture through the relay of sign-value. The "superstar" phenomenon of academe is a mode of control, where the acquisition of prestige and a prestige-driven sociality generates its own economic/cultural subpositions; the "pet" projects of the grand moguls of Capital — vanity architecture — are mirrored in the redundancy of cultural projects, none of which is allowed to pass into any category with a whiff of "non-prestige" attached to it. Economic prestige, cultural economics, prestige culture, economic culture — all the permutations add something to the following discussion. It is a matter also of framing a transition from the myth of the scholar as scientist (discovery of universal representations) to that of a bureaucrat of language: "an immense social domestication . . . techno-structural rationalization that has as its effect the corruption of all the categories."[62] (Not that there is ever anything "pure" about that promiscuous . . . category.)

The context is more or less as follows (so long as one understands "context" in terms derived from pragmaticism [Peirce], as something active). In the 1950s the University of _____ at _____ emerged as the dominant educational institution in Southern California. There was no opposition from any constituents (legislature, faculty, students) to the *research* model that served as the machine (organ plus energy) of retraining many of the professionals providing one service or another to the growth of the region, its development in the extended sense of the term. Its training hospital, as well as enormous outlays for other "hard" scientific analyses, became the model for large increases in FTEs in the humanities, social sciences, arts and letters. Relations between "hard" and "soft" knowledges had achieved a mutually satisfying reduction — to the question of how these latter areas could be made to "look" and "fit" and "conform" to a scientific model of their practices when, precisely, no one in their right mind could consider *acts of reading* to be anything but conceptual. Is there really an identity between, say, the best philosophical writing and science? The demoralizing reiteration of "humanistic knowledge" as subjective furthered the notion of making the "softer" knowledges "scientific," hence the emergence of Freud and Marx, normal sta- tistics, comparative theory, in competition for statist funding. Western historians, for example, have waffled (not to give waffling a bad name) over this essentially territorial problem; "history" is scientific through the reference to archives, narrative at the level of form.

Now by the mid-1980s the university had developed or achieved the status of national ranking required to justify its "needs" for increased positions, a sure sign of capital success. This meant that its history de- partment received funding for many new, specialist "posts" (e.g., social history of Southeast Asia between 1850 and 1980; Native American his- tory, 1750 . . .), these specializations becoming an index of success. The university encouraged this "scientization" of nonscience while the upper administration aggressively sought an increase in "endowed positions" purchased by benefactors. A more "scientific history" may or may not generate more hypotheses and debate about the (putative) significance of past-present, but it did create more security for investments regardless of source. Scientization heightened the status of signifiers of value (e.g., a "deep" interpretation, a "significant" contribution), which in turn pro- vided the verbal "charge" required to keep the entire mythos intact. Say- ing this tempts me to say further that the academic "tests" that matter are ones that prolong real-mythic processes of exclusion/omission: the controls placed on the number of academic "posts" ensures certain *non- discussable* criteria from consideration in decisions of appointment and hiring. Most needed is a sponsor — whose value is undisputed — who can take one's work and convince others — who often cannot read it on their own — that its narrative completion (closure) and scholarly apparatus synthesizes into a supersign of scholarship or "research activity." One enters this "public realm" as having managed to survive in a monop- olistic system (Baudrillard) of intellectual equilibrium. When Habermas calls for intellectuals "to make conscious a murky reality," he must pre- suppose that he has a rule of criterion such that "to make conscious" as concept is beyond challenge. But is one describing "scientific" events at that point?

Part-time positions were "collected" across the disciplines of arts and letters and funds "pooled" to "superstarize," that is, give the department visibility in order to attract the very best qualified graduate students and other scholars. Some 114 nontenured part-time scholars saw funding for their specializations disappear between 1985 and 1988 (or so). A docu- ment with the forbidding title of "The Allocation and Use of Faculty Resources in the College of Letters and Science" (December 16, 1987) allows one, concretely, to link onto, what I am calling the assemblage where the high university exposes its policy toward appointment of various faculty "grades." From lecturer to university professor, one is ranked: ascent and descent are accompanied by rules; for example, lecturers may teach at any level of instruction but cannot vote in an academic "senate" on policy affecting their job security (or lack thereof). This document overcodes; written by university lawyers, who can double as legislators in the State Assembly, it authorizes another document, which protects the concept of research value.

This document, whose full title is "The Call: _____ Summary of Policy and Procedure, Lecturer Series, 1987–88," governed the continuity of year-to-year temporary contracts into something resembling permanent appointments; in 1987, after seven years of such "service," I was informed by the chair of history that I could apply for the improvement of one-year contracts into periods covering three years — this because of complaints filed by the local union with state agencies. If I did not apply for this improvement, I would be forced to leave the university since there was a state law that limited the number of continuous one-year contracts allowable. Thus, the first set of relevant terms is: temporary and permanent activated as a bind: "up or out" is its street value. Metonymic to this was the university's bind: it desired to concentrate and centralize funds from within its system so as to "drive" the "superstar syndrome," the acceleration of "writings with standing" without which the high university could not continue to modernize its reproduction (or give signs thereof). Funds from Central University Bank were unavailable, but there were numerous one-year-contract people whose change to permanent three-year contracts would "spoil" the further concentration of "high-powered knowledge" and decrease the required star sign-value the administrators deemed necessary for fund-raising from yet more authorities. It takes no theoretical insight to figure out this power play, which all the political factions — including internationally famous left historians — played to the hilt.

Now take up the particular deformation: the public research university is able to have a scientific "humanities" because tenure is that kind of contractual tie that carries with it the *maximization of concentration*, a form of production where the knowledge required in the future is supposed as already on the way to us, now. In this "Call" (literalism, allegorism, Protestantism) tenure is defined as "faculty members of professional rank who have demonstrated their ability both in teaching and in research or other creative achievement."[63] Now the referent of this rationale is another rationale: a Hegelian code. This beneficent conjunction of teaching and research — tenure — requires that it be in opposition to what is inferior, to what would initiate the effect of a disjunctive nonsynthesis, this nontenure, which has already been indicated in the sense of the expression "temporary." Tenure and temporary, security and non-security, pivot on the success of the "have demonstrated their ability," and are thus subject to other enunciations that would make good on the definition. "Temporary" was spoken of by the Officer Corps at _____ in the following way: from the same document, what is inferior are those positions attached to a "flexible temporary faculty . . . *pool*" (my italics), whose "three-year lecturerships carry responsibility for teaching but not research."

On the one hand, then, temporary, flexible teaching and, on the other, permanent, definite teaching *and* research. The semantic difference settles on the affirmative based upon a conjunction — the duty of the final "and." The extra "and." The surplus "hand." The "and" of "pool," the knowledge reserve army of the modern university.

A "post" thus disappears, reappropriated by the bureaucracy of professors. Here is the rationale, delivered by Dean _____:

> Under the Memorandum of Understanding with the AFT [my union],
> lecturers with six or more years of service can now be considered only for
> three-year terms . . . [but] such a term of service cannot now be
> guaranteed for the position you hold.

There is no "post" to occupy: it had been only temporary all along; it had to be converted into a permanent — tenurable — position, but to do this, the history department would have had to make the argument to the officers that the "post" was tenurable, since it was not a matter of my credentials. The history department decided that the subject of the "post" — modern historiography — would not convey to others the requisite sign-value of research.

Interventions occur; letters and conversations are exchanged. But the temporary funds were moving toward that "superstar" void, for there is more to say from the officers. The precise reason why no funds were to be allocated for my field of specialization is that it was said that this field lacked "scientificity." There's no reason to *academicize the cultural field of historiography* because the dual officers — provosts (rear and above) and departmental "chiefs" — agreed that practices of "historical thought" were expressed through the normal practices of any "scientific" historian. Historiography was likened to the ether of "doing history." The argument was made that "Sande Cohen works directly in this field, which is as special an area of expertise as the history of the French Revolution," but after one officer acknowledged a "need" for a three-year department commitment to that area, another plainly asserted the obvious: "it is hard to believe that in a distinguished faculty of nearly seventy historians, only one is qualified to teach a beginning course in historiography" at the upper-division level. Indeed. This little Platoneme merely reminded the history department of what it had "proved" through its own practices: "history" is what every historian says it is. This was softened, shortly after someone in the department reflected on my case, into another enunciation by the provost that historiography "is not required by the major; it can be taught occasionally." But the meaning of this also highlighted another, more problematic, one: the only course that in fact had any possible semantic "commonality" with the cultural usages of the concept of "history" presumably communicated by my colleagues was rendered inoperative as a "scientific" category.

Which is to say that no war machines of any sort were activated over historiography.

One last encounter with this (university) state apparatus, for one is entitled to file an appeal: there is a clause in one's contract for this. The University of _____'s Academic Senate is compelled to offer a grievance commission. Convened the following year, it consisted of three full professors, none of whom was a member of the history department. They found in my favor, particularly that "this decision [to not make a three-year contract] was made for reasons other than academic judgment," that is, political and economic motivations had in effect "evicted" intellectual and pedagogical ones. The review panel further pointed out that my replacement "is a non-ladder [nontenure] track appointee for one year." The process of exploitation had begun on a fresh recruit, or perhaps historiography had finally become attractive (a cultural plus-value). The officers responded by rejecting the appeal panel's power to enforce its findings — I was free to litigate; they were free to ignore the "body" of their academic "senate." The union voted to support litigation of my case in the amount of three thousand dollars (one day's time in an expensive California divorce case) and filed a letter on my behalf with the president of the university.

Six months later (April 1990), the provost at same institution publicly announced that one of the contributing reasons for the enormous deficit of the university was its "aggressive recruiting" of "superstars"; this had occurred, in particular, by collecting the funds and having "dishonored some temporary faculty contracts."

Concluding Remarks

To those interested in such matters, I would say that the passive-aggressivity of professors toward language is telling; it is in practice impossible to dislodge the bureaucratization of the concept of "research" in the nonscientific disciplines of the high university. The "research" model is undoubtedly a colossal piece of narcissism.[64] As Lyotard has argued, "knowledge" of the "humanistic" and "critical" types is produced for exchange; the status of its "use value" is adrift in what is, at best, contested argumentation.[65] But so much academic product is carefully entrenched in what Baudrillard has called the "tentacular, protuberant, excrescent, hypertelic . . . the inertial destiny of a saturated world," that is, cultural overcoding; this overcoding ensures that both academic writing and instructional "posts" remain subject to the controls of statist forms and language.[66]

Tenure is ended or "released only at the time of resignation, retirement, or death."[67] The "Call" says a lot. Production of the permanent becomes one with permanent production. Subjects must signify, but especially to those who would transport ideas to *sign-forms* that appear authoritative, conclusive, appropriate, and the like. The subjectivity required for this was found, according to Adorno, in a sociolect whose jargon "marks the adept, in their own opinion, as untrivial and of higher sensibility." In this they are self-ranked, their "discourse" not addressed to the real but to an already-controlled linguistified consumer who is too often another academic "producer."

So what is one to say in the face of these same officers who proclaim "need after need," a veritable chasm of needs, wrapped in the papers of "the university's mission"?[68] Mission impossible: to disentangle the conjunction of an unreal psychology of "need" and its remilitarized control overseen by "academic officers."

3

Habermas's Bureaucratization of the Final Solution

Introductory Remarks

I turn now to a contentious and impossibly concrete yet never entirely specifiable topic, the event known as the Final Solution. My objective is to show, through a close reading, some of the differences that matter, particularly the cultural formations by which this event has become image and concept; my aim is to disorient contemporary criticism's extractions of cultural use value. In the light of what has been said in chapters 1 and 2, this cannot be a matter of criticism having any straightforward linkage to the Final Solution, but of a thinking which has to again evoke thinking out of the foggy stew of progressive morality, transcendence, history, becoming what Nietzsche called strife against "the power of the actual" (Final Solution reduced to our giving narcissistic interpretations). This strife is perforce, as thinking, not to "drag their generation to the grave, but to found a new one" (Nietzsche, *The Advantage and Disadvantage of History for Life*), which is a matter of not allowing criticism to become "final," or affirmatively, to help create the more difficult notion of Final Solution discourse as a "first-comer" in an event that we cannot "own." By drawing out the different stakes of the arguments between Habermas and Lyotard on the cultural theorization of the Final Solution, how such arguments engender cultural and intellectual controversies, it will become immediately apparent that the view of language-as-representation is like a (s)takeout, hauled into the machinery of use value (Final Solution as a test of one's historicism, one's right to politics), and this can be compared to those arguments that emphasize the plasticity of the signifier — hence the Final Solution as a not determinable name and thus potentially use-less. Was the Final Solution a modern event, and are today's questions motivated by that modernity or by something else?

Habermas's Model

Historicism has been variously defined, but I would like to start by suggesting that we consider its major nineteenth- and twentieth-century articulations as attempts to achieve a cultural "timeless time," an image that holds categories such as origin/result together. Historicism as a centering device always overcodes one or more absolutely continuous lines, even if there is room for discontinuities. Allan Megill has said that this sense of historicism is shared by writers as divergent as Lyotard and Maurice Mandelbaum, a mainstream academic historiographer. Historicism enables one to "take account of the number of moves around the dial the hand has made by the end of the period of observation," the sense of which renders an image of an unavoidable presentation handed down by "history" that braids past, present, and future in the here and now.[1] Words such as canon and tradition and critical opposition presuppose historicist setups. One is anchored to both a date and an image at once; one starts one's narration by setting the clock at a metaphoric dawn — time "counts" because the historian imputes this clock to the events recounted. (There are restorative countings, apocalyptic ones, and so on). As a cultural arrangement, historicism is severely pressured when Capital is exceptionally dynamic, or when the economic genre itself becomes sublime, that is, "a finality of antifinality and a pleasure of pain" (consumerism), which produces for many an unreal sense of "history," for example, the perpetual nonpresence of a consumerist utopia or the perpetual manipulations of neurotic politics of virtually any sort. As I argue in chapter 4, it may well be that Capital exterminates "history," not to put too fine a sense to it.[2]

Habermas's contribution to the historian's debate over the Final Solution resulted in the publication of *The New Conservatism*, and it is that text I shall analyze. Habermas's contribution was anything but a continuation of the historian Saul Friedlander's call for "a new style . . . to be introduced for the purpose of historical description. . . . the duty of the historian may well be to forego the attempt to visualize, precisely so that he can fulfill his task in terms of documentary precision and rendition of the events."[3] Although Friedlander seems unaware of the repressive sense of "documentary precision," its ordering of a demand, Habermas shows no intention of allowing the practicing historians to establish the criteria for the Final Solution's becoming a stake in the determinations of public history. On the contrary, Habermas does not waver in connecting historicization and visuality, a mode of classical German historiography in its concern with national, monumental narrations. For Habermas, the visual connector between narrativity, the Final Solution, and the present is secured in the following way:

> Today the grandchildren of those who at the close of World War II were too young to be able to experience personal guilt are already growing up. Memory . . . has not become correspondingly distantiated.
> Contemporary history remains fixated on the period between 1933 and 1945. It does not move beyond the horizon of its own life-history; it remains tied up in sensitivities and reactions that . . . still always have the same point of departure: *the images of that unloading ramp at Auschwitz. This traumatic refusal to pass away of a moral imperfect past tense that has been burned into our national history entered the consciousness of the general population only in the 1980s.*[4]

This long citation makes extensive cultural claims. The immovable stases of time — "fixity" and "does not move" — are sutured to a present urgency, whose philosophical expression is that of a negative identity between past and present. The psychological series comes forward as a nondistance, the self of then and of now connected by irresolution. What happened then, the "unloading ramp" — projected as the material basis of the entire problematic — is embedded in a continuity of not-forgetting: the sense of "has been burned," the "traumatic refusal." These luxurious synecdoches (*pace* Hayden White) of pain have not blended with an objective past; narration has not been able to do its job of simultaneously closing the black hole of the past and serving as a foundation for the future.

The citation privileges the psychological dimension, designated as the "traumatic refusal," the inability of the present to engage with unacceptable images. The past is not past, and it cannot put itself "out" — like a memory that ricochets in the nondirection of displacement — and Habermas wants this understood as decidedly nonmetaphorical.[5] The "unloading ramp," this putative universal image as seen by the victims and culturally burned into all subsequent members of the German nation (through the cultural intervention of West German television), is the result of the assertive force of a statement that does not want to be challenged; unsayable by Habermas is this projection of an archaic "philosophy of history," what can be called the *universality of inclusive traditions*, established by the imposition of psychological negative continuities on all levels of contemporary German relations. In my evaluation of what Habermas's discourse performs, it is very much the issue that he is recoding *conformist* elements of historicism, in particular the very demand that the Hegelian and idealist categories of "all" and "everyone" serve as linchpins of representation and understanding.

Past and memory are thus the vehicles of the psychological phrasing that counts in the present (establishes the present under the signs of psychology, e.g., "traumatic," "burned") and the one that holds to account the writings of culturally engaged historians, German or otherwise. Every attempt to represent the Final Solution as something normal, as not exceptional or as repeatable, calls forth denunciation by Habermas. The time continuum accessed by psychological trauma is treated as a universal/national fact, as the substance of psychological judgments. In effect, the question of collectivity, of "national history," is treated as an unproblematical extension of individual feelings; this move legitimizes the demand for a therapeutic political culture, one which, as the authors of *Anti-Oedipus* scrupulously argue, re-oedipalizes as it relentlessly superegoizes. *The New Conservatism* insists that there can be no really enlightened national public culture until the melancholy of the survivors is recognized as determining that "the survival of all of us stand[s] under the *curse*, in attentuated form, of having merely escaped . . . an intersubjective liability . . . for distorted life circumstances."[6]

This "curse," which can be multiplied to include the cultural politics of the American treatment of the Indians, the Spanish treatment of the same, the former Soviets and "their" Asians, Israel and the Palestinians, and so on, satisfies one of the key conditions of Hegelian Freudianism (where the Marxian element momentarily is placed in suspension), for "curse" renders a powerful symbol of negative identity. The institutionalization of "working through" this negative identity offsets a society that day by day becomes more fractured in terms of capitalist dynamics. What are the true stakes in making attitudes toward the Final Solution *the* dominant present issue of German cultural politics? In addition, Habermas seems unaware that the invocation of the philosophy of "history" is problematic all along; it is not a question of getting the appropriate philosophy of history set up as a control code, but of whether any such philosophy is appropriate to the very thing called Final Solution.

The New Conservatism asserts that the "unloading ramp" at Auschwitz "put a whole population, as it were, under a compulsion to reflect." The telos of this particular oxymoron (on which Habermas's prose is silent) is to rehistoricize public life, in which intellectuals would essentially eliminate distinctions, such as they are, between thinking and psychologization. Their engagement in collective "therapy" for a curse, asserted as the form of German collectivity, in effect would signal the success of exterminating intellectuals and their resurrection as administrators of state therapy. This proper activity could not, of course, be subject to negation; as another form of the Hegelian code of a "negation of the negation," future intellectual-political involvement is anchored to the *result* ("curse"), the substance of a new German "historical consciousness," one that would be finally Western and not itself "exceptional" (e.g., antirational).

It seems to me weird but true that Habermas is encoding nothing so much as the desire for the West to have some sort of normal, that is, therapeutic form of social relation, which the new cultural historiography might emulate. Even if that were the case (but it's too unreal, since nothing Western is not filtered through sign-exchange, including criticism), it unfortunately involves regression to the level of an invoked organic form, here a recoding of an unreflective use of the term *milieu*:

> Our own life is linked to the life context in which Auschwitz was possible not by contingent circumstances but intrinsically. Our form of life is connected with that of our parents and grandparents . . . through a historical milieu that made us what and who we are today. None of us can escape this milieu, because our identities, both as individuals and as Germans, are indissolubly interwoven with it. . . . We have to stand by our traditions, then, if we do not want to disavow ourselves.[7]

The "curse" that has fallen on the "people" now is transformed into the "milieu" of an identity already formed in the past and that cannot be "disavowed" without a wholesale plunge into unresolved materials; the citation above calls back that entity named "German" and it must retain its particularity, no matter what. What is exceptional cannot be "escaped." This metapsychological "curse" may never be "reparable," but it can be "treated," as it were, by "historical reflection." There is thus an *irreversible* demand made by Habermas, which is directed against what, in another place, Peter Sloterdijk has called the "radical ironization of ethics and social convention . . . as if the general laws were only meant for the stupid."[8] That is, Habermas proposes the reinvention of a national life controlled by a "gaze educated by the moral catastrophe" of the Final Solution and which will preclude the fragmentation that Sloterdijk says is an irresistible construct of modernity as such.[9] In place of ordinary "history," it is a question of an extraordinary liability and psychologically based moral economy, a mixture of law and ethics by which to dissolve a past that blocks "our path like a locked door." To borrow some terms from *Anti-Oedipus, The New Conservatism* invents an organ— the "German people"—and combines it with an energy machine— "traumatic refusal"—requiring a machine of rehabilitation in order to collect and glue the pieces together. This cultural machine works as a recentering device, within which "cognitive meanings, moral expectations, subjective expressions and evaluations must relate to one another."[10] In the face of the shatterings performed by the Final Solution on value, on meaning, on law, and so on (or by modern Capital in the present), the category of intellectual is disengaged from any possible antimodernist argument. The demand of "must relate" serves as the device of this inclusive disjunction. One could read *The New Conservatism* as theorizing a state-building negation of those who would disavow enlightenment or cultural modernism.

So *The New Conservatism* recodes one of the constant figures of modern European historiography, the unquestioned image of German identity; the iteration of phrases of the type "our national life" are ladeled on everyone regardless of actual differences, opposition, nonidentities, with the German language serving as one vehicle of such continuity. This is a contemporary version of the burdened will, of a past experienced as a perpetual sadness, a negative epiphany of being stuck as a latecomer.[11] Because contemporary Germans, regardless of generation, have yet to "synthesize the initially competing images of the good and the bad parents into complex images of the *same* person. . . . The weak ego acquires its strength only through nonselective interaction with an ambivalent environment," so there can be no allowable negation of the implied therapy that intellectuals must effectuate.[12] Or again: "In adults the need to defuse the corresponding cognitive dissonances is still alive." The projection of these needs, of a speculative faculty of psychic synthesis, necessitates a language that can detect the satisfaction and frustration of needs. This, of course alludes to the "ideal speech situation," which would ensure the survival of what Habermas calls "the supply of motivation and meaning" to limit illicit power plays and "merge elements of public education, social welfare, liberalized punishment, and therapy for mental illness."[13] Thus the German dilemma of a "corrupted effective history" requires the merging of critical therapy and its grafting to redemptive reflection so as "to reclaim encumbered traditions."[14]

What is offensive, then, in Habermas's contribution to the "historian's debate" concerning the Final Solution is precisely this multiple reduction to critical usefulness for Germans now, for everyone, and, by extension, its claims on Western intellectuals. Acceptance of the reductions summarized here serves as the litmus test of one's current "reflexive, scrutinizing attitude toward one's own identity-forming traditions"; those who refuse this overall reegoization are thus barred from the door of cultural significance, cultural and political difference. I do not believe that it takes much "counterreflection" to note that Habermas's program also *deproblematizes* contemporary relations, which cannot "properly" be taken up until the Final Solution is resolved by a historicotherapeutic model. Historicism continues to set social priorities.

Historicism writes the meaning of the name Final Solution and its date, 1942 plus. The result of the Final Solution is the "curse" that does not end. The Final Solution is at once the origin of a contemporary burden of reconciliation — the "blocked door" between present and past — and the substance of a collective critical self-examination mirrored in a universal uniqueness of Germany now: "no one can take our place in the liability required of us."[15] Thus, "Germans" receive the archaic or premodern Hegelian category of an *unacceptable narration*, where the "spent" cultural forces of religion, philosophy, and sociology have now given way to psychology.

Just as *The New Conservatism* asserts that there are no grounds for normalization of the Final Solution, it emphasizes that there are no convincing grounds for the formation of a post-Enlightenment social critique. As neoconservatism practices moral neutralization of the Final Solution, so too contemporary *dissident* critics, those who reject the historicotherapeutic model, are shunted off to the dark side of modernity; in his comments on Heidegger's Nazi connections, Habermas affirms that as contemporaries, "we share a life-context and a history with others [and] we have the right to call one another to account."[16] Those, of whatever cultural or political persuasion, who stand outside of this negatively inclusive "life-context" are encoded as irrationalists, for in not accepting the model of "a society based on communication . . . limited to the formal aspects of an undamaged subjectivity," Habermas rails that there is no alternative to enlightenment: "it is of the very nature of the Enlightenment to enlighten itself about itself, and about the harm that it does. Only when this fact is repressed can the counter-Enlightenment present itself."[17]

So the neoconservatives of historical normalization and the postmodernist critique of the West are stitched together in this rejectionism. Both the repressive integration of the former (with its stress on normalization of tradition as a means of softening capitalist overdevelopment) and the deconstructive pragmatism of the latter (its dystopian force) are linked by their metonymizing slide into "one-sided" perspectives. Enlightenment set forth as something endangered thus repeats Freud's gesture of calling psychoanalysis a discipline under attack. *The New Conservatism* cannot lose in a politics based on psychological needs that no "mere" critique of politics, culture, subjectivity, or self is allowed to affect. Once again the intellectuals are empowered so long as they stay in the precut grooves of providing resocialization with concepts, theory, sophistication, the seductions, one might say, of bureaucratic integration.

It is crucial to note that where the exception of the Final Solution offered opportunities for cultural learning, contemporary Capital is presented as virtually normal in terms of its determination of social contradictions. Just as the memory of the Final Solution allows for *no break* concerning "our more sinister traditions,"[18] or negative continuity, there is *no break* from Capital, which receives an affirmative continuity: "reformed conditions of employment retain a position of central importance."[19] Capital is acknowledged to be a source of crises, but in a telling phrase, Habermas says that the goal of capitalism — as of the welfare state — "is the establishment of forms of life that are structured in an egalitarian way and that at the same time open up arenas for individual self-realization and spontaneity." This is an academic madness: suppressed is any trace of the idea that Capital is asocial in its constitutive forms. Habermas saves the possible experience of a finality in which "hope" is directive and willed, and damns only the means of the "legal and administrative . . . practice of normalization and surveillance" of advanced capitalist practices.[20]

In my opinion, the exceptionality of the Final Solution is anchored to the nonexceptionality of Capital. That capitalism be given the capacity of providing for "a higher level of reflection," as Habermas puts it in *The New Conservatism*, is disturbing. Why isn't capitalism — which makes mincemeat of real argumentation by its homogenization of signifiers, accomplished, for example, by the media's ordinary excessive displacement of analysis or the marginalization of unfamiliar cultural and social voices — rendered more critically?[21] There are disjunctions between capitalism and democracy that are not raised by Habermas, particularly the atrophy that today defines the latter. Why is the economic mode so accepted in the first place as an unalterable form of social relation? Why is criticism so often an opposition that acts under the identity of a "loyal opposition"? Why so much acceptance-repetition of playing politics? Why the nihilistic politics of affirming the necessity of reducing cultural practices to those of reformism? Habermas's interest in the cognitive *control of dissidence* is ominous, since those who argue for any "normalization" of the Final Solution are lumped with those who make up the new "antiproductivist alliance." We are told that "the old and the young, women and the unemployed, gays and the handicapped, believers and nonbelievers" might reject a "productivist vision of progress that the legitimists [of Capital and the welfare state] share with the neoconservatives."[22] This semiotic "machine" aims at cultural transcendence: it is a rationalization of the irreversibility of Capital's power to clear away what limits it. The intellectual's role can only be that of smoothing the effects of being reactive in the first place.

Finally, the parallel between the "exceptionality" of the Final Solution and the crises of contemporary Capital is that both have a similar referent: learning, enlightenment, reflection. Habermas's language targets the category of the dissident — those who argue for the normality of the Final Solution (neoconservatives) and those who argue for the impossibility of reflection as adequate to contest Capital (the young conservatives, whom Habermas equates with postmodernism). The former do not accept a "detached understanding [which] liberates the power of reflective remembrance and thus extends the possibilities for dealing autonomously with an ambivalent tradition,"[23] while those who reject liberation *within* capitalism are said to deny a "reflection and steering," which means rejecting the new utopia of communication — "the formal aspects of an undamaged subjectivity," the "democratic generalization of interest positions and a universalist justification of norms."[24] The realized nihilism of Capital is thus displaced, just as speculative psychology submits every German for whom the Final Solution was not an experience into a "need" to reflect upon. In a sign of disturbing value, Habermas calls again for a German youth that would be sensitized by its reflection upon "history," but, as Nietzsche pointed out in *The Advantage and Disadvantage of History for Life*, such "sensitivity" usually means internalizing realities and experiences that can never be "theirs" in any but an abstract and secondary manner ("the world-process and the personality of the earthworm").

In sum, *The New Conservatism* contributes to the debate on the Final Solution by setting aside the repeated crises of modernity insofar as they are not allowed to call into question enlightenment and critique.[25] The image of the "unloading ramp" at Auschwitz carries an enormous cultural-political agenda, but it does so through the language of psychological historicism, which gives present-day progressive audiences a stable cultural anchor.

Lyotard's Notion of Dispossession

The effective cultural and intellectual context for Lyotard's consideration of names and images attending to the Final Solution are those writings where Western historicism (*The Postmodern Condition*) and philosophy (*The Differend*) are discussed without reduction to consensus, ground, foundation, or other cultural apriorisms. The acceptance of a sign-form or articulation mode such as that of speculative dialectics (where illicit notions of continuity and discontinuity regulate semantics) is challenged by Lyotard's notion of "dispossession," which G. Bennington and R. Young call a conceptual move: language deployed as directly productive of provisional conceptions of "history" and "society" and "theory," and not a language that, it is claimed, results from "history" and company.[26] Fastening onto an evaluation of modernism that stresses, regardless of the division of experience, its relentless "shattering of reality," itself a force that does not allow for cultural recuperations, modernist processes are seen as irreducible to the language games of critical practice. The form of intellectual life that Habermas outlines as *normative* is theorized by Lyotard as *impossible*: there is no such thing as "normativity" when it comes to producing conceptions, ideations, figurations whose "business," to put it strongly, is never to reduce itself to the demands of politicized agents of cultural reproduction. Every (academic) stabilization of interpretation is challenged by Lyotard's version of an objective pragmatism, which sets off from a kind of "listening" (but irreducible to the ear) to events, objects, and texts rather than interpreting them according to the dictates of meaning. Criticism and art-making are linked by activating differences in all directions at once instead of synthesizing consequences according to the "logics" of historicism.

"Dispossession" has a number of senses, but it refers to events that suspend memory functions of consciousness from being the subject of traditions, disciplines, and interpretations. "Dispossession" burns up forms: the concept acknowledges that things occur that make it impossible for language to represent; this surplus of the signified does not allow for the basic historicist reduction, namely, a representing document. Of course there are many nonlinguistic realities: but who said "historical writing" could ever reach out of language, since it is exactly *a* writing? Lyotard, like Kant in this regard, acidifies one's wanting to "desire history." *Ecce historia, ecce academia.* So it cannot be said frequently enough that the narcissistic capture of language occurs as soon as one puts the notion of representation forward as the guarantor of the interpretability of criticism.

Nonetheless, one's disseizure of meaning through insights that may not "add up," or someone's refusal to agree with an oedipalizing evaluation, or a painting's frustration of one's subjective expectations (by, say, the steady dissolve of perspective, which only takes place later, but a later that in turn corrodes the stability of early), or the momentary appearance of the sublime are examples of the dispossession of historicizing, narrating, reducing, demanding. An "it happens" can "happen" unconnected to acts of thought anxious for what has "already been thought, written, painted in order to determine what hasn't been." Without conceiving this conception, which cannot be fully presented, there would be nothing done that was not automatically inserted into what we already thought. "Dispossession" is antithetical to phenomenologies of meaning because "it" already supposes something sublime, excluding the ascription of "formal commonalities that are constitutive for reaching any understanding at all."[27] As was emphasized in chapter 1, much of contemporary criticism epitomizes a surplus of possessive seizure insofar as it promises the form of answer for problematical phenomena. Unlike sociological and historicizing criticism, "dispossession" opens onto what "remains to be determined, something that hasn't been determined before."[28] From the perspective of modern Euro-American intellectual arguments, "dispossession" is not a Platonic reminder of the "counterculture" but a figure of uncontrolled presentation (which is not reducible to presence). One is not dealing with absence and nothingness, in which a relation is thought to lack meanings to be restored — as in psychoanalysis or the Sartrean version of existentialism (*Being and Nothingness*)[29] — but with "disarming all grasping intelligence," a "protection of the occurrence 'before' defending it, by illustration of commentary." Thinking itself shifts from a fanatical dependency on representations to experiences whose reasons are not relevant.[30] Modernity may itself be theorized as "dispossessive" insofar as more and more segments of it are "ruled" by aleatory factors, which are nevertheless utterly determinate (the working poor).

The near-epithetic "no consistent symbols" is the way Lyotard puts it in considering the systematic suspension of identification, including its negative variety (e.g., Adorno's aesthetic theory with its notion of art as a "martyred witness" to suffering).[31] (My regression to the negative indicates the power of reduction.) In Lyotard's arguments in "Freud according to Cézanne," an essay richly suggestive for considerations of cultural criticism, "dispossession" sets aside the privileged representation of tragedy, the machinery for the elaboration of Oedipus or the subject of identity, the positions thereof. Oedipalized paintings, for example, lodged in the space of a "hallucinatory representation and deception" and subject to the truth-value of psychoanalytic statements, today encourage the desire to achieve identification and the release of an "incitement premium," the interpretation thickening the linguistic reductions of things to words. Such works (there are lots of academicized art objects) and (words) are believed to raise "the barriers of repression." "Dispossession," on the other hand, would construe, in this case, painting "to be itself an object, to be no longer a message, threat, beseechment, defense, exorcism, lesson or allusion in a symbolic relation, but rather an absolute object, delivered of transferential relation, indifferent to the order of relations, active only in the order of energies, in the silence of the body. . . . Both desire and the fascinated gaze are spurned."[32] "Dispossession" refers to practices wherein objects do not symbolize but instead materialize possible movements of bodies and forces and relations of all sorts; thoughts and feelings and desires do not connect desire and history or thought and sociality, but *exteriorize* and sidestep the collective sociological ego.[33] Even such dinosauric works as Seurat's *La Grande Jatte* (as described by T. J. Clark) instance extremes that upend one interpretation, everyone's narrative. When "dispossession" is active, according to Lyotard, it modernizes: suspended is any "final solution" that presents itself as the way to achieve an artistic goal or a social end or a verbal consensus.

In the matter of language, "dispossession" is enacted as a "differend," an aspect of which is familiar in everyday life as the expression "perhaps," a pausing of conversation (and departure and . . .), which is heard as epistemic uncertainty. John Tagg discusses the "differend" as a thinking that has pulled back from any consensus, which complicates our pragmatic ability to conceive interesting ideas, a spacing.[34] As the differend, dispossession will be like the "unstable state and instant of language wherein something which must be able to be put into phrases cannot yet be."[35] Silence, vague feelings, pausing, postponements, refusals to judge even the most "obvious" of errors and faults, keeping one's subjectivity out of the way for the "reception" of regimes of possible signs, and constant delay in affixing names situate "phrasing" within a virtual bind of (1) the "impossibility of indifference" and (2) the "absence of a universal genre of discourse to regulate" events.[36] One is always making phrases that are incomplete; there is always surplus of content and form but also nonboundaries, different forms of which are connected to Capital (e.g., very rapid credit withdrawals) and to cultural productions (e.g., the Final Solution as an unknown genre). "Dispossession" is not a link to the persistence of social amnesia but part of the physics of modern action. Nothing could be more "dispossessive" than Capital's extermination of possibles, reduction of other modes of becoming, the binding of language to economy and not to an expansion of things to say. Saul Friedlander, criticizing the critics of Habermas while ranting about the "historical relativism" ushered in by Hayden White, misses the point entirely about modern Capital in describing it as the "constant impingement of functional rationality" on the "life-world," as if hysterical dependency upon money and job by everyone in the world were a mere impoliteness instead of the cold-blooded terrorism it actually is.[37]

The concept of "dispossession" as "differend" implies that the Final

Solution cannot be entirely cognized by phrases, which is exploited by "revisionists" who deny its having taken place (Faurisson). But the issue is less truth than the nature of the wrong and its silence. The disturbing problematic is whether the Final Solution can be "phrased" in the register of a *result* of German or Western history. Habermas's use of a speculative, historicist model, that which he calls the utterly nonspeculative *fact* of "our sinister traditions," encodes speculation through psychology and creates the illusion of a "state of being," one that has supposedly been delivered to us by "history itself." For the readers of a "differend," this entirely displaces the Final Solution as a cultural and related problematic.[38] The couple "speculation/result" would anchor present consciousness in a social determination from which there would be no more phrases: the criminal state, the terror of racism, the reactionary psychological formation of modernity. In short, the notion of "dispossession" makes it more difficult for any of us to claim any use value, cultural or otherwise, concerning the proper name that now goes by the signifiers Final Solution.

The Differend sets aside the overcoded Hegelian straitjacket of speculative determinations. The incessant integration of negative universals is not tenable, for all it does is to concoct passive memory as the dominant form of cultural pedagogy. Instead, Auschwitz "would be the proper name of a para-experience or even of a destruction of experience" rather than Habermas's "pluperfect past that will not pass away." The latter is based upon a model of "continuities of German history," the "sinister traditions" mentioned earlier.[39] For Lyotard, this notion of the "sinister" is another cultural deus ex machina, inventing negative continuity, but too remote from events, since the phrase-structure of the death camps annihilated every phrase that the victims could link onto; amidst the "solitude and silence" of the victims, there were not "sinister traditions" but repeated and varied acts of violence and mayhem. The question is not whether a "sinister tradition" was "revived" from the past (which was then never "past"), but how to express "shame and anger over the explanations and interpretations — as sophisticated as they may be — by thinkers who claim to have found sense to this shit."[40] The conflict is between a historicization *for the present* and what can be said now by which to resist historicization of the Final Solution. What is called into question is the actual nihilistic structure of our demand for a representational system, one that would give us the narcissistic but self-destructive satisfaction of what Karl Bohrer has called a "falsely objectified tradition," meanings that block the articulation of a heterogeneous past *and* present.[41]

Lyotard asks us to imagine that a cultural formula for "Auschwitz" as thought by Nazi phrasing might take something like the following shape: "It is a norm decreed by *y* that it is obligatory for *x* to die," and that this death has no sociality left to it, since it is not a question of there having been alternatives, options, discussions, reasons, or even rationalizations; the formula manifests an unmodalized "You must die," which entails "Your right to life is not recognized," and because of this, there is no *after* reason to it. Scary as it may be, the Nazi phrase-regimen managed to absolutely *depsychologize* itself, and in this sense, the Nazis practiced a countersemiotic: their speaking, phrasing, is not something we can restore in a form that answers our "why" questions, including survivors' and critics' "recountings of all kinds."[42] There having been no norm fulfilled, satisfied, or even broken by the individual deaths of the Final Solution as spoken by the Nazi phrasing, the acts of murder destroyed even the proper name of death; in this sense

> Auschwitz is the forbiddance of the beautiful death. . . . The canonical formula of "Auschwitz" . . . would be, if we focus on the SS as "legislator": That s/he die, I decree it; or, if we focus on the deportee as the one "obligated": That I die, s/he decrees it. The authority of the SS comes out of a we from which the deportee is excepted once and for all: the race, which grants not only the right to command, but also the right to live, that is, to place oneself at the various instances of a phrase universe.[43]

No action by a Jew could link onto Nazi interpretations; they were caught by the other's narration in a place within that narration, which annulled existence a priori. They were dead within the SS narrative; Nazi stories had already been murderous, which "dispossesses" our attempts at analyzing Nazi "psyche" and "culture."[44]

The most extreme threshold of this challenge to meaning occurs when we reflect that what allowed Auschwitz "to happen" already "dispossessed" it of pegs for after-interpretations; Nazism shares this dangerous feature with other, even progressive, events of modernity — a generalized "dismantling of the bastion of signification."[45] Again, that suggests that no space is left to us for a Habermasian "history of the German people" as that which allows us to have some kind of intellectual closure, for the event in question was itself a conjunction between a racist phrase-regimen and an institutionalization of the type SS. There are no continuous links to the present: that was the whole point of becoming Nazi, *whether we like it or not.* Instead of retaining general terms like "history," Lyotard's countermodel "dispossesses" positive and negative histories based on either the psychologization of "becoming normal again" (*The*

New Conservatism) or Habermas's "exceptionalism," which relies on the psychology of debt and curse.

So the encoding of the Final Solution was itself a masterwork of death to language. Jews and others were not ordered to die according to the "logic" of SS "discourse" or because of something "in" German history. They did not have the "right to life" in the first place, since the racialist narrative of the Beautiful Death was precisely that which decreed that their "death is legitimate because one's life is illegitimate." In such "thinking," serial numbers "naturally" replaced individual names in the eradication of names, which suggests an SS metaphysics: "This death must therefore be killed, and that is what is worse than death. For, if death can be exterminated, it is because there is nothing to kill. Not even the name Jew."[46] There is no pseudolegitimation from the SS by which we can access their "unconscious," for there is no point at which Nazi and Jew intersect in a manner that would establish figures of identity, or even disidentity. As Lyotard puts it, "Dispersion is at its height. My law kills them who have no relevance to it. My death is due to their law, to which I owe nothing. Delegitimation is complete."[47] Frighteningly dispersive, negative, and analytic, the machine set in motion by the Nazis engenders no room for a critical thinking to come along and make sense. The insistence upon memory and the cultural obligation to transmit knowledge of the Final Solution to "youth" are only reactive formations *for ourselves*. It becomes precisely impossible to derive a generalization of the effect that Freud called *Nachträglichkeit*, where a past has not "passed" but continues to work within a future-present toward the presentation of a decisive "that's it." Given the "dispossession" that obtains between the phrase-universe of Nazi and the objectless nonsubjectivity of the Jews as spoken by Nazi discourse, the only connection between such divergence would be that of myth (including the psychoanalytic one, which would establish negative "mirroring" or "disidentification" or psychosis between Nazi and victim). The Nazi as the "failed child" and the victim as the "trapped infant" or "agent of capitalism" or "organic disease" could only refer to our fantasy of symbolizing and appropriating some cultural use value for ourselves, whose referent is our narcissism of continuing to pretend that there is sense.

Is there anything, then, that necessitates historicist categories? To what would they be applicable? The "unloading ramp at Auschwitz" gives an image of the fright experienced by victims; it certainly introduces a television-inspired image into the oversaturated image pools of contemporary society. The power and horror of the image is such that it is directed at those in the present who would "forget." But from the perspective of "dispossession," the Final Solution is not an event that we can reduce to images for the consensus, or need for consensus, of cultural politics. This precludes any "general history of Germany and Nazism," as Nazi murder revealed or disclosed no "universal" whatsoever (not even concerning mass psychology) and its victims experienced nothing by which we, now, can narrate what their deaths were "sacrifices for." Stripped of the positivity that results from such extreme negativity, bereft of Hegelianism, Nazism reaches us in a manner that makes it impossible to be sure which concepts *really apply* to those events. In such a feeling-scape, instead of postulating "curses" and images and cultural "liabilities," it would be better to maintain skepticism: to challenge the Final Solution as it today becomes institutionalized as an academic discipline.

After all, where is the concrete linkage between present-day Germans and the Aryan, savage narrative of the SS? How is it possible that present-day Germans born after the collapse of Nazism and who are not racist have to come to terms with the supposed "past that will not go away," as Habermas insists? Is it to be supposed that *all* Germans now, in not practicing "historical remembrance," are potential racists? And if that is so, if the potentiality of racism is the referred yet exorcised part that actually informs Habermas's model of cultural criticism, then why doesn't *The New Conservatism* address that topic instead of putative "universals" of German history and culture?

Conclusion: Myth and Criticism

The savage narratives of Nazism are criticized by Habermas after he reduces them to the imagistic evocation of their criminality. It is doubtful whether Nazism is reducible to criminality, a category of law. I believe it is wishful thinking to postulate law and its breaking as a foundation for understanding this limit-event of representation. Similarly, law and concepts of criminality will not help us address the question: Why did the Americans drop *two* atomic bombs? Notions of criminality are not the issue and signify, in fact, an agenda of nostalgia — the criminal, after all, has been judged and society has, in that judgment, been vindicated.[48] Nazism made law irrelevant; it showed law to be an ambiguous formation within modernity, irrelevant to one of the active forms of the modern state. This implies that enlightenment after the fact can be inappropriate to what happened, by deluding subjects that names and interpretations have value by the demand to "remember." They may not. Habermas's "unloading ramp at Auschwitz" would culturally empower an Everyone to possess the Final Solution in a manner that renders it no longer argumentative, since the image and name of the "unloading ramp" operates a priori as object and limit on other images and, in fact, governs the power to image.

What does the phrase "German history" mean? Or "German people"? Or "German nation"? It is highly implausible that these terms stand for actualities, save mythic ones. Lyotard's *The Differend* offers something else; that we consider modern events as active in the register of splitting apart and recombining such "wholes" as "German nation" or "German people," constructs that were mythological in 1933. The reiteration of "German" smacks of a deictic mytheme, an overcoded cultural wish-projection. Of course Habermas is correct to set aside the false "normalization" of the Final Solution, but at the same time this negation of the false supposes that the "true" belongs to a psychological "recognition" — which supposes "consensus" in the here and now by every "German." The "unloading ramp at Auschwitz" would be an encapsulating image and, far worse, it would preside over the legitimation of cultural politics now. I do not see how intellectuals should allow their work to serve culture or politics, especially at the cost of taking sides with the dominant players. Is there a sense to the Final Solution that "reflection" can take hold of, apart from these overcharged psychologemes; if anything needs to be explained, it is not the epideictics of the Aryan "beautiful death" but the contemporary language game(s) of psychological historicism.

Put another way, in the word-conflicts over the Final Solution, Habermas practices a dangerous game: he does not see that modern Capital may be "dispossessive" of the very "reason" he wants to establish. On the one hand, terms such as "German" or "reflection" or "life-context" are intended to convey certain social and linguistic negative continuities when connected to the "exceptional" aspects of the Final Solution ("our sinister traditions"). These overcharged terms are also connected to affirmative predicates — mourning, remembrance, and "detached philosophical thinking" — an amalgam intended to signify an enlightened perspective. There is thus a negative and positive of "continuity." But this enlightenment turns out to be an affirmation of myth, where the West is defined in empty terms (a formal recourse to law, but since it is unaffordable, is it still law?) and where every cultural/political move that is not enlightened is negated. The affirmative myth-judgment concerning the West as a model of positivity obscures the counterjudgment that Capital is not aligned, safely, with "fundamental liberalization."

Because Habermas does not consider Capital to share the semantic-real space of irrationality, he rejects the so-called young conservatives (Derrida and company) as antirational and antimodern, and hence irresponsible, critics. It seems to me that if Habermas were to consider Capital within the semantic orb of criminality (which is already perhaps reductive), it would dismantle the construction of the Final Solution as an event of both "exceptionality" *and* "learning," this because to acknowledge the "civilized nihilism" or the "acceptable criminality" of Capital would mean a nonmediated encounter with *facts of the present*, and such "facts" would make it impossible to encode the Final Solution as "exceptional": if extermination of the "human countenance" is Nazi, then why isn't Capital another form of this overall Nazism?

As opposed to Habermas's endeavors to salvage modernity by separating into categories such as criminal and enlightened, Lyotard's critique suggests that the Final Solution is not intrinsically attached to any "historical" mode of comprehension. Dispossession and the concept of a differend remind us that modernity is not itself a necessarily "historical" phenomenon. An analysis of ambivalences and dangers built into modernity (e.g., the "normal" asociality of Capital) might show that the Final Solution pushed its own dispossession beyond limit, beyond "speculative dialectics," by its connection to a mythic narrative, which, paradoxically, resulted in "Silences, instead of a *Resultat*." The real fright concerning modernity is that it still expands in the political and social-economic spheres, while the cultural and critical ones are trapped by premodern belief formations like that of training consciousness to react.

The next chapter, "The Disappearance of History," will take up in a more detailed manner how it is possible to maintain (if it is) a contemporary sense of "history" in the light of the ambiguity of modernity treated as a cultural construct. Following some remarks by Matei Calinescu from his *Faces of Modernity*, in particular his remark that "Modernity . . . appears as the history of the battle to give value to the present," the chapter considers what the grounds might be for any linkage between present (contemporaneity) and "history."

4

The Disappearance of History

Are "we" today still able to give credence to the concept of a sign of history?

Lyotard, *The Differend*

Introductory Remarks

The idea of a "disappearance of history" is treated here as a concept relevant to discussions of cultural criticism inasmuch as it refers to the *ambiguity* of "before/after" in establishing precedent, rank, hierarchy, the force of argument. As a concept concerning reality, "history" is invoked by dominant players as a strategic move and will be treated here as an essentially politicizing construct: "history" is involved when subject groups are engaged in the formation of a state, a government, codifications of sense, desire, and power. As I trace some conceptual reasons for the "disappearance of history" from contemporary Western societies — its noncontact, so to speak, with newer "reals" — the suggestion will emerge that none of the compelling actual problems one *could confront* are themselves "historical." Put in the strongest terms, if it is unimaginable to give, once and for all, a material sense to "history," then is there any compelling sense to the constancy of any "name of history"? There are no "historical realities" in the same way that one can argue for financial or psychological ones (but even these terms are suspect, for reasons we shall see). How does one come to acknowledge that "historical consciousness" is of no use in trying to make determinations as to "what's going on," that the concept doesn't even work, that it's a lousy machine? This is not just an issue of the irrelevance of "before/after" when applied to public life, or opposition to the widespread belief that there is a Western cultural gestalt attached to "history" such that the present is perforce a "historical" phenomenon. I start out from the linguistically informed judgment that "historical consciousness" is a form of law and order, based upon the construction of a typical historian's narrative, and, as a corollary, that it is metapolitical to that extent, that is, not restricted to one political classification. I go on to trace various appearances of its "disappearance" in some contemporary cultural theories, particularly social and aesthetic areas. The flow of this essay moves between the "disappearance" of plausibility belonging to this order-form and suggestions about emerging structures of Western Capital that are difficult to characterize in narrative terms. Capital is understood here as having plunged university-based thinking in academic sign-value, maintenance of the flow of scholarly performance as *currency*.

Drawing upon Barthes's classification of myth-forms, an initial cultural, linguistic figure of historiography is that of the insider's tautologism, a form emptied of all traces of nonidentity. Here is a piece of it from an erudite historian in which the assimilation of narrative and history and truth and mystery and more sketches a mythological system of absolute wish-projection:

> Narratives are historical in that they are not arbitrary, inasmuch as they
> are true, that is to say, historical. The "truth" or authenticity of a
> historical narrative—if we strip off the subjective categories and points of
> view of the narrator—is, like the *je ne sais quoi* of 18th century aesthetic
> theoreticians, or like Kant's "intuition," evasive, incapable of isolation, yet
> ever present; triggered—we do not know how—by "things in
> themselves" that we cannot define except to say that they are, and are of
> necessity.[1]

True to its assertions, the quotation is most active in the register of cliché. The "are" asserts itself as a primordial concatenation of the faculty of judging, which is presented as an entirely unambiguous practice. Nothing is argued; every security for "historical thought" is tied to the form of assertion, that is, it remains removed from expressions that open it to other sides, perceptions, arguments, or ideas that one may not control. That's just the first sentence. In the second, "truth" and "authenticity" get married, after they are first domesticated; this makes room for the final clause, where now that cultural forms—language—are exterminated, the holy religiosity of narrative power is confirmed by "things in themselves." The historians must be collectively mad if they circulate such phrasings as anything but sad indices of a depressant profession, which elevates a irresponsible attitude to linguistic disputes into a license to practice.

In this chapter, I explore some of the reasons why a "historical reason" is a reason for laughter, reason considered attached to what Antonio Negri, after Spinoza, has called "the savage versatility of being" instead of the command centers of academic institutions.[2] In addition, if Capital ceaselessly redynamizes social relations, where all the "historical clocks" are transformed into hourglasses on their side, then how could the obvious absurdity of there never appearing in person this "historical reason" manage to linger on? Capital, if it thinks, must think of every raising of the name of "history," in all its forms, as the epiphany of the triumph of a spirit world, the past that is waiting for us to "close it." This idiotic projection into the past of its being turned toward us is just another figure in suppressing what historical writing despises: those "strange flows which circulate" (Deleuze), and not in ways that return to Hegelian, Marxian, and Freudian conjugations.

A "disappearance of history" begins with the shift out of time-consciousness possessing an "objective" or "subjective" identity with capitalist-driven times. Since these times are derived from nonsynchronous movements and actions, as in a "vampiric" or zombie-like time (shopping), or accelerations that outstrip the capacity for storified times to "intervene" (small-scale exterminations of reflection), it has become unclear exactly what "clocks," instruments, meters, beatings, and more *could* matter. Institutions, including those of the criticism market, require that one learn to pay attention to lengths (time codes), repetitions (structures), and processes (directions), since these forms are directly creative of labor and cultural socialities. Codes such as precursor-affiliation, sometimes confused with precedents, or narrative confirmations (one has a recognizable past) are fundamental to the stability of, say, the rehistoricization of American political "history," and account for an extreme psychologization of feeling, which can dominate social "understanding." But can the narrations of political and social roles (the hero, the fool, the marauder, the dope, the bully, etc.) be as interesting as the actual sociality between, say, progressives such as Jesse Jackson and the masses who supposedly see an alternative in another well-to-do politico? Considered simply at the level of narrative descriptions, is there not — as I will suggest below — something like an actual "sinister kitsch" (Baudrillard) that prevails over any "narrative history," whereby Jackson and the media ceaselessly position the other for use value in the other's deployment of images? It is legitimate to ask why one would bother to historicize such politics when there is more to "marvel" at in the contacts, the linkages, the couplings themselves.[3]

Let me continue these introductory remarks by saying that what finally intrigues me is the impossibility of "historicity": to fully "historicize" (contextualize) complicated phenomena of the present-future is intellectually futile, since the more one embeds the "real" in narrated context(s) the more that something will—if it releases any active energies—show itself to be unamenable to our narrative designations. Something can be narrated—historicized—that has been already reduced, by signs (language) to social control. Intellectually, it is more stimulating to postulate that there are forces, acts, syntheses, possibilities, effects that are independent of us yet no less actual for our being unable to directly narrate them:

> names with regions of intensity that provide the impetus toward other still more intense regions, stimuli of one sort or another that set in motion another journey altogether, stases that prepare for other breakthroughs, other movements.[4]

An objectifying force is inherent in any formation that is trying to live, to express itself, to modify itself, and it does not matter whether one is referring to things, people, signs, indices, paragraphs, or mountains, for the effects are different from "historical" narrativity, whose *invariance* (of form) cannot place phenomena "in variation . . . without beginning and end." Instead of the "je ne sais quoi" of our straw historian, in which it is supposed that *equations obtain* between event, consequent, reference, interpretation, and the like, it is rather that a phenomenon narrated is finalized and hence uninteresting, and this *wording* in advance of expressive forces is unstimulating.[5] One antidote to "historical consciousness" is linguistic skepticism, but so is a life active in diminishing as much as possible all "politics as usual," which is the overcoded referent of "historical thought." Stories of decline can themselves initiate decline (but do not have to); expressions of desires irreducible to "history" are also, perhaps, irreducible to "historical" effects and functions.

From another angle, it can be said that what is disappearing today is the mythos of academic form—that modern "historical consciousness," as an exclusionary and hence political identity, is adrift. That it never existed in an identity with its own name is acknowledged, as Stephen Bann has pointed out, when one considers that this consciousness only appeared *as* the effect of "recreating the real." When one speaks about having a "historical sense," one really means being able to "recreate" some event or other. This massive secondary elaboration, this overdeveloped Western function—"recreating the real" by means of narratives, dioramas, epic cinema, and literature—is disappearing both as normal practice and as an increase of revisionism. Does revisionism really express the exceptionality of the normal? Revisionism tends to an identification with new powers: "We have been excluded and deserve the center" is often the fatality built into its thought.[6] Revisionism, as contrasted with wholesale transformation of all the elements of meaning, continues the passage of culture onto the control of bureaucracies of meaning — schools, galleries, museums and so on — whose luxurious reactivity stands out against "general society" and its skidding toward "infotainment" and worse.

But at the same time, historicism (general form) is also a precise structure in Western culture's attempt to position itself in, and for, the future. Hence it will not disappear. This has a technical or epistemic aspect. Historicism may be said to involve the following: (1) it signifies views that assert a nonpast "past" or the continuity of now and then; (2) this assertion of continuity also territorializes, or tries to, a playing field in which claimants must put forth "historical" justifications or find their "games" discredited; and (3) the future is forced to "resemble" the new entity, the *passed-present*. The cultural "logic" of historicism aims at a reduction of conflict to *a* politics or *a* social model allowing for the drawing of straight lines, but such "logic" holds only for those who *already* require it. Formally, I would like to stress that "historicism" requires a "past" made into a function of an extreme cultural determination: conflict must have a distinctive form — it must take place within language unchallenged as representative and representing. The name "history" ensures that no "living" struggles are recognized until compared and reduced to an exchange "with the past." Any event can be historicized; no event comes to anyone as "historical." Historicism's function is that of giving credentials to interests whose actants receive the advantage of time in the here and now; one comes credentialed — one's claims and counterclaims receive the cultural plus-value of being regarded as serious and justified *simply because* historicism passes onto events and renders them significant, as worthy values. The additive factor — that one has a name, which renders the subjective pole objective — guarantees the spacing of articulation; and one has no claim, no right, no subjectivity, no power because one's names are not recognized by the existing "historicist" encyclopedia.

Historicism's reductive equations — whose typical form is that of a past recognized by present names, which in turn equals the construction of a future that resembles the present — thus de-space interesting "presences" (what Nietzsche called the dissolution of "aura," and what seems, in that way, to have stimulated Walter Benjamin). Such destructive equations appear (to some) to embody an attitude of hatred and contempt for any "presencing" that cannot be immediately plugged into existing "uniforms" and identities. Because of this control factor, it is useful to remind oneself that Nietzsche called "historical comparisons" the "walking lie" that scorches the terrain of "superhistorical" creativity.[7] The historicist discourse is something to be feared, something to practice a creative paranoia against.

The narrated past is given to Western readers as something objective; the mode of its telling — linear perspective, appropriate literary plot, resolutions of conflict, absence of subjective markers — concocts a falsely "objective" *future* the instant the referent/object slips into a reader's linguistic unconsciousness. Because the typical historian's narrative is a writing that does not invite argument, is the historian not also a "helper" in providing chronic narrative "doses" that delegitimate unrecognized claims? Narrations whose language overcodes necessity become the suppression of alternativity. If there is an ethic to this chapter, it is in trying to subvert the conjunction between choice = history, to disengage from the rigid satisfactions of "history."[8]

What follows brings into consideration the argument that the concept of "history" is moribund as a cultural construct, which leaves it open as to how pastness as such is to be presented (Nietzsche: "There could be a kind of historical writing that had no drop of common fact in it and yet could claim to be called in the highest degree objective").[9] More affirmative is the fact that this judgment opens onto the further discussion of events where the "disappearance of history" ceases to differentiate, ceases to pose the terms of description, and where "something else" occurs. The line of argument is consonant with what Collingwood called "to fasten upon the difficulties and obscurities . . . involved" in thinking itself: "The philosopher therefore, in the course of his business, must always be confessing his difficulties, whereas the historian is always concealing them [to impress and convince . . . bombast]."[10] The ethics involved is a matter of sidestepping becoming the ancestor of a future decimated in advance by having an overwhelming past to contend with: there's an impossible idea, of a present that did not add to the burden of the future. It seems also, in an introduction, to suggest that dehistoricization might equal ahistoricity, experiences for the future that do not diminish a future's possibilities. To try and not injure the future? What kind of idea is that? Perhaps this means nothing more than experiences in suspension from a freezing immersion in sign-valuations, new joys and new terrors with which to occupy ourselves. Make something of all the muck. In the same way that J.-J. Goux has argued that the social logic of currency does not align with one's affective sense of money (what one thinks one is worth), so too no version of "history" maps experiences for the future — without thereby destroying the difference of the future. I will remind the reader throughout that every calling up of the signifier "history" plunges one into mostly uninteresting mythologies.

Hence, "disappearance" is mobile enough to connect with setting aside of use value to the concept "history" and also, I will argue, to refuse the vanity of comparing oneself to "first," "last," and other syntagma of time-rank, that remarkable institutionalization of seniority; this "disappearance" is an opportunity to break the line of temporal models of integration, notably the incestuous couple of nostalgia/utopia, one of the molding forms of competition over precursors and ancestors, one of the malevolent evocations of time as something wasted. This critique of historicism is intended to include psychological versions, like that of Habermas, which would subject a reinvented Everyone to the pedagogics of reinstruction at the altar(s) of what went wrong with the West. All in all, it takes up the Nietzschean challenge that forgetfulness is part of that life "continuing and eternal," which differs from the "scientific, the finished, the historical" by virtue of not being a negation or rejection of all this "secondhand life," and in not being that, allows for not returning to the "world-process and the personality of the earthworm" given to us by historians.

Modernity, Temporalities

I begin by pursuing an implication of Bataille's remark that the concept of "history" was pulled into flux along with other elements of the "foundations of things"; the modern, which is this "fallen into a bottomless void," frames the "human being who arrives at the threshold: there he must throw himself headlong into that which has no foundation and no head."[11] This existentialism without a subject is challenged, without possibility of revocation, to not become enfeebled in the face of reactivity. Invoking "history" to locate oneself only generates the illusion of a distance from the *actual surplus of the nonhistorical*, for the actual world of one's life is composed by this surplus of choices and effects.

Modernism so considered is not a process but more a maze; temporal modes such as a "cumulative learning process" (Habermas) or the "disciplining of the body" (Foucault) or the appropriative and directive powers of the modern state (process, function, objective direction) are continuums, positive and negative, which hardly account for the active aggression and temporal dislocation of, say, the development of advanced radio technology in the homogenization of sound. The "improved" hearing of the "silences" may well be contained by a larger, overall reduction of those "sounds" to our recording devices. The modern, after it is reduced to straight, parallel, geometric (even if plural), and multiple lines, provides for intellectual comfort — it makes modernity understandable. The lifeline of middle-class marriage may well have cut through an ambiguous promiscuity, or the emergence of computer "patience" might actually erode "productive time"; what kind of narrative form can claim that it summarizes less than it complicates? Sad to say, what is compelling from the perspective of cultural ruminations is that the Final Solution is an example of an uncontrollable line: was it archaic and modern? Charles Levin has connected modernism to a "postmortem effect," the "success" of "a psychology of the after-image, a hermeneutics of life as lack, castration and death."[12] This suggests a modernity that is more restabilizing than historicizing, one whose strongest lines are creating some really weird angles (the working poor).

To some, the term modernity fits into a preexisting "historical" register, particularly that of a one-way linearity, a future becoming more and more subject to human decision making of every sort. It was Kant who presided over a nature that could only come under our scientizing protocols (all our capacities must be, can only be, developed to "perfection"). But this aspect has given out as sustainable for the organization of "historical knowledge," and modernity has left the historians high and dry. The modern orgy of destruction of the "ties that bind" identities and oppositions has eaten through all the expected results and goals; "despite isomorphisms and isotopies, no formation provides the model for another," writes Deleuze in suggesting that modernity might be thought of as a deactualization of the integrating and unifying narratives, even of some antinarratives of sociality.[13]

What matters here, I think, is that an important time effect of a "disappearance of history" has already occurred, namely that "history" and time are not necessary to each other, that the finalities and names of the former are only forcibly made to cohere with the events and occurrences, movements, of the latter. We could generalize a remark made by Phillipson in considering Duchamp's art-making in terms of a "general theory of art," namely, that "art in its very concreteness already fragments all systematising theory." Without making this into an axiom or rule, it could be that Capital is the nonsimple form of this accelerating fragmentation.[14] In any case, the concrete, which fragments instead of serving as the raw material or base of syntheses, allows one to consider serialization and other temporalizations as already agrammatical in terms of their inability to provide figures for modernity. Being does not speak to us in the form of *our* "historical sentences." This is particularized in noting that the classical pattern of historicity has dissolved in the general difficulty of expecting to "learn from" exempla and norms, generalizable exceptions, and other combinations of time processes. Relations between dating and naming are *both* tightened and loosened. If the lines to the future are themselves more and more fractured, then it is control of contextually "hot" sign-values that oversees the transformation of consciousness, including the activities of artists and intellectuals. Can one "join history" today, as so many believe? Or is it rather that one "links with" functional situations whose effectivity is *completely* absorbed by the reproduction of circulating sign-values (e.g., image-value, exchange-marker, negotiating-term: what signs have been put on you which another "reader" desires to deploy for their larger practices?). No series can make another signify an irresistible, datable memory: architectural monumentalism or military conflicts or avant-garde literary experiences do not express the force of temporal recentering; there is more to remember, while nothing determines the meaning of *another memory*.

Reinhart Koselleck, in his estimable *Futures Past*, notes, with much intriguing evocation, how modernity dissolved "millennial expectations" of a break with temporality — cultural modernism as a negation of discontinuity, the impossibility of another peasant's war (for example) — and was replaced by the temporality of "prognosis," a general form that, under Capital, recodes synthesizing reintegration: "weighing the probability of forthcoming or nonoccurring events" was another way of producing various controlled temporalities, since "the prognosis implies a diagnosis which introduces the past into the future. This always-already guaranteed futurity of the past effected the closure and bounding of the sphere of action available to the state."[15] Classical exempla or canonical signifieds gave way to both the unique event and philosophies of history whose purpose was to "tie and bind" the plurality of series of events into ever-comprehending wholes. As exempla were systematically annulled by an increasing derealization of possibilities (it has been a very long time since significant numbers of people grew their own . . . raised . . . built . . .), it was "historical narrative [that] was expected to provide . . . unity."[16]

But Koselleck projects this unity — or explains its supposed existence — by holding fast to links between "history" and mutable structures, which are the referents keeping "history" from dissolve. "History thus shows us the boundaries of the possible otherness of our future."[17] He does not take the logical step, which is bluntly "there," and challenge the signifier in and of itself. For if "history" shows what is *formally* the structure of the future, then the "future" is not "future" and the past is not "past." Saving a sense of "historical consciousness" *at any cost* seems to me to be importantly connected with the inability of constituting differences "off the lines" of narrative linearities.

Shifting to the terrain of events, one could argue that it is the emphatic pattern of named "historical experiences" as experiences of dissolution —

the "rusting" of America comes to mind — that render "history" as conceptually suspended. "Historical learning" of the prognostic version gives way to an *overflowed consciousness: a regime is installed — the future never happened*. Differences emerge that are unrecuperable. A senselessness of "historical reason" captures it from the inside, and this pertains to what is distinctive about Capital. For isn't it arguable that modernity is "like" an impermanent permanence or a "transitory eternity" insofar as it surrenders so quickly to dehistoricization by Capital? A flood of money one day, somehow, the regularity of scraping by "all the time." One in five Americans in 1991 changed jobs, were at some point unemployed in a system whose saturating norms are precisely those of Capital. Does one narrate a "history of" housing since 1945 or describe its becoming a sign-value, a trap, a desire, an uncomfortable refuge? Valéry believed that for his generation "history" was a "poor" guide to the future. This already old idea, always dreaded by the historians, appears today to minds once sure of emancipation, liberation, fulfillment (Lyotard), now nullified by nonhistorical events that are built at the outset as things undecidable: contemporary experiences do not cohere with "history" as their conceptual sense and may not be reducible to a time spun out of an integrating consciousness. In short, "history" may more plausibly be said to intersect with an enlarging *perversion*, itself characterized by the unfolding of moments neither "neurotic" (where time is displaced) nor "psychotic" (where time stops), but instead "a defensive linear subjectification," a k a the demand for culture.[18] The stockbroking life idealized as (past) sensory thrill, or the intellectual seized by nostalgia for "real work," or the academic endlessly politicizing so as to make marginal cultural experiences "central" to everyone's daily life. Seemingly impossible conjunctions replace "history": a lottery effect of the social or the boredom involved in the "service sector" of the economy render, in different ways, images of an ahistorical life.

All experiences can be historicized — made to serve as retroactive links in a chain of succession, reduced to blocks of time as so many impediments to the arduous tasks of creating a different future. The result, of a surplus of unnecessary or mythic precursors, would establish the rule of no precursors without history = no claims to the future. Modernity has taken up the historian's implicit challenge and has answered back, in many ways, but in every case with the response that the future is threatened. We cannot use "history" in situations where the future is "postreal," to put it somewhat too glibly; it is a pretense, then, to suggest that somehow there is continuity across the lines of past, present, future. The pretense has itself become an archaic capitalist commodity. Indeed, the expansion of contemporary "historical knowledge" with the addition of social and feminist and labor "histories" also co-occurs with the virtually complete "dumbing down" of Western youth.

"Has Happened" and Capital

The stabilizing force of "historical consciousness" — a "before and after" assigned to each series of experience, each series given a commanding subject, each subject given a necessary fate/outcome — has made capitalism a valid and legitimate "historical subject." This is a mental disaster: how can any rational person not laugh hard at the idea that capital entered the world isomorphic with a benevolent "historical" narrative? The West "needed" the world, Braudel uttered in his revision of Historical Orphism. What sustains Capital is the grafting to it of a philosophy of history derived from theopolitics, the unity of now-then-will be, whose "living present" synthesizes a transcendental subject and references an otherness on both sides of the "now." One is *stuck* in the equation between "history" and "living present." Precapital equals something undeveloped (humanity, individuation, positivity of science, etc.), which occurs as soon as Capital is narrated as a subject whose performativity is definitely one of synthetic goals, directions, forces, desires, outcomes, attributes of will and intention. There is self-legitimation built into narrative definitions of Capital. The "narratives of foundation" of Capital (e.g., Braudel's projection that the introduction of banking "fulfilled" a *general* evolutionary "need") have been reinforced by the socialist acceptance of capitalism as a necessary conveyor to a better future (what is socialism without "history" to look like?). "History" in these terms is riveted to the promulgation of some collective identity, while Capital performs immediate *deidentifying* operations: they drop dead at work in Japan and within months of retirement in the United States. Even in right-wing narratives of American nationalism, the idea of the United States is already unrecoverable. "Historical" narratives usher in the consolations of interiorized, controlled images of an "all-encompassing Being" (Deleuze). Capital is in and of itself destructive *to* that very "historicity."

That conjunction unwraps the body of "has happened." This was the elementary category of modern historicisms, the stickiness of an event that cannot be gotten round, the unquestioned assumption that some recognizable narrative form was then necessary in the telling. But "has happened" has definitively "lost" its status as material for cultural prognosis. What succeeds it is *chronicity* projected as representative "duels" with time (e.g., the struggle of Germans to "reconcile" with the Final Solution, a nonevent that has, interestingly, a similar structure to that *reactive status* like the Aztec lore that forecast, retroactively, the coming of the white gods who would/had to devour them). The "historical consciousness" postulated by Hegel, in what were exquisite passages of time as the other, of chronos as contest, of fate as gravity, and the like, are driven out of the social by formations of contemporary Capital. *The contest gives way to generalized testing.* "Has happened" follows the general flow of reality: the rhetorics (*pace* Hayden White) which authorized that "yesterday" slides into an identity with "founding" and "basis," or that the present lacks something and so needs "providers," gives way to what the Althusserians called cultural overdetermination, but which is really an enormous nonintersecting oxymoron: absolute contextualization in which no "historical" expression holds for any other context. "Has happened" does not anchor models of historicized time in a social system that is always "onto" the next turn, the next anticipation, the next pause, the next speedup.[19]

The historicist category "has happened" does not demarcate a special cognitive moment binding for understanding. It was supposed to give rise to the *narrativized comparison*, the precursor, the precedent, a situation of normative determinism: the imperative order of a "do this" because it stands continuous or discontinuous with a "do that." Converted to the plus-value of marking time, the filling of a space *stretched* over time, *tradition* was the *referent* and function of narrative followability, given at least one comparing/compared relation. Narrativized by statist syntax, "has happened" demarcated a "once," the singular, something nonrecurring, the "real uselessness" of the past outside itself. Another name for this was contextual "aura," a very ambiguous concept which we have transformed into a vulgarity of "loss." A self-transcending present (oxymoronic in its core), "has happened" was pressed into generating the lengthening and shortening of temporal continuities, at the expense of otherwise "unbounded" or partially "free territories," not yet under the control of a time-based spatial reduction. Historiography was injected into grammar. I have in mind here Fredric Jameson's notion that "collective time" takes away the "sharpness and pain" of individual death — a "community time" is/should be established as a "lightening" of the slowness (= agon) of dying. Such an idealization of unity would seem to disallow a noncommunity dying, replete with *unofficial* values. People may not like the difficulties of not having "has happened" as automatic cliché at their disposal, but at least there's an inventive aspect to it.[20]

Further, "has happened" was converted into a statist "history" by belief in a subject of final resort, some which or who that can be set against the materiality of "universal variation" (Deleuze), and an infinity of noncoinciding logics. Dispersion negated. Such an inward pull relied upon what can be called contests of symmetrical couples: capitalism/socialism, progress/decline, and so on, the function of which was to grind a potentially unlimited number of distinctions away so that the comparative "method" can operate without difficulty.[21] This supposed an enormous hermeneutics supplying "interpreters" with sanctified events (e.g., ranks, grades of "has happened"). An event brought to the "bar" of comparison is stripped of its force. As Nietzsche suggested, we locate a "cause" from "behind"; in doing so, we block those past transformations in which what was selected and not selected as motivations threatens our interpretations. "Has happened" acknowledged that we're doing the interpreting and that this did not interfere with the event "getting through."

In the orbit of what can be called official narration, a statism still commands "officiality" and encourages the continuation or repetition of what Lyotard calls *narrations of the unreal*:

> Once the givens are established, a new genre of discourse is required, one whose canonical phrase is *What can we do?* This phrase is not without analogy with what Kant calls an Idea of the imagination (intuitions without a concept) . . . scenarios or simulations. . . . A multiplicity of possible, probable, and improbable stories are told heedless of their verisimilitude.[22]

Lyotard goes on and argues that such phrases serve to "silence one's interlocutor," insofar as "What can we do?" also contains criteria for delegitimation of rules that would threaten the games. Statism appropriated a monumentalist treatment of "history," in particular the nationalist stories that are today seemingly less virulent than stories of "crisis" and denunciation. One of the characters of ahistoricity is the suspension of the subjectivities implied by these stories. Operating across verbal and visual media, "has happened" was linked to narrative prescriptions whose linguistic expression marked out the "true being" of "progressive" subjects. Habermas, while acknowledging problems with the "self-image" and "self-understanding" of the modern university, nonetheless monumentalizes "the communicative or discursive forms of scientific argumentation," delusionally treating the on-again, off-again *occurrence* of that description as the real subject of the university, a proposition that places *nonlinguistic* and potentially uncontrollable linguistic effects under the medium of universal speech. Is it a "historical" issue who controls the university, or does a discussion of this belong to another sphere altogether? "Has happened" — behind and ahead at the same time, this magic of temporality, this ecstasy of narrative form — can only be effective in the mythic atmosphere of beliefs that hold that all subjectivities of the collective are properly constituted. "Historical culture" ensures that Capital is never narrated in the nonsubject position (of uninteresting waste, for example); the issue today is whether "has happened" can be stabilized along its classical functions.

The negative identity of "has happened" enforced a high-bourgeois cultural configuration: it condemned one to be socially and culturally futural as present and past were absorbed by a narrativized or storified "history." Temporal deferral and purpose were connected in the seme of "later," which, as a code, ushered in the doubleness of obligation/ anticipation. This domesticating aspect ruled, by whatever temporary overcoding, that American Westerns positioned the Indian as doomed/ self-destructive, a negative precursor, an "earlier" with no future. There is not enough room in the future: even this is projected through the "has happened." Each past's "is happening" transformed into an "it has happened"; and a story told by someone about himself or herself is obliterated—John Wilkes Booth becomes Son of Sam becomes Sirhan Sirhan, the story of assassins reduced to that of insane men, whose "good" addressee can then *switch off* more difficult ideations. In modern historiography, *names as identities are preserved.* Or in psychological lingo, a malleable and castrated past is used to make immediate judgments where complexities are reduced to story forms. "Has happened," in its semantico-emotive aspect, territorialized on the body of contestability. It is also, as a cultural form, part of the "melancholy haphazardness" of an unwilled future as described by Hannah Arendt.

Let me conclude this discussion of "has happened," this cell form of modern "historical thought," which is now itself caught up in the jeopardy of meaning. "Has happened" occurs in semantic variations that say exactly how action and force have been reduced to familiarity; in this way, it supports the construction of narratives that can be read as final. Whether passive/aggressive reactivity ("We were taken unawares . . . ", "If we had known . . . ") or assertive disjunctive ("Truman had no choice but to order the second bomb"), "has happened" prevented, by acting as a prescriptive form, the nonhistoricity of events from appearing. In Deleuze's terminology, the nonhistorical involves

> becoming the child of one's own events. The wound is something that I receive in my body, in a particular place, at a particular moment, but there is also an eternal truth of the wound as an impassive, incorporeal event. . . . *Amor fati,* to want the event, has never been to resign oneself, still less to play the clown or the mountebank, but to extract from our actions and passions that surface refulgence, to *counter-effectuate the event,* to accompany that effect without body, that part which goes beyond the

accomplishment, the immaculate part. A love of life which can say yes to death.[23]

Isn't this what Carlo Ginzburg rails against when he threatens to castrate historians if they break through "realism" and think that "historiography . . . creates it own object"?[24]

Where any such superhistorical *amor fati* threatens the identity that every event = a narratable result, "has happened" tried to close a potentially dizzying circle of uncontrollable meanings. Its attendant *cultural economy*, in which there is a "normal" expansion of revisionism, especially its institutionalization (e.g., Holocaust historiography: was "it" the German "curse," as Habermas puts it in *The New Conservatism*, or was modernism responsible, as Bauman argues?), is utterly opposed to the uncontrolled release of this Deleuzian "countereffect." Given the vast resources of narrative language, "has happened," in de Certeau's words, "constantly mends the rents in the fabric that joins both past and present. It assures a meaning which surmounts the violence and the divisions of time."[25]

As writing, being written, saying, stating, denoting, and so on, "historical discourse" creates a *seam*, which is nonmetaphorically a verbal shroud provided by Western culture for subjects who already identify with the reactivity of "processes" (like shopping, as Fukuyama describes it). Each political version of "history" would characterize different stitches, as it were, in postulating a "falsely objectified tradition" (Bohrer). "Escape" from forms of "official becoming," of saying something that is not appropriable, or not easily, by the codes that ceaselessly level and flatten the plane of action and reduce life to the reproduction of domestic politics with its precise local power games, is something the historians are unable to think. Ginzburg, who denounces at every occurrence the name "effective," does so with no consciousness but that of literary idealism, a k a elite Philistinism, when he quotes what he thinks is the foundation of "historical thinking," one's being "a slave of the thing in itself."[26]

Instead of this mythic alibi, the "disappearance of history" is an opportunity to "conceive the present, to affirm the notion of the present," with the history machines turning in the void.[27]

Narration, Criticism

Here it is a question of mapping how narrations are both authoritarian and implausible.

It was Orwell's generation that remained antagonistic to the big ideas of Truth and Right and National Community, which were often enlistment campaigns in someone else's war. Using naturalist imagery, Orwell emphasized a criticism that would pull out meanings that have sunk their "roots into all the fibres of the human intellect" (Humboldt). Orwell was an optimist when it came to the linguistic apparatus. The near-total bombardment by images and signs makes it impossible to share the strategy of "uprooting" today; rationalizations and critiques attendant on the "field" turn in a conceptual system now irrelevant.

Intellectual difference from the devices of historicizing has to suspend strategies of resistance. Nonhistorical criticism is undoubtedly going to have to invent many devices around what Barthes called the "writerly," that is,

> the writerly text is ourselves writing, before the infinite play of the world (the world as function) is traversed, intersected, stopped, plasticized by some singular system (Ideology, Genus, Criticism). . . . writerly is the novelistic without the novel, poetry without the poem . . . writing without style.[28]

"Historical resistance" in forms suggesting a desire for ownership — to "take over" — gives way to an *achronic persistence* of states and conditions notable for their boundaries and limits, their thresholds and risks, whose ends and goals are already dehistoricized. Contemporary Capital has not ushered in narrations of strife and reconciliation but a *rush* to conclusions that are not ends, maxi- and minimizations (the mania to stay middle-class; the derailing of work by means of socialized dis-ease [stress]). Repositioning replaces narrative conclusions.

What does resistance "look like" to, say, someone abusing power in an institutional setting, where the force of law stands as the barrier to confrontation? How does one resist a power play whose very structure is committed to the taking of power while being in opposition to it (the liar)? What has "history" ever said about such phenomena?

Phrases like "the founding fathers," "the legacy," the "master" have become immediately laughable as matrices of narrative order. Bush and Castro mirror each other in a parody of Lacanian theory; they give off symbols of an insipid imaginary (pork rinds, baseball), not a narrative origin (pork rinds and baseball are both of an industrial system); they disclose a semantic pertinence activated as pseudohistorical referents. How is it possible to argue for the objective subjectification of "historical narrations" in a scene where T-shirts operate as "personal cultural dictionaries" of an immediate unsociality?

There is a choice to be made between narration and criticism, and this concerns possibilities in a debureaucratization of one's thought-signs. Narration is inconceivable without the modality of exotactic doing, composed of "having to" (must) and "being able to" (can); "must" and "can" are often contrasted with a mode of endotactic being, made up of "wanting" and "knowing." The first, when "translated" into "historical" expressions, emerges in statements where distinct subjects are linked together by such phrases as "finding themselves under fire, they returned . . . ," whose cause is a matter of acknowledging some time-prior necessity condition (Humean "habit"). The statement "Kissinger believed he was acting as any tenured professor might in ordering the bombing of Cambodia" activates or modalizes the desire of a subject, the professor as warrior, Kissinger, and embeds this implicitness by appeal to the "normal" condition of being-a-professor, which already includes the capacity of acting in that way. Implicitly, the "doing" involved releases, as Danto has put it, an event or action noteworthy or relevant to a subject because it may disclose some sense of a past and some part of belief about its copresent world. Semiotics draws one's attention to the discursive inhabitation of the present in which a past is *deproblematized in the mind of the present reader*, and which perforce also *performs* a present inoculation. The expression "deproblematized in the mind of the present reader" saturates the act in a life-world (*pace* Habermas) in which it is virtually impossible not to identify with its affective gravity. Kissinger had to: his "want" and "knowledge" need not appear as in and of themselves open to criticism. Hence Kissinger is "historical," but the mode of presenting this will in fact be "hysterical" on account of its repressive omission, this melding into a single story the events of professorial "bombing" and military codes.

Here is an example of current rehistoricization that draws upon a psychoanalytic recoding. It seems to me to be a fair instance of territorial expansion, of suppressing a cultural problematic of narration. Rosalind Krauss, a tireless critic in the demystification of modernity — she esteems the argument that "postmodernism" makes for a more extensive self-consciousness of modernism — has recently called for setting aside one of the dominant paradigms of modern art history, Gombrich's model of "relational cryptograms," because of its inadequate theorization of painting. Gombrich could not and did not accurately construct modern painting as a "function of desire operating in the register of lack." That is to say, Lacanian phrases were not employed by Gombrich. According to Krauss, the modern crisis of monumentalism in art and criticism follows upon an internally fractured artist-subject, whose confused sense of self produces works that systematize their negative desire for mastery and thus produce their own "blind spot." There is something uncanny about

modern paintings, which the Gombrich model prevents one from acknowledging. Because of the Lacanian codification of what Krauss calls
"presubjective otherness," experiences of futility that arise from ambivalence toward one's prior dependency (or the unconscious thinks according to the rules of pessimistic psychology) are themselves the explanation
of painterly "blind spots," and so this theoretical factor allows for the old
art history to be replaced by the new "negative science" of art history.
Lacanian theory lets us theorize these "blind spots" of the subjective neu-
rotic-inclusive attempts to see and be seen; Krauss goes so far as to accept
the Lacanian metaphysics — "You never look at me from the place from
which I see you" — and draws the conclusion that this allows for narrative descriptions of this problematic — even displaced — as worked out
by artists. The critic is saved by theory, the latter reduced to a secure
system of a negative recoding of "historical" identity.

Now the "crisis of the subject" has great use value in rehistoricizing.
The assertions that a painter such as Ingres was painting what amounts
to autoplagiarized confusions of interiority, that the bathing paintings by
Ingres were obsessed with Raphael's *La Fornorina*, a "substitution com-
pulsively multiplied," and that "fetishism begins in the realm of the
scopic," supposes that the painting's evaluation by different audiences is
accounted for by one *control code* (Lacanian statements). Further, it is assumed that art history is itself fetishistic-scopic, while art theory is not.
At what point do these assertions pass out of the "blind spot" that theory
is already a "seeing," as well as serving to reessentialize the idea of the
fetish? In denying argumentation over Lacanian theory, Krauss puts out
of argument the model whose negativity (the subject as lack) is somehow
thought to be conclusive evidence. The "defeat" of Gombrich (Oedipus
again) by this unanalyzed Lacanian model shows that rehistoricization
can envelop any area of cultural criticism.[29] Narration can regain its privileged status in the "disappearance of history" when it receives theoretical
infusions; the cutting edge of criticism requires "theoretic narration." Art
history: prepare for colonization by the metaphysics of antiseeing!

Defended as the signifier of "real resort" ("Always historicize," demands Jameson), "historical" narration is not connected to, is not an
opening onto, cultural problems. It adds nothing to an ethical term like
"good" to say "historical good," just as it adds nothing to a temporal
semantic unit like "an impossibly boring bourgeois avant-garde" to say
something or someone is part of a "historically impossibly boring bourgeois avant-garde." To say that capitalism is a "historical" phenomenon
may be important within the practices of an intra-academic competition
to maintain social credibility; but "historical capitalism" adds nothing to
our understanding of labor depression or "junk bonds." To say, drawing

upon political categories, that the utopianism of socialism is based upon the "historical experience of the socialist movement," as Aronowitz does, means that some culturally idealized past experience of socialism has been projected onto collectives, which themselves do not exist.[30]

Why the Signifier "History" Is Not Communicative

In Habermas's communication theory the political formations of the signifier "history" intersect those of a culture devoted to production and consumption. Habermas has strongly asserted that "a communicatively achieved agreement . . . is propositionally differentiated. . . . Processes of reaching understanding aim at an agreement that meets the conditions of rationally motivated assent to the content of an utterance."[31]

"Rationally motivated assent": the purity of the concept has nothing to do with being engaged with someone else in a dynamic exchange; this reduction, momentarily congealed as signification, to the controlled instance of "agreement" supposes that people are schoolchildren who have to be taught how to get along. Further, Habermas seems unaware as to how such "rationally motivated assent" can be given to mythic utterances or to contradictory ones: there is no place in this system for dealing with absurd yet everyday language. The communication of assent, achieved by examination of the validity claims of rightness, truthfulness, and sincerity, remains an academic idealization; that one can, in a seminar, say "yes to no" and "no to yes" does not obtain in an *effectual context* where a judge's legal orders enable police powers to be activated so that a timber company can maximize its clear-cutting. If it takes, as it does, fifty thousand dollars to get a case challenging academic officials to court, then it is clear that "rationally motivated" is so severely limited a concept that it fails to "deliver" a precise difference. This "historicism of understanding," which makes language subservient to the goals and ends of "rational understanding" and worked-out agreements between mutually recognized "players," supposes that conceptualism is itself directional, that is, aims at or tends toward a *conclusion* or satisfaction or fulfillment. Those uses of language, those phrases and formations of "marginal" "use value" and diminished "exchange value," which do not "count" or give an "account" of their desire and interest (i.e., do not offer themselves upon the plate of cultural goals and ends), are simply effaced from consideration by writers like Habermas.

Communicative functions cannot coincide with "historical enunciations," and there are functions of language that resist rehistoricizing. In being placed in the subject position of a sentence or as the implicit subject, "historical" statements perform the memorability of the noteworthy.

Statements of the form "that is the way it was," which establish for some now that "this is how it is now," immediately exclude *indirect discourse*, whose variability is much more fluid and productive. "Historical speech" is set aside every time thinking ignores the event of a "first" who has seen or witnessed or claims to be continuous with those who have (the research mythos); movements that go from "second to third," "neither of whom has seen," involve one in senses that are never final, complete. As order-words, as commands, "historical statements" do not allow for precisely an argument on their construction.[32] Adherence to order-forms of narration, that they are workable and efficient despite events that suggest ahistoricity — the recent savings and loan debacle in the United States comes to mind — supposes that every event is already a narration, precisely *not* an event at all.

Why is it that close reading of historical narratives *always* loosens their plausibility? Or, to put it in terms familiar to readers of Hayden White's *Metahistory*: if one does not read "history" in the "light" of its obvious literary composition or its pseudolegal treatment of "evidence" or its astonishing acceptance of precedents, then are such texts readable at all?

No final agreement is possible between pragmatically based groups and individuals concerning "rational ends": what counts as the meaning of a phrase cannot be communicated across the contextual differences. Those who insist from the high university (on down) that "historical narration" is of the type "cultural mediation" have to show that any such "mediation" is not itself already implicated in the power plays of academics. Why should an effect of the divisions of knowledge — the positioning of "historical narration" as a recollection (reterritorializing, recoding, renaming) — be treated as necessary for "mending" (de Certeau) divisions? Phrases such as the "will of the people" (which had spoken or was about to speak), or that refer to some segment of the social as about to realize itself (e.g., the end of art), construct their own model readers, an ideal audience. What are the *noncommunicating contexts* that establish the authority of "timed" events — "first" and "then" and "now" and "when" — as comparatives within the persistence of capitalist disorders?

On the Way to Uselessness

In all cases, the signifier "history" is unthinkable apart from the cultural use value of integration, including such designations as "countermemory," "counterhistory," and the like, which are concepts of restoration, recuperation, and realignment, or signifiers of balance for new groups that have already internalized the "being of opposition." That social and economic modernism was successfully integrative motivated the Structuralist insight that the conjunction of passive and neurotic subjects accompanied the great (uneven) "heatings" of Capital. Lévi-Strauss used the term "creative disequilibrium" in arguing that modern narrations were aligned with the function of the "cooling devices" of culturation, a process studied in some detail by, among others, the Lotman group (which emphasized that the shifter function could take place at virtually any level, that is, "correct" and "incorrect" paintings vying for new audiences). The demand for images that are "eternal yet bearing a date" (Barthes) and that deaccelerate or unnecessarily speed up movements, conveys us to and from our compromises (academia), modes of control (law), reductions (science), and wastings (politics). Academic culture is even "cool" to the point where its surplus repertoire of images provides for a reinvention of the *list* as one of the forms that replaces general narrative history.[33]

Is the "cooling" function itself a thing of the past? Is it not arguable that the equation between taking "sides" and "historical positions" is being replaced by a cultural "logic" of management that is more effective than a narrative of choices? What happens culturally when people refuse to differentiate between a "historical" choice and a choice as such? Ben-Gurion stated that he would choose to save half the Jews of Europe for liberation in Palestine over saving all the Jews for a liberation in England: where is the difference between a "historical" selection and a selection so absolute? Was Ben-Gurion's rigid anti-Englishness the expression of a "historical" awareness or the rejection of this awareness? A historian writes that today "history" may be used to "derealify," that "history constantly probes and challenges, mercilessly exposing unwarranted assumptions and dashing the finest hopes of warriors and peacemakers alike." So does redlining; so do bad credit reports. Why not instead postulate an *incapacity* belonging to the distinctiveness of the signifier "history," such that no one can, in Lyotard's words, "place himself or herself in the position of an utterer on the course of things"? Final Solutions, saving and loan debacles, mass emigration, worldwide evictions, and so on: these hyperphenomena are already superhistoric, in and of themselves derealizing.

After History: From the Irreversible to . . .

Nothing resembling images of progressive liberation is achieved in the "disappearance of history." Everyone is entitled to put forward claims for representing the "truth of" some past-present conjunction that is felt to have occurred. The historians will continue to recode and struggle against any "breakthrough" where relations between past and present are articulated outside of their professional control. As a group, historians are committed to modes of thought and presentation with which they socialize *uncoded* readers: this "ordinary educated reader/public" is, at best, the prisoner we call students, forced to read what they are given (in this they are really creatures of an unnamed laboratory, who cannot select what they consume but are constantly examined as to the success or failure of their consumption).

Although academically produced "history" perpetuates the *mythic irreversibility* of its narrative categories — aim, result, effect, outcome, determination, the nonpresence of the present — projected onto the existential inchoateness of temporality, at best "after-history" may intersect possible ways of introducing modalities of *reversibility*. The idea of reversibility takes its sense from current arguments concerning use and exchange value. One of the strongest formulations is found in Baudrillard's critique *Forget Foucault*. He points out that as "economic reference loses its strength, either the reference of desire or that of power becomes preponderant," both of which ensure that there are nonshattered categories that bear one to the future. Baudrillard had the nerve to suggest that Foucault's interest in power and desire was still conditioned by historicist defenses, by a last category of historicism, called the

> ultimatum of *pro-duction* in the literal sense of the word. The original sense of "production" [Baudrillard gets caught up in the historicist virus] is not in fact of material manufacture; rather it means to render visible, to cause to appear and be made to appear: *pro-ducere.* . . . To produce is to force what belongs to another order (that of secrecy and seduction) to materialize.[34]

If economic "history" is unable to carry strong narrative lines, then try another series: irreversibility is the very point of cultural socialities — identity in time. There are all sorts of "last tales that are still being told."[35] In the face of this virtual rush to irreversibility, the question is, What would it take to *undo* this? "In the name of" what interests would reversibility be established? In a situation where "accumulation, progress, growth, production, value, power, and desire itself are irreversible processes," are there any conditions for difference?

What is possible in terms of the category of reversibility is first suspending "counterhistorical" demands and instead formulating ways of connecting to the "implosion" of the West's normalizing ideologies, those of the family, growth, the self-consciousness of art, and so on. It is not a question of possessing the real or of taking charge of it — the cultural businesses of recoding — but rather of "secretly ruining and dismantling it while simultaneously insuring that minimal continuum of pleasure moving across it and without which it would be nothing."[36] More patient than mere patience, more temperate than ordinary ease, more angry than . . . — these inventions of contemporary seductions indicate, to a fair degree, the extent to which ahistoricity has to find ways of living; it is not a call for parody or just intensive critique, the strategies of obviousness, but for not producing more of the same "transparency principle," which Baudrillard thinks "governs" the third-order real, the simulacra.[37]

The reversible and irreversible are an interesting couple. In this context, one might reread, for example, the rapture with which Foucault closes his *Madness and Civilization* (1961), and compare it to a Baudrillardian reading. Where Foucault could postulate a modernist crisis in which it was argued that the texts of Artaud, Nietzsche, and Van Gogh effected or inaugurated the existence of an impossible truth of madness — a society having become arraigned by its works of art, a society that could put itself in an essentially reflective position to its own banished and grotesquely expressive waste or residue, and hence open to change — Baudrillard envisions this:

> The more art tries to realize itself, the more it hyperrealizes itself, the more it transcends itself to find its own empty essence. There is vertigo here as well, a vertigo *mise-en-abyme* and stupified. . . . Duchamp's . . . ecstasy of a prosaic object transfers the pictorial act into its ecstatic form — which henceforth without an object will spiral in on itself and in a sense disappear, but not without exercising over us a definite fascination. Art, today, merely practices the magic of disappearance.[38]

The Subject, overcome by the consumption of someone else's delusions, suns itself on the Nietzschean rock and is prostrate after each cultural feeding; it feels the murmur within itself of its own superfluity. Art, liberated from its interpretive and mirroring function, becomes a moment in the generalized "exterminism" that is Western *posthistorique*.

The mirroring that represents the return of openings or moves for a more beneficial social outcome, Foucault's hope against hope, is replaced in Baudrillard's account of a present being driven by the emergence of a "third-order" simulacrum, incarnated as perpetual displacement, a real oxymoron, which leaves no more "space" for the "concept of history" to be deduced as sufficient and necessary in making sense of events:

> We are witnessing the end of perspective and panoptic space . . . and hence the *very abolition of the spectacular.* . . . We are no longer in the society of the spectacle . . . nor in the specific types of alienation and repression which this implied. . . . There is no longer any medium in the

literal sense: it is now intangible, diffuse and diffracted in the real, and it can no longer even be said that the latter is distorted by it.[39]

The rhetoric of this is of course "apocalyptic," assuming, that is, that there is a "historical" that is *unquestionably* narrating preparation, a straight line of finality in resolving problematic social relations[40] — the sense of hope from madness that Foucault supposed loses sense and purpose outside of the myth that critical art = counterhistory = continuity. In an earlier formation, of signs emancipated from nature (the disappearance of landscape), an individual was integrated into the game of a generalized equivalence, which was thought of as a temporalizing change (e.g., repression of spending = accumulation).

Inherited as a structure embedded in terms like industrialism, with its expansion of subjectivity that runs parallel to the development of objectifying forms (e.g., anonymity and city centers), this second order was code by code replaced by an exchangist culture, which is less integrative than it is the operationalization of specific laws of value entirely immanent to themselves, a society of nonnarrative *tests*. Hyperfunctionalism. This third-order simulacrum is structured by the "precession" of models, "where only affiliation to the models makes sense, and nothing flows any longer according to its end, but proceeds from the model, the "signifier of reference" which is a kind of anterior finality and the only resemblance there is."[41] This ordering, now ascendent — or hyperreal — reduces "history" to the status of an idealized and sentimental "dialogue" (which never happens), swept aside by material transformations having merged with operations of economic intensification and social fragmentation. The Trump Tower manifests a generalized narcissism of Capital, its own "counterhistorical" dissolution of symbolics replaced by strategic signs. *Being positioned for the future* is the only position (posi-tronics: the new future of science?). The promissory note — social contract — of a linkage between past and present and future, irreversible and binding, gives way to a *nonhistorical, nonsubjective chronicity*.[42] The becoming-lingering in which nostalgia and utopia cannot turn any mechanism. Important here is the declension of identifications between morality and times; for example, one cannot justify the equation between archaic and bad or demise of enlightenment and regression.[43] This potentially delirious and unexpected lack of justification between morality and time leaves open a number of irreconcilable arguments, on which more below.

In what can be called high industrialization, the exchange value of the concept "history" rested on insights into moral and aesthetic choices that sustained one's social identities.[44] Each periodization could be converted, as it were, into a hierarchy, a rank, a mode of inclusion/exclusion. We have seen this semantic-cultural power, for example, whenever the equation was disclosed that youth = inexperience, or, symmetrically, that old age = inability, rewards = later, regrets = now, and so on. Such relations limited the playing field, a control on who was empowered to throw the dice. One exchanged the possibility of experiences radiating from a here and now for position in the world of use values (career, advancement, increase in material satisfaction), based upon inclusive productivism, where the "history" signifier could stop on the "in between." Each "between" was a transition whose existence was bound up with the paradox of not being except by "giving rise to" something later, something after. "History" made sense in a context where codes regulated the precise value of early and later. In his magisterial *Savage Mind* (1956), Lévi-Strauss noted that the "originality and distinctive nature" of "history" were to be found in "apprehending the relation between before and after," where the connector "between" marks a nonoccurrence but produces an iterable, serial repetition. This "between," which reached its apogee in Dilthey's elevation of "empathy" to pure method, whose aim was to "get between" intention and outcome, sustained continuity, since among its social actants were politicians and professors who facilitated, as it were, that no "between" slipped out of "line."

Hannah Arendt, writing a trenchant critique of what she took to be the dilemma of "historical consciousness," stressed that in a technocratically driven order like ours, where legitimation is reduced to acts of "starting processes" (i.e., being a "player"), technology had proved irreversible in creating problematic effects while it satisfied the demand for "hypothesis making." So many processes have been started with such nonnarrative consequences that the present now resembles an insane jumble of arbitrary, contingent actions *made* into so many "traditions" and roles, which yield, quickly, to replacement. In a negative judgment concerning such processes — any and all — that competed as mechanisms of "historical transformation" (like class conflict, racial ideologies or, excessive individualism), Arendt pointed out that the overall process of "world alienation" had devoured belief in the given and rendered "meaningless the one overall process which originally was conceived in order to give meaning. . . . Neither history nor nature is at all conceivable." Arendt's assessment: present actions are transformed into devalued "betweens," a "melancholic haphazardness of the particular had caught up with us."[45] Lyotard has pounced on one of the more dramatic philosophical possibilities of this negative seduction borne along by this "melancholic haphazardness":

The expectant wait of the *Is it happening?* as silence. Feelings as a phrase for what cannot now be phrased. The immediate incommensurability of desire, or the immediate incommunicability of murder. . . . The suspense of the linking.[46]

In a world more and more tending toward oxymoron and similar setups, it becomes use-less in a practical sense to conjure "historical" talk. If the conceptual "disappearance of history" is itself *nonhistorically irreversible*, that is, built into societies whose rigid control of futures to come is at issue, then "historicity" cannot but disappear.

As intellectually compelling versions of "history" like those of Hegel, Marx, and Freud disappear, there is joy insofar as terms are released for a multitude of affects disengaged from the compulsion to "have a usable past." There is no doubt that the micronarratives of "ruin" will increase, and it is true that nothing can issue from this but more degraded psychologizing. But many types of energetic work will show that once dispossessed, "history" cannot represent the denominator in a politics of division (e.g., friend/foe); instead, as interests voluntarily emerge or come forward, where various pasts are drawn upon by their lending values for the emergent, there might be less the reestablishing of governments and states (of all sizes and kinds), and more tribes, cults, sects, and so on, dividing and subdividing in the wake of the implausibility of "official" pasts "saying" the future. Events that do not answer the interrogations of politics.[47] Many subjectifications, many reobjectifications, not necessarily supporting positions in the various wars *for* position.[48] Instead of historicizing for, say, either prolife or prochoice groups as if these were the "choices" provided by "history," one might subvert the lineup. Deleuze provides an optimistic sketch of this possibility:

> To think means to be embedded in the present time stratum that serves as
> a limit: what can I see and what can I say today? But this involves
> thinking of the past as it condensed in the inside, in the relation to oneself
> (there is a Greek in me, or a Christian, and so on). We will then think the
> past against the present and resist the latter, not in favor of a return but
> "in favor, I hope, of a time to come" (Nietzsche), that is, by making the
> past active and present to the outside so that something new will finally
> come.[49]

Making a difference that does not so much negate and oppose an existing reality as it does makes the latter irrelevant also involves a radical transformation of critical work, so much so that it, too, will have to be produced:

A thing, an animal, a person are now only definable by movements and rests, speeds and slownesses and by affects, intensities. There are no more forms but cinematic relations between unformed elements; there are no more subjects but dynamic individuations without subjects, which constitute collective assemblages. Nothing develops, but things arrive late or in advance . . . from the middle, to be always in-between . . . the imperceptible . . . and all of a sudden, a decisive gesture so swift that we didn't see it.[50]

This is not what Simon Schama means when he insists that "history" is something "of contingencies and unforeseen consequences,"[51] which is anchored to empirical "philosophy of history." It is not a question of affirming contingency or any other category as a basis for criticism, but of a writing that slips away from agents and agencies, subjects and contexts, further away from reconciling knowledge.

Lyotard has elucidated as well as any contemporary author what it might mean to reinvent for oneself a different form of narrativity, one that continues to alienate from command structures and order-words. Rather than the obsession with remembering something one has not experienced — the substitution of word-things for things that may not have happened at all, which establishes objective delirium — an alternative is that of the "pagan," whose effectivity performs creative forgetting, in a telling that is neither subjective nor objective:

While being a relay . . . in the simple fact of relaying something, there is precisely something that gets forgotten. . . . the forgetting of what is being repeated . . . makes for a nonforgetting of time as a beat in place. . . . nothing gets accumulated. . . . the narratives must be repeated all the time because they get forgotten all the time. But what does not get forgotten is the temporal beat that does not stop sending the narratives to oblivion.[52]

How would movements, in what would then be entirely uneven cultural worlds, be calibrated with official rhythms?

Walter Benjamin, desperately in search of a spiritual transcendence of the past to set against present powers, preferred to remain with the myth that "the past carries with it a temporal index by which it is referred to redemption. There is a secret agreement between past generations and the present one."[53] It is a question of turning one's back on all such satisfying melancholia, even the tragic sublime, and setting aside the feeling structures that accompany "historical consciousness." The distinctness of various *tellings that dehistoricize* is discontinuous with Benjamin's realization of the past; one's senses cannot be construed as dependent upon an obligation "to remember" without reinventing the "look of officiality" (rhetoric control) all over again.

Modernism Again

Bataille wrote that the "reasonable conceptions" associated with "closed systems" such as historicism are overthrown by realities of an

> immense travail of recklessness, discharge, and upheaval that constitutes life . . . [which] has meaning only from the moment when the ordered and reserved forces liberate and lose themselves for ends that cannot be subordinated to anything one can account for. It is only by such insubordination — even if it is impoverished — that the human race ceases to be isolated in the unconditional splendor of material things.[54]

Bataille's challenge is that of a modernism that did emphasize the invention of insubordination — from Kafka's Yiddish to Beckett's silences, from the gazing-machine at the Folies to Ryman's disrupting of canvas, from the most lurid garage band to Lévi-Strauss's antipathy to psychologism, and beyond.

Insubordination cannot compete, however, with the more legitimate, and hence familiar, "death" industry, to put it somewhat bluntly. I mean that we are saturated with announcements of various ends and modes of ending. If painting, for example, has "really" been dealt multiple "blows" by photography (or the ready-made or Dada excess or Futurist nonrationality or feminist deconstruction), certainly someone has written the "definitive" narration. That end and crisis are ladeled over modern art by many critics is not structurally different from "affirmations" of life that come from the right, since in either case one is dealing with the joining of periodization and exclusionary disjunctions. Consider the work of Lothar Baumgarten. Here is a well-received German conceptual artist who works in photography and film, who writes and constructs installations where text is an integral part, and where effects are generated which dovetail with language, with criticism. In various European and American installations, many devices are used that are directly "historicist": the mixture of European imperial marble floors with Amazonian rivers concocts a version of the "raw and the cooked" where the dominated and the dominant are brought together, as in a reminder of an unpleasant past; the combination at the Paris métro of Napoleonic names placed under names of the victims of French colonialism was worthy of any progressive narration. In monumental public spaces — two large rooms at the Los Angeles County Museum of Contemporary Art in 1990 — Baumgarten engaged the contestation over "public history" by first setting out a "strange history" of Indian/Anglo relations. Using the walls as maps and signs of multiple sites of conflict, where Indian names and rail lines suggested the forgetting of Indians and the abandonment of the rails by whites, Baumgarten tries to make thinkable the Western exclusion of what may or may not be Other (Sequoyah's alphabetic system suggests something "other than other" since the exclusion of Sequoyah by nineteenth-century whites was an exclusion of sameness — he wanted Indians to have the white power of writing). The landscape/past conjunction is put forward as visual semes, in colors, lines, words, sizes, juxtapositions — continuous with vocabularic and encyclopedic systems, word/image/ and sense/referent articulations. In this way the past is put off as a single determinate meaning, the semiotic markers an opening to the site of the here and now. In addition, there is reinforcement by way of the idea of the destruction of the panoramic loveliness of "the West."

At its best, as when Baumgarten can set up one's ability to ponder the difference and distance as well as proximity and mixing between Indian trails and industrial rails, over the "t" which is then not just "t," Baumgarten gives us epic conflict without spectacle. There is no "death of art" here. This is of some intellectual interest, achieving the effect of "superhistory" without its moralizing narrative form and without an explicit politics of the present guiding one's interpretation. In some texts of this artist, it becomes virtually undecidable whether "history" is available to the visitor of the installation (an ambiguating "history" predominating) or whether a sense of the autonomy of "art" can be maintained if one singular "t" performs so much differentiation.

Perhaps artists have an easier time alienating "historicism" than the historians do in allowing for an alienating "art." The art historian T. J. Clark, for example, laments what he calls the "blanking out of history," which he says has accelerated since the Impressionist era. He writes that "the circumstances of modernism were not modern, and only became so by being given the forms called 'spectacle,' " which involved the bourgeois destruction of the patronage system as well as eradicating critical aspects of "popular" culture. Painting was "positioned" to register the capitalist absorption of radical expressions of working-class groups, but in fact the intellectuals presided over a deradicalization process, and turned into a near impossibility a painting that would criticize the "new order." In submitting to the "system" by evading the class-power axis of Capital in the formation of the modern city, painting "painted" the "unhistorical spectacle" of leisure and entertainment becoming routine. Clark describes the petite bourgeoisie as passive and castrated before modernization, and who then become the audience *for* "spectacle"; painters such as Manet who continued to visualize the marginal did not have any *political impact* on class struggle. Impressionist painting and beyond is compared and measured to the *historical consciousness that could have obtained at the time by political thinkers.* The painters who refused to "confront" bourgeois order thus, according to Clark, *dehistoricized themselves.* Modernist painting = depoliticization. Depoliticization = "historical" failure. Indeed, then as now, petit bourgeois intellectuals belong to the narrative trajectory of doom, carried out on the equation between the aestheticization of modern art and deradicalization. In this scene, modernism is handed back to psychoanalysis — the Freud-to-Lacan transfer — and the language of lack, castration, and absence gives *present historicism* its "realism."[55]

Another critic argues for an internal construction of painting, one that seems to allow for the potential uselessness of painting as an ordinary "historical" phenomenon. Painting only really becomes "modern" when confronted with not being at all, as in all "strong moments," so "history" is irrelevant to all painting, which wills its own contest with time. Where Clark's version of historicism sees painting as having fallen into fetishism on account of its lack of "historical consciousness," this version depicts "modernist classics" as masterworks whose temporal field is quasi-achronic as well as supercontextual, on account of a "self-reflexivity achieved through the agency of the impersonal."[56] This argument maintains that today it is pointless to "date" (modern) painting, after painting has been shown to have only one, endlessly repetitive test, that of "existentializing experience"; in place of a next period — ours — delivering an "end to painting," painting must deliver itself from its "end" within an antireflexive social order that turns the "end of painting" into another commodity.

The pertinent question raised by modernism and criticism is, How far can one go in painting or any other medium in putting forward ideations that expand some present rather than enclosing it within a historicization? Rather than painting *receiving* its determination from "general history" (the one that is saluted) and keeping its audience calibrated to its modernity or lack thereof, a more interesting argument, it seems to me, is that some paintings (texts) are *events that suspend relations of continuity.*[57] Where the emphasis of "to historicize" falls on that of determinate negation (paintings cut out their own relation to temporality; they practice a continuous periodization, which they themselves establish, and increase "historical consciousness"), presentist "dispossession" has to actively invent concepts in a *radicalizing* directed against even present trends. In this schema, the present is set against itself, not compared with a past reduced to our comparisons. As Lyotard has put it, the primary experience of this sense of modernity is not its representation of the "present" as a "historical reality" but the occurrence of events "without rules in order to formulate the rules of what *will have been done.*" Works of interest concern an immediate future as a contested site rather than incessant nagging about "how the present came to be."[58]

On its own terms, the category of modernity gives rise to cultural insolubles, not satisfactions of "history," since the *constant* unevenness of potentially incomparable processes sets up many sublimes, many experimentations, as well as many nostalgias and utopias. As the American schoolplace is undone as something contained by narratives of pedagogy (if schools cannot protect children from violence, then the story-forms of learning collapse), there can be as many events as there are undoings, the latter almost certainly integral to any critical sense of contemporary society. Consider Capital's making *immaterial* past and future in denarrativizing acts: in passing from school as subject of discipline for training/learning to its function in the selection of "life-styles," suspended is anyone's dominant narrative of "schooling." Is Capital in this way modern or more than modern?

Leaving Is Not Psychological

The "disappearance of history" means that "historical consciousness" has been replaced by all sorts of new modes, including *diagrams* that suggest radical deterritorialization (e.g., Derrida's genre-effacing "readings" of Hegel; real street punk with its noserings) as well as regressive verbal reterritorializings (e.g., academic "thick description" whose forming is displaced by the exotica of the materials).[59] At a minimum, it seems almost honest to stress the achronicity of dominant social forms. This avoids projecting a symmetrical reversal represented in the normalization of "decline," which seems to be the reflex when the social does not "move forward." A "nonhistorical contextualism" (or is that already too orderly?) suspends the conceptual apparatus of narrative "histories," including that of decline: "I used to" says it all syntactically — the energy of regret, the runoff of despair.

When one begins to move from linearizing oneself according to the timings of various labor clocks (e.g., careerist timings), there are also events not driven by the "cuer and the cued . . . [the] tune in a relation of redundancy."[60] That is, instead of direct confrontation with the powers that be, one might imagine a "disappearance of history" as a freeing of one's mind from a burdening weight now acknowledged as unnecessary. This was already a "superhistorical" idea in Lucretius's *On the Nature of the Universe*, where it is suggested that rather than thinking as conformity to other's opinions, by the pressing subjectivisms of hope and despair, there is "the mind itself [which] does not feel an internal necessity in all its actions and is not as it were overmastered and compelled to bear and put up with this."[61] This would be a strengthening of nonpsychologism, which, like various states of achrony, leaves the cover of temporalized proofs, its "ego ideals" of past and future, which make the present something desperate. Time as something regular is itself a massive irregularity; simply consider, for example, the timings allowed for by the authorities of our university systems—by unions, managers, deans, provosts, and so on—and which determine the time frame for teaching. The fifty-minute or one-hundred-and-fifteen-minute class—to say nothing of the timing of "passive memory" or the minor ecstasy of the stand-up lecture—already overcodes thinking by lists, the scarcity of depth reading, the subcodings of how much time a lecture is worth. Such sequencings—the list as result, the honor as reward—reestablish a continuous bond between childhood and education, a continuity also made between the ranking of students by teachers and "read" by employers. These are socialized figures of integrations "on time," determinants for "living on line," the correct sequence laid out in advance, series by series: birth, school, work, death.

Since the historians cannot help us with delinearization, the latter might be thought by its difference from order-words,

> such that a body or a word does not end at a precise point. . . . Whatever the breaks and ruptures, only continuous variation brings forth this virtual line, this virtual continuum of life, "the essential element of the real beneath the everyday." . . . one should bring forth the order word of the order word. In the order-word life must answer the word of death, not by fleeing, but by making flight act and create. There are pass-words beneath order-words. Words that pass, words that are components of passage, whereas order-words mark stoppages or organized, stratified compositions.[62]

To keep to the example: instead of teaching = frustration of ideals or teaching = identity of the failure of ideals, *a*historicality upends these anchorings in favor of a dismembering of norms, a setting off of unpredictable effects.[63] Paul de Man, emphasizing that to separate fiction and fact already supposed an uncritical acceptance of mimesis, also noted that reading as the constant frustration of extracting results from language (answers, references, resolvings) generated unacceptable uncertainty. What I am suggesting about temporality is consonant with de Man's remark that tropes are not necessarily "patterned on a non-verbal entity": there are timings that know nothing of origin and result, beginning and outcome—but they have to be invented.[64]

Earlier, I cited Hannah Arendt, who called the oppressive sense of many pasts intersecting and going off in a succession of future-presents the "melancholy haphazardness" of experience. Processes that might begin cannot, and events that can begin do not: such was the fate of mass society. This sense of the traditional idea of *context* unravels a dominant linearization acting as the through line of change. The academic repression of this "chronosmosis" requires one to consider events in the self-consciousness of time. The nonpsychological effect of "disappearing" from the historian's subject-positions is to acknowledge that no sense of direction can be valued except as a move that works like an ordinary tool: instead of speculation whose dominant effects intensify an already psychologized reality surrounding public life, Arendt suggested an active critique of ends and goals, their being short-circuited by a language that never identifies with atrophied time valuations. The significations of ascent or descent, lineage, heritage, and so on, are, then, challenges to make something more of them than their preexisting nationalist, privatist, exclusionary, castrating symbolizations.

What is conceptually stimulating about such arguments is the emergence of what can be called qualitative noncomparable temporalities, events detached from the codes of an exclusive successivity where seizure of the now sustains desire and anxiety based upon aestheticized figures of *possessing history*, of

> interactions without resonance . . . trapped in a thousand little
> monomanias, self-evident truths, and clarities that gush from every black
> hole . . . rumble and buzz, blinding lights giving any and everybody the
> mission of self-appointed judge, dispenser of justice, policeman,
> neighborhood SS man,[65]

a holding to the incomparable is to disenchant the future, to not harm it, in reproductions now. Ahistoricity suggests an extreme problematizing of the future. In this it is bitterly opposed to the "historical players," who have a stake in maintenance of the category of the same that legitimizes lines of continuity.

It is a question here of creating connections that support neither identity "with" nor nonidentity "from." In place of such persistent modes of resemblance, where the new, old, traditional, recent, anticipatory are conjugated by phrases like the "new tradition," the "contemporary classic," the "alternative space," where temporal resolutions are sustained, the category of resemblance must itself be shaken. We cannot expect to meet events that come from elsewhere (even the other in oneself) while joined to "their final combination in a common chord."[66] Instead, an infinitive mode, an exuberant alienation of naming, seems better in creating events "outside what is recognized" (Lyotard). Does this mean that radical modernist experimentations are everywhere, nowhere?

The pre(-)texts or narrative scripts that we deploy unconsciously (or not) are put out of reach by treating events as an *excessive being* that provokes one to "respond to a case without criteria."[67] Strangify: never "historicize." What matters is to effectively amplify the energy required to not succumb to the evasions and stupidities of one's epoch, regardless of what this "looks like." No doubt such disidentity may be fetishized, might add to the development of mere cleverness in the exploitation of the large and small codes that run through us (which can occur in academic appropriations, e.g., the "study" of graffiti). Gerald Graff calls for a rehistoricization of the teaching of literature, for fulfilling the psychological demand that "people need a sense of what an institution as a corporate body stands for, in order to be able to enter — or to want to enter — into its issues, methods and modes of talking and thinking."[68] On the contrary: the institution can only survive by withholding what its "corporate body stands for," since *that* is precisely what is at issue. Universities cannot speak to their own participation in the destruction of events without undoing their "need" and control structures.

"Posthistoricity" implies an "after," hence recoding. Instead of this term, which is too straight, without curve, one might jam (the idea is Barthes's) all the terms of transportation "from . . . to." In aesthetics this has been called "cross-modal experiences," which scatter every sociologic interpretation of art.[69] Whatever terms one uses, one should not misidentify "antihistory" with a (Nietzschean or other) craving for "health." In *The Use and Abuse of History*, Nietzsche proposed that a past can be judged only from acts that "stand higher than that which is to be judged," where one "can explain the past only by what is most powerful in the present," propositions not of "health" but of a surpassing of what the past *can say*.[70] One "disappears" *to* oneself, loses oneself not in ways fully known, hence is not absorbed by tragedy. Easily misconstrued as a myth of presence = satisfaction, ahistoricity is rather closer to

> the "holy no" become creative and affirmative. . . . the will to power
> ceases to be fettered to the negative as the *ratio* by which it is known to
> us, it reveals its unknown face.[71]

"Posthistoricity" is not psychological: one is not resubjectifying.

Deleuzian "Untimeliness"

Baudrillard's and Arendt's notions of a "negative history" leading to the concept's extinction, its not being applicable to a profoundly antihistorical capitalism, belong to (relatively) rare academic endeavors to depict "history" as the mythic discourse Structuralism (and related analyses) said it was (some notions of which are found in ancient Stoicism, modern Formalism, Futurism, impersonal poetics, Spinoza's nominalism, Constructivism, and so on). What I would like to do is to elaborate on the transformation of concepts into devices that subvert modeling a visible, collective "past." The discussion here of Deleuze pursues what Kristeva has called a "splitting subject in conflict who risks being shattered" by getting too far ahead or behind of socially acceptable timings, but which has left a self-destructive desire for reconciliation, for unity, for ideal models. It is a matter of relinquishing expectations that posit reconciliation. In particular, Capital never operates by making things work well, and it directly demythologizes by

> fits and starts, by grinding and breaking down . . . dysfunctions . . . feeding on the contradictions . . . on the crises . . . on the anxieties . . . and on the infernal operations [they] regenerate. Capitalism has learned this and has ceased doubting itself. . . . No one has ever died from contradictions. And the more it breaks down, the more it schizophrenizes, the better it works, the American way.[72]

One is not dealing with what Martin Jay calls a "poststructuralist" "play of non-identity and difference [treated as] a superior state of being," a "quietistic politics," and an "escapist" writing.[73] The rigid inflexibility of such epithets, in particular the charge of *elitism*, is a ploy by which the university left makes negation a way of protecting itself from this very "charge."

The citation from Deleuze reminds us that the temporalities intrinsic to Capital are already extralinear: paranoid states (work before pleasure) have been made virtually natural, where psychology represents the sign system of thinking "the last," where an ineffectual "spontaneous dynamic" of natural desire or an "impossible revolution" saturates choices in mythic times, that is, pure ineffectuality. It is a question of a "plane of immanence," which does not so much offer a means of resistance as it implies

> reverse causalities or "advanced" determinisms, decoded innate functions related to *acts of discernment* or election rather than to linked reactions; and *molecular combinations* that proceed by noncovalent bonding rather than by linear relations — in short, a new "pace."[74]

The question here, asked in different ways and undoubtedly with no definitive answer, is, What does writing connect with — what is its outside? Again, one sees that separation from "historicity" is not easy, that it raises the ante on everything that can be said to be "cultural."

Consider the example of the passage from inert words to movements of a diagrammatic sort, which Deleuze has evoked in suggesting making pointless the binary codification of everyday existence:

> Virginia Woolf's Wave, Lovecraft's Hypersphere, Proust's Spider Web, Kleist's Programme, Kafka's K-function, the Rhizosphere . . . no longer any fixed distinction between content and expression. . . . We no longer know if it is a flux of words or of alcohol, we are so drunk on pure water. . . . a flux of food or of words, so much is anorexia a regime of signs. . . . No longer are elements on one side and syntagms on the other; there are only particles entering into each other's proximity, on the basis of a plane of immanence.[75]

Isn't this another way of saying that it is not the job of "nonhistorical thought" to claim what is "timely"? The material question is whether untimeliness can be taken to new highs and lows, to accelerate it or slow it down to the point where it *does something* other than promote linear causalities, which are always "behind and ahead" (before and after) of necessity-forms. In other words, the category of the "untimely" raises the question of a dislocation from the concerns of the going players. Consider the new structures of labor, and then ask what kinds of writing are possible. Capital has already "busted" or dehistoricized the "family" as fact and as model in the United States, but it also recapitalizes itself: excessive work ruins children-parent relations, and culture industries administer dosages of sense and reterritorialization — therapy, educational policies, even "blockbuster art" for the poor. Relinearization in the withdrawal of "history" is a disaster; the "untimely" is not some expected "on the other hand" (the clock is ticking again), but rather stepping out of the enclosures of time-forms that have convinced us that time is itself scarce:

> The nonhierarchical work is a condensation of coexistences, a simultaneity of events. It is the triumph of the false claimant . . . but the false claimant cannot be said to be false in relation to a supposedly true model, any more than simulation can be termed an appearance, an illusion. . . . The simulacrum, in rising to the surface, causes the Same and the Like, the model and the copy, to fall.[76]

Narrative trajectories quit turning us to the arcs of destiny: the "history" of the transition to Capital and to a not-yet-better socialism is not sustainable when the fall ceases to be registered as collapse, catastrophe. Untimeliness — which embraces "defamiliarizing, de-oedipalizing, de-castrating; undoing theatre, dream and fantasy; decoding, deterritorial-izing . . . a malevolent activity" — is at the limits of any "social science," where no one's "history" rules.

Modernity, considered in the obscuring "antilight" (smog, haze, klieg lights, grocery stores at midnight) of capitalist desocialization, constantly smashes norms and standards, as if an alien social physics set out to "drive the event back to the border" (Lyotard). The "untimely" and "his-toricity" remain in unalterable contrariety on account of the latter's com-mitment to the speculative game of redemption:

> The great story of history has its end in the extinction of names (particularisms). At the end of the great story, there will simply be humanity. The names humanity has taken will turn out to be superfluous, at best they will have designated certain stations along the way of the cross. This universalism and this pure teleology is not classical in the sense of Antiquity, but modern in the sense of Christianity. "Philosophies of history" are forged around a redemptive future. (Even capitalism, which has no philosophy of history, disguises its "realism" under the Idea of an emancipation from poverty.)[77]

The historians tell us that we will fall into a becoming-Beirut, with its asyntactic atemporality, if we stop taking their medicine, these periodic dosages of redemption. Lawrence Stone tells us that the historian always knows how to tell the difference between what is a forgery and what is not, and so the historians do want to rule, as Deleuze reminds us, as legislators of usable models and copies that would repress simulation.[78] There will be no forgeries. That's important, to be worried about forgery.

New "historical subjectivities" want an "identity with" the Same (tra-dition), with "inclusion" in the "new." This "organization of the chaos" establishes a distinguishing narrative by means of which it can "feel" itself to be "historical" (instead of alive).

Making subjectivity different, on the other hand, is not an institution-alization of negation and opposition. It is not based upon what the Stoics called the commemorative sign — those signs "having been previously observed in conjunction with certain other phenomena, e.g., a wound in the heart with death, *remind* us at every occurrence to expect the same conjoined phenomenon" — but upon insubordinate signifiers, those Stoic *lekta* or propositions whose proliferation creates the situation where "the same singular proposition can never be expressed twice. Every serious use of tenses involves at least a tacit 'now' and so 'My left eye-tooth is aching now' will not express the same proposition twice. Thus singular propositions become as fugitive . . . extremely short-lived."[79]

Paintings and books and individuals become so many *arrangements* insofar as they are connected to another outside, the one that forestalls closure on an inside. The prison is real. An arrangement has to elaborate relations to surfaces, which it has to define (e.g., the smoothness of erudition, the break of an idea), plateaus (e.g., the logic of surplus, the "either . . . or . . . or . . . or," which Deleuze proposes), valleys (e.g., the water holes of ideas, city walks, anonymous places), rifts (e.g., the chasms of interpretation, tending to actual irreconcilable values), plus internalities, machines, sometimes relayed through language, but mostly mixed up. This is language on the spot — including theory — where the only "timeliness" that matters is that of a generalized bricolage; no one series commands the others, and there is no inventory of visible roles to play; the "unhistorical" is plugged in. The real is not prepared for linguistic expression; chances abound to escape the terror of only knowing the "face . . . as an overcoding of all of the decoded parts."[80] Instead of the Good Reproduction, the concoction of an "untimely event" has "nothing to do with signifying, but with land-surveying and map making, even of countries yet to come."

It is now widely accepted that culture as such expands by producing figural contiguity with what is not-book, whose symbols "pick up" and "reflect" and "alter" (and . . . and . . .) the semantic structures and codes of worlds. The book imitation of the world punctuates different forces, and acts as One that stands for Two, which gets its object "right" (or "wrong") or story "straight" (or "crooked"). This Platonic "heritage" surfaces as the apparatus ensuring that reading = the fanatical reduction of thinking to that where "the mind is alone and engaged with being" or the immediate force of language as order. Its cultural presentation is the incessant axiomatization of a rule of arbitrary identification by overcoded exclusions — where the "thing" defines away a potentially uncontrollable difference. One is free to sue in a system of laws so as to raise genuinely complicated matters of collective importance, but one cannot afford it; one is capable of scientific work, but there is none; one disagrees with a master or mistress of some highly delimited territory, and one is banished. The suprapolitical decision that an image or sense is a good copy or not legislates acceptable "copies" and unacceptable "simulacra." The former are authorized by resemblance to a model (which is transcendental); the latter are not authorized since they come forward without precoded credentials.[81]

What Deleuze calls rhizomatic (ahistorical) acts first by that Nietzschean move of shifting to the "unhistorical," to a device that can serve as the tool which neutralizes, here, the Platonic control on the power to select. We know that this is the terrorist demand: "make sense or shut up." The challenge thrown up by this Platonism requires actions that render the form of equational logic, positive and negative, impossible: "an encounter of dialects, patois, argots and special languages. . . . language stabilizes around a parish, a diocese, a capital. It forms a bulb . . . [whereas] the rhizome type . . . can only analyze language by de-centering it onto other dimensions and into other registers."[82] In some works by Lewis Carroll, Deleuze recasts this nonreduction of meaning either to propositions or to things by emphasizing Carroll's work as an active paradox, expressed "sometimes by a hollow word, sometimes by an esoteric word, and sometimes by a portmanteau word whose function is to fuse and ramify these heterogeneous series." "Slithy" is an "inframeaning according to a fluid and burning principle that absorbs or actually resorbs the meaning as it is produced." Some of Carroll's poetry, then, managed to connect "to eat and to speak" in ways that to write so as to distinguish the surface of language was to eat or consume expressions. Even if it's at times a narcissistic adventure, it's radical, it shows forth one of the innumerable ways in which passion is articulated.[83]

Instead of a "historicizing grammar" that keeps everything together in claiming that what has succeeded deserved to endure, another mode of the chrono-obsessive, there are Kafka's *Letters* and *Diaries*, for example, with their vacating "any proper or figurative sense" and movement toward "a continuum of reversible intensities," where language is not symbol, not wordplay, but where "the words themselves are not 'like' the animals but in their own way climb about, bark and roam around, being properly linguistic dogs, insects or mice."[84] Kafka's use of "Yiddish" was the stranger's way of allowing for the event of "ordinary German-state madness" to shine forth; instead of recentering for the conflation of every material force to those of "historical agency," these radical instances of writing expand events, which are antireductive:

> Even when it is unique, a language remains a mixture, a schizophrenic mélange . . . an absolute deterritorialization . . . this . . . sober syntactical invention, simply to write like a dog (but a dog can't write—exactly, exactly).[85]

Bereft of cultural ideals, even that of a satisfying opposition, one might prefer a writing that remains "fragmented, without anything lacking: eternally partial parts, open boxes and sealed vessels, swept on by time without forming a whole or presupposing one . . . denouncing in advance every organic unity we might seek to introduce into it"; instead of impossible academicized ideals, writings that attempt "to trace the field of immanence," an immanence turned to the future, to "the sound of a contiguous future, the murmur (*rumeur*) of new assemblages of desire, of machines, and of statements, that insert themselves into the old assemblages and break with them."[86]

Nihilism, History

Platonism is a trans-"historical" political technique whose power appearances are perpetually revised in the return of imaginary formations: monumentalism, with its attitude of a controlled release of expression, or the neopsychoanalytic "discovery" of fourth or even fifth "drives," instantaneously saturating an event with a dose of verbal significance.[87] Platonism is what one thinks with when one "knows," in advance, what things "look like," the emergent pressured and forced to fit with and conform to the already-existing weight of already-known sign-systems, the reactive force of *ratio cognoscendi*.[88] In it the visible and the sayable are fused in a manner in which words are not remotely connected to "password" formations but captured as orders and commands; that is the success of *political rhetoric*, that words become things instead of multiplying more word and thing differences, and that things are spoken nonetheless. Platonism is the defeat and cleansing of language of its possible simulacra. Language prevented from being a trigger for the senses, language that cannot *deculturize*. In place of the becoming-extreme of a present, Platonism *authorizes* a present-subject to absorb contradictory appearances, validating authority as a figure that separates essential predicates from unessential ones without owning up to what is occurring. In *A Thousand Plateaus*, Platonism is treated as the very form of politicized discourse insofar as it is based on the order of negative identity, not separating from the model and falling into *figments* (phantasma). The negative but inclusive disjunction of like-by-like rules judgments as to what is *not*-like. The "order-word" maintains the stratification of language, its segmentations, their latent sedentariness, each an aspect of a power block; the psychoanalytic reduction of surrealism, for example, to the singular "deciphering of the unconscious" is tantamount to ordering surrealism to "be denotative." Or everyday life shows that most people do not "read" legal discourse as a militarized sign-system, but as "reasons" in movements away from violence.

Cultural nihilism dominates when one must contest myths so as to engage "the real." This nihilism is overwhelming in the form of past foundation-myths, which *anchor* here and now *away from language*, in past performatives. Nihilism as language joins "the power of dialectic with that of myth" (Deleuze). Since a claimant must "appeal to foundations" in order to contest the duration and iteration of tradition or innovation, a successful "appeal" has to, in some sense, defeat how a present power setup removes itself from contestability by its precoded advantage. In Plato's system, "well-founded madness or true love" is (circularly) established as legitimate because such madness is connected to dormant memory of its idea and so (it is claimed) fits itself into a device for returning; sensuous love is excluded because it is barred from making such a claim insofar as it lacks a mythic foundation to control the metonymization of its effects. Rational myths — an oxymoron — are inscribed in the linguistic relay as "*a criterion of selection . . . according to which different men within the City share unequally in the mythical model.*"[89] Academic historiography remains Platonic to the extent that it is unable to think itself in difference: there is so much that it is unable to say.

Concluding Remarks

"Historical consciousness" and language are linked by a number of reinforcing devices, placed in cement to strengthen it, including the claim that "history" and "narration" possess shared attributes of the same substance, namely, general representability. Both assume a descent from the lineage of making visible in figures that which has not yet been said but which has already happened, anterior to its representation. It does not matter very much whether one stresses the "scientificity" or the "poetics" of this type of code, since both aspects are indices of a larger organization, that of the control of events by possessive interpretations that are unable to reconstruct their own rationality and, hence, limits. The political aspect of language is intimately bound up with the control of the "givens" by existing "players" and their overall semantic presentation. It is impossible to think of a "historical consciousness" that did not demand that thinking now first take up the supposed objective or proper "burden" of the cultural "inheritance"; it is unthinkable to suggest the "disappearance of history," because then we might confront more of the surplus which itself supports all of modernity. In Deleuze's words:

> There is no general recipe. We are finished with all globalizing concepts. Even concepts are haecceities [thisness] and events in themselves. What is interesting about concepts like "desire," "machine," or "arrangement" [or "history"], is that they are valuable only as variables, and as they permit a maximum number of variables.[90]

There are many "machines" that set up an identification with social roles and secure a future by dint of their claim to know how power has worked in the past. Oppositional criticism is easily converted into institutional criticism. The ability to "speak" between now and then, then and this, pro- and preleptic, pause and action, affects each of us; but the deofficiation and depoliticization of links between "history" and functions of criticism should not reinvent "before and after." In Paul Veyne's phrase, we are not "sucked into the abyss of the infinitesimal" because "historical" thinking, of any version, slams a door on some possible abyss of the present. The same — as plot, as truism, as script — generates the narrative effect that contingency and chance are epiphenomena and that there is no inner void or interval between meaning and itself. The code of "before and after" reestablishes social order.

What I have called a "disappearance of history" concerns the possibility that reality — as modernity — itself makes "history" an increasingly archaic connection; nonetheless, as language, this relation belongs to a semantic control code, whose purpose is the historicization of experiences, their verbal reduction to the games and rules of the existing players. I have not minimized how difficult it is to engage in a critique with this formation, but it is disappearing. As it does, so appear possible transformations without "history."

5

Criticism and Art Events: Reading with Lyotard and Baudrillard

Introductory Remarks

In a review of recent historical scholarship on the demise of the Old South, C. Vann Woodward evokes continuity between the "living memory" of past participants while the "full illumination by history [writing]" of its story accumulates. On one track, memory moves toward the past of actuality *and* toward extinction in a future, while on another the historian is to get "behind" the "curtains" that have obscured this, and presumably any other, past. Historical writing is that future which rescues the becoming-inert of memory: "open sesame" is the phrase that Nietzsche used to awaken one's countermemory of the flooding of that internal "ticking away" that constitute's the social's determination of cultural debt. Memory must "die" for "history" to exist, but memory "lives on" as "history." Memory is a "phrase" that is not subject to language in the important manner of itself really passing away. This absolutely impossible phenomenon, memory, spiritualizes by vesting sentimental affirmation in some palpably fearful image of loss of the past; doubled as an insecurity toward the future, cultural memory "orbitizes" commemoration, and, to my mind, evokes a particular American "apparatchik" desire: the professorial construction of a narrative purpose tied to a mythic social consensus, where negativity in the present (e.g., current racial stresses) will be overcome through declaring negation as definitive. Richard von Weizsacker, the president of Germany, is applauded for uttering the following piece of state terrorism: "Anyone who closes his eyes to the past is blind to the present." "Anyone who" says it all: or else! Always the order-words from this destroying "historical consciousness," always its demand for death. Weizsacker's phrase sounds serious, but is senseless. Does it mean that if one "opens one's eyes the past is not past"? To disperse the terror of loss, Woodward offers negation; better to say that the historian brings *memory to the surface so as to inflict pain*: that *x* is not over. This pain is neither horrific nor sublime, but a re-working of an existing program of social hope. Through images that traverse and unite affective, perceptual, and action images, the pain of an awful past ("lynchings") is connected to a less-than-pleasant present ("discrimination"). The function of such images is to override the power of cultural mythics and the dispersion of indices (signs — for example, Is the government a friendly player or not?). *The function of such images is to integrate criticism, to restrain social conflict within the realm of a "historical possibility," the reality of which is social impossibility.* "Keep struggling," or a stream of redundant clichés, is the basic form of this "historical culture," regardless of the particular ideological "voicing." The present is *relatively* fearful, and would be worse without the labor of historians and their "incomparable comparisons."

Historians need to work, of course, but it's peculiar work, since historians often promote fear of life as their work. Perhaps this is the normal terrorism of an essentially business culture, where political-economic considerations are constantly exerting negative pressures, to "make" something of negativity, a *rehabilitative* attitude. Leslie Berkowitz, director of the New York University Humanities Council, has gone so far as to say that "Americans . . . fear . . . they have had no past." Fear of what did not happen?[1] This crystallizes the process of psychological "dumbing-down": a liberal Platonism, which reinvents a modern soul, in need of . . . everything. There are not enough historians to "fill that need." In another context, the art historian Benjamin Buchloh tells us that we ought to, at times, beware of parody, which, because of its "ambiguity and balance [that] can be tilted at any moment from subversive mimicry to obedience,"[2] weakens one's sense of "historical consciousness." Parody does not allow, as Buchloh puts it, one to "reconcile" the current working artist and the ideological (de)formations of capitalism.

All these calls for more "historical consciousness" assume an exchange of one incomparable with something else (then = now), and often involve the further claim that one is handling two time-separated negatives, as Woodward does at the beginning of this chapter. The double negativity is redundant to the extreme, since "then and now" are brought together as the Same. Such "consciousness" sets up a culturally satisfying need/pain — as in the "lack of a past" — and reconfirms the "need" for expanding an image stock. Every neighborhood devastated by transformation shall have its "historic" remembrance. Such "consciousness" appears to always, or virtually always, reinforce the existing images of conflict drawn by existing players. It is notorious that American novelists can elicit a comparison to Melville by setting a male and a boat in a large stream of water. Apart from reinforcing existing subjectivities, such "consciousness" also speeds up the degradation of objects, the ceaseless rescripting processes that follow upon the more direct modes of social ravaging ("mourning" over nature after the success of chemistry in ruining soil). The past is hardly in a transitive, contestable relation with us. In short, Woodward and company represent a profession where it is widely believed that one exchanges, in the sending and receiving of official history, images (of continuity or discontinuity) that affect one's sensory apparatus — a motivation for tying oneself into the practices of the going players.[3] That one has no choice is made out to be a benign necessity. Given what was argued earlier, I think this to be a highly precise mode of psychological police statism, since it involves exchanging identificatory images for thinking up definitions, using (reduced) definitions to motivate actions, relying upon suspect clusters of favored and disfavored epistemes, methods, likes and dislikes, and so on.

In this chapter, I propose to take up the topic of "historical consciousness" in relation to works of art and art criticism. The assertion that such works/criticism must be "historical" in order to be representative will be challenged. In addition, I will explore what some of the alternatives might be to the incessant politics of criticism. This will, perforce, require saying things about the term "postmodern," which will figure here as a *narrow and precise* term, not at all as a term to demarcate a "historical period."

First, let us evoke the range of the topics and some of the cultural issues at stake.

The modernist paradigm (e.g., analytic Cubism, Brechtian theatre, Godardian cinema) is falling apart: the "modern classics" are being overthrown, decentered; the following citation explains first what is in "dissolution," and then offers a description of the effects of this temporal process:

> The modernist paradigm — with its valorization of myth and symbol, temporality, organic form and the concrete universal, the identity of the subject and the continuity of linguistic expression — foretells the emergence of some new, properly postmodernist schizophrenic conception of the artifact — discontinuity, allegory, the mechanical, the gap between the signifier and the signified, the lapse in meaning, the syncope in the experience of the subject.[4]

Everything from the beginning through the second dash is not modernism at all, but *Hegelianism*, the reconciliating thought-form of State

Workers of the Soul, the State-Speak that has the function of providing people with the signs of presentistic decline: the activities of consumption and "struggles" for "mastery" supply unity. Under what conditions does Hegelianism equal modernism? The definition of modernism as a type of organicism does not explain why or how Pudovkin, for example, derails the official party line in *The Heir of Genghis Khan* (1928), where, by overloading the ostensible narrative with a documentary mode, the viewer is encouraged to think of life forms *outside* of political reductionism. The competitors for state power, the Reds and Whites, are undone by the Yellows who, through their evocation of feelings and affects that cannot be comprehended by political agents, withhold something from politics. There are all kinds of "positive" instances of texts that have practiced, or tried to, something different from what is here called modernism and postmodernism. What would Jameson make of Fritz Lang's *Manhunt* (1944), in which the supposedly negative terms from the citation above trace something else, someone's becoming-unknown-in-action? Isn't the "hero" in this film stripped of all "organic relations" (to class, country, street), and does he not, instead of trying to kill Hitler as a representative of the Good Side versus the Bad, become open to chance and multiplicity, even if this means becoming nonmemory? The closing image of *Manhunt*, the leap from the plane, might be an instance of taking up an indirection and not an "organic" restoration of order. Jameson's list of negative terms for the second set is foolishly automatic; but "postmodernism" is not a temporal marker except as it is forced to do that job: as the effect of the magic "foretells." It may well be that what is called modernism already precludes all these straight lines.

Have existing players in art-making and criticism, art theory and its "history," any choice but to appropriate pain, memory, image, icon, every variant of feeling and thought or semiotics at the limit, in trying to create momentary pauses in the homogenization and socialization of the West? Are there any processes, degrading or enhancing, that are not already overcoded by mediations of image and sense (families, ethnicities, patois, argots, student and workers' groups)? In the current conflict in the United States between artists and their supporters and the American right (e.g., Jesse Helms), isn't it now the artist/intellectual who is capable of turning such conflict into "sign-value," another "last surplus" extractable from negative socialization? Or should one say that academics are in possession of a special will to write: representation über alles. The unthinkable is that one forgo "historical" comparisons in the first place. Consider the claim, for example, that painters who cannot account for their "historical" modernity are guilty of cultural disavowal, for where "neither . . . original implications nor . . . subsequent development" are "acknowledged," there necessarily results "the formation of the fetish."[5] In disputes over the present shape of equating history and reality, those who deny the reality of *this* actual interpretation of the past are doomed to psychoanalytically deny "history" (= denial of reality). It is hard to imagine larger demand structures of culture. Here, as Buchloh puts it, only art events that negate fetishization can generate a "new collective culture," one that is symmetrical with the hope that an academic treatment of problems has moved away from the (presently) overvalued (i.e., the fetishized). In this case, consonant with right-wing strategies of symbolic mastery, the left is willing to embrace continuities that it "knows" will not disappear; in so doing, it brings about those continuities, which is an apriorism "after the fact," or *hyper*oxymoronic. It wants its "own history," its heroes and villains: the left "needs" an ever-contestable signified of "history," just as, disastrously, the right does. I am not saying this as a liberal, but as a demythifier of context manipulation.

I am arguing that making "historical consciousness" a "player" in the evaluation or production of works of art, when such consciousness is itself a political-cultural code, projects discursive and existential anthropomorphisms of hopeful delusion, at best. Closer to the worst is that "slave of the facts" attitude put forth by Ginzburg. This reduces works of art to objects of control. Thinking, in the sense of effects that relay, as in a passage of real changes in perception (e.g., a verdict is delivered, a lie is manifested, something cannot be taken back), and which is not an imaginary or symbolic rhetoric whose purpose is to substitute identifications for the prehension of things, is denied in being reduced to metaphorical language.[6] All of this concerns the logic of cultural expectations: if one believes that most art-making today is "fetishistic" if it "plays" without denouncing, say, surface, then does one also expect some "historical rupture" with this kind of making? What is the difference between a "rupture" and a "historical" one? Does the latter come into play whenever one wishes to exert control? Is Bataille's "my father slaps me and I see the sun" a psychological phrase, while Jameson's "history hurts" is one of realism?

Cultural Models

A more concrete analysis might begin with those circulating classifications concerning "culture" made by Bohrer, Lyotard, Huyssens et al. concerning the sense attributed to terms such as "avant-garde," "reality," "history," audience, and so on. It is obvious that one is dealing with terms (or superterms) whose referential status is cloudy. There are as many definitions of the "avant-garde" as there are arguments concerning the reach of the idea, from Calinescu's apocalyptic model to Lyotard's version of immanentism (the former preserves a military coding, while the latter's "avant-garde" effect is not governed by "preestablished rules" or is a cultural guerrilla war). Bohrer has proposed a distinction that is worth taking up in considering art insofar as it comes under cultural and social criticism. This is the distinction between cultural attempts to "realize history" versus those of a "historicizing reality."[7]

To the first category belongs the activity of intellectuals for whom critique of and objections to present-day society are based upon a "reading of history." This "read" supposes continuity between one's "rightness" in criticizing the present, or some segment of it, with an Enlightenment ideal of reason, which both precedes and follows each negative or affirmative judgment; the cultural goal of to "realize" (e.g., make manifest) a social, political, aesthetic model believed to be continuous with both the past and the future legitimizes one's playing now. It is a radically tautologic setup: only those who affirm a verbal model that remains out of discussion are eligible to critique the present; only those who in the present will act in an enlightened manner are "rational." For example, to some in this group, the "revolt" or "liberation" of the 1960s — a moment often reduced to that of pop and/or camp in the arts (there are other reductions) — shows that the category of the avant-garde had reached "historical exhaustion," and so, in order to remain phatically related to an idea of "progress," the remnants of the older high-modernist avant-garde, with its demand to negate the negation of the separation between art and life (Peter Burger's argument in *Theory of the Avant-Garde*), thereby shifted to the liquidation of its own category. Critiques of the 1960s in effect "read" their own period in relation to a theory of history. In a situation of reification, the autonomy of art is regressive, and the vehicle of negating this regression is the self-liquidation of the avant-garde. Burger has suggested what this was to exclude: any critique carried out by the distribution of Nietzschean effects (e.g., "denial of history," metaphors are only metaphors), any practice that did not "clarify this crisis" (of modernity, of the power of capital) was declared reactionary. "It [such a critique] remains bound to an irrational concept of life that stands opposed to a rational organizing of social reality."[8] Or, if that is not absolute enough in equating ahistory with irrationality and nonrightness, the Enlightenment alone allows for the correct socialization in which we are *reparented*: "The conflict between a narcissistically omnipotent and a factually impotent self demands reconciliation. . . . Since the chosen father is dead, everyone is entitled to imagine himself as the only legitimate heir. But regression is not an acceptable fate, especially for intellectuals."[9] For intellectuals, the Enlightenment is our parentage, a *socius* that takes the place of ancestry, heir, tradition, and other ineffectual samenesses. It sets up another image of the family as appropriate for identity-in-opposition, another mytheme in the belief in cultural criticism.

It is important to note that what is imagined as decisively intolerable in this model of "realizing history" is the permanent separation of spheres of life; Habermas, who has proposed that the instrumental, the moral, and the aesthetic be taken as distinctive spheres of one life-world, argues that they can be brought together through a will to communicate. This supposes that capitalization processes allow for this communicative element of dialogue, a rather fearsome leap of tenuous states of mind. Past critical movements, such as Dada, must be redeployed so as to contribute to the "safeguarding of realms of experience and forms of life that are threatened with being eroded, undermined and washed away by the dynamics of economic growth and bureaucratization."[10] Dada, with its juxtaposed montage of symbols plunging the viewer into disruption of "seeing," does not transfer to the present, having been appropriated by subsystems such as advertising. The current avant-garde has learned — or must be willing to learn again — the "historical lesson" here, which is that its earlier failure was partly due to its abandonment of "historical consciousness." The Duchampian strategy of signing a ready-made and sending it to the gallery may have helped to dissolve the idea of an individual/unique artist; such provocation remained restricted to art, both intensifying its lines as a sphere of life and ultimately encasing it within those lines. The avant-garde of the 1920s is "historical" in Hegelian terms: it raised the self-consciousness of a contradiction to the surface, and, as a model of a Good Past, it is worth studying. It has been realized as a "historical category." The argument of a "useful history" transferred to art has it that art is to fuse with pedagogy in the *reappropriation* of the past, of its significant works of art, so as to use them in an illumination of the present. The path of "betterness," a conventional form of enlightenment, can be pursued through the communicative channel that sustains the "dignity of modernity, the dimension of a non-truncated rationality" (Habermas). Artists as different as Glass, Beuys, and Haacke should put forward the experiences of present reality so as to expose the present as something *blocked*, which cannot fulfill the promises of reason without students and others becoming aware of their "historical subjectivity." "History" is held to be necessary for social reconstruction, but the modern avant-garde interest in shock and assault on received ideation is not "useful" in and of itself. In effect, "realizing history" supposes a contemporary reduction of claimants.

On the other hand, the category of a "historicized reality" is evoked by Bohrer in order to sidestep or bypass the route of any "historical form" thought to make sense, a priori, of experiences. Here the operative concept is the actuality that there is not and cannot be a "universally applicable theory of history."[11] The form of a supposedly Enlightenment "progress" or directive telos is unreal in a scene where "phone sex" is well on its way to being legitimized as a way of making money, anchored in a "sensibility" that sees this practice as one item in the category of "release." Or junk bonds. Or the persistence of functions such as district attorneys for which there is no rationale . . . I am thinking here of Lyotard in particular, for whom art-making in a present does not "liberate from history" but frees its effectuality from the mythos of "historical terror," which is that of being used for the old ways "of the mere presentation of things driven away by the generalization of the media and the closure of thought on itself."[12] Drawing upon a mélange of terminologies, Lyotard's version of a "historicization of experience" can only move toward an *expansion* of temporal movements that lessen the powers of future and past on the present. "Impulsional movements," which do not lend themselves to refurbishing narrative order, are preferable to the predictable beating of political factions. This is not a question of promoting the antichrononyms (decline) nor celebrating, say, the insipidness of the arhythmic murders in the film *Joe*, one that immobilizes and one that accelerates the viewer out of real time, both of which rebuild narrative order:

> Both arhythmies are produced not in some aberrant fashion but at the culminating points in the tragedy of the impossible father/daughter incest underlying the scenario. . . . these two affective charges do not fail to suit the narrative order.[13]

The arguments in favoring a "realization of history" evoke sememes of discontinuity (e.g., references to "postmodern" as equal to after, later) reabsorbed in an established narrative (e.g., "learning processes" that may have gone "awry" but can be set on course). To "historicize reality," on the other hand, would upend the psychological "drag" that makes of discontinuities something to fear, suspending altogether narrative order. The narrative myths, these no-matter-what narratives that "history makes sense," of rational change (the plus-value of reason), direction in history (the plus-value of Capital), taking one's bearings in criticism from collective transformations (the plus-value of the "whole"), "hang together" as elements of a politics whose power or cultural force is based upon rational evaluation threaded to a self-protective psychology of reaction.[14] In essence, the argument for "realizing history" supposes that capitalism is all along marked by the temporality of "preparation" for a future that will, and hence must, be more "social" than now; Capital is imagined as something necessary, if immature — psychologized — and what is blocked out is that Capital is always asocial (Baudrillard's critique, which I will take up later). Bohrer goes so far as to say that individuals and groups who do not go along with psychologization sentence themselves "to designated reservations."[15]

To summarize: in the name of "realizing history" critical texts link up with progressive elements of mass/consumer society. Critical works are supported if they postulate an ethic that is energized by emerging elements of a new culture (e.g., ecologism, feminism) and can forge links in popular culture (e.g., punk, rock and roll, television, some sports activities) in superseding old culture (modernism). "Realizing history" causes the reduction of all relations to those inside the Western family: no outside. On the other hand, those who would instead "historicize reality" are thought to have abandoned utopian perspective in favor of conceiving one's "epochal feeling." The strong versions or texts associated with high modernism offer crystallizations through which important experiences were made contemporary realities.

These cultural "logics" are based upon a mixture of diagnosis and prognosis — categories themselves conceivably set aside by modernity. Isn't to "historicize reality" also to "dehistoricize" in the sense that story lines change? But isn't this, in turn, contained by an overall rehistoricization, which is fundamentally narcissistic? Consider the phrase "alternative culture." In the area of theatre, for example, the ideas of Artaud (the West as a sleepwalking culture, madness as intensity) — which were not cemented to "the enigma of pleasing forms" (Lyotard) — were "liberated" in the 1960s. Yet instead of serving as a plus-factor in a radical understanding of existence, they gave way to the familiar tactics of irony and pessimism toward change associated with the dramaturgy of Pinter, Wesker, Orton, Bond. Where Duchamp and the Cubists employed a suspension of satisfaction, isn't the "normalization" of movements such as neoexpressionism a challenge to the notion of art as difference? In cinema, the 1960s work of Godard, which was experimental in every aspect of the medium, has given way to the reinvention of a psychologism associated with Fassbinder or Wenders, directors for whom cinema registers a kind of "speechlessness" before the monumental triviality (oxymoronic) of everyday life (one thinks here of the opening of Wenders's *Paris, Texas*, with its desert-rat figure who repeats, in extremis, the return of the "hero" in the opening of *The Searchers* [1956], the quest for a family). Although a few directors (e.g., Herzog) are relentless in their depiction of the present as a catastrophe — a joyous one of sorts, since one has nothing to draw upon, from either past or future — it is quite uncommon to think of cinema in "alternative" terms, its "shocks" having been entirely absorbed by interpretations or cordoned off in art schools.

Let me go further. The category of "realizing history" reads the present as a continuous segment, each prior temporal break an episode in a story that precedes present and future. Retrospectively, the Enlightenment forms its parentage, and prospectively, the near future is focused upon as the site of various sorts of social and cultural "fulfillment." Its political limit is the groups, coalitions, and alliances formed for a strength not possible to any specific member, and which reterritorialize what Capital has deterritorialized (e.g., artists for the homeless). The category of "historicizing reality" — which is really dehistoricization in the sense of making the present incomparable (if possible) — whose practical doing begins with effacing the semantics of "history" as automatically providing the forms of reality, belongs, then, to the future. This means that one is not engaged in art-making so as to symbolize an idea, but is challenging symbolic reflection "in favor of authentic acts."[16] "Authentic" is notoriously difficult to explicate, but Bohrer has in mind practices that bypass the traditional categories of an ethicopolitical utopia that "guides" one's strategies of critique for a challenge, which might be considered "existential": works that press against and dislodge, in whatever sphere, "a falsely objectified tradition."[17] Critical acts irreducible to recognized agendas at least suggest presentations of the "posthistorical." In a decimated present, which is constantly pressured to embrace a past of nostalgia and which thins out future configurations, the term *invention* maintains a "pragmatic aggressiveness" toward existing games and codes, rules and formations. In *Cinema One*, Deleuze brilliantly expresses this acceptance of discontinuity at the level of understanding:

> The most "healthy" illusions fall. The first things to be compromised everywhere are . . . the sensory motor links which produced the action-image. Realism, despite all its violence — or rather with all its violence which remains sensory-motor — is oblivious to this new state of things where the synsigns disperse and the indices become confused. We need new signs.[18]

Historicization and Theories of Art Criticism

I want now to move closer to making distinctions between a contemporary, historicist left perspective on art-making and then juxtapose its terms with those suggested by considering Capital as something "ahistorical."

One critic tries to represent modernism by giving it a negative histor-icization. It is said that modernists desired an "immanent critique" (of form, effect, means) in order to avoid "the declining legitimacy of the liberal capitalist worldview." Modernism was defensive, an ideological reaction in which such holistic notions as the social disappeared in favor of examinations of fractured spheres. Aesthetic valuation was driven, inexorably, by artists making work that amounted to the success of fe-tishistic experimentation, which polluted every aspect of the creative processes, with the sole exceptions of an ethics for the future (socialism) and an expanded criticism now (judgments that signs foretell a different future). (Bad) capitalism is made causal to (of) (bad) art, the latter rec-ognized in its "inward" turn, which parallels the "outward" triumph of the commodity form. All of this, in turn, became the conditions for more "historical" deformation (e.g., the "neo-avant-garde"). For Buch-loh, the "neo-avant-garde" is an all-too-strong version of "the gridlock of depoliticized consumption and consumerized politics," which are "cut off from the production of use-value."[19] Here artist and purchaser are linked in "a futile repetition of symbolic liberation." Critical knowledge of the *direction of history* ("declining legitimacy") establishes the ranking of artworks, leading to the (enthymatic) conclusion that Joyce's *Finnegans Wake* is equivalent to analytic Cubism, which is equivalent to a Griffith film, and so on: they have the same social effect of evading some aspect of the social drama.[20] The artist as critic has "penetrated history"; one "knows" the continuous form of the process — perversion by Capital — which serves as a use value to guide one's sensibility toward "liberation" or "revolution." Criticism demands agreement on the intellectual deter-mination of reality: or else. Baudrillard offers a succinct statement of what is involved in this cultural postulate of making the "long-term" perspective of "history" one's criteria for art-making and social criticism: "When Marxism takes up its critique it does not question this retrospec-tive finality."[21] The latter corresponds to

> the aim of ideological analysis [which wants] to restore the objective
> process; it is always a false problem to want to restore the truth beneath
> the simulation. . . . all discourses of *truth* [are] always good, even and
> especially if they are revolutionary, to counter the mortal blows of
> simulation.[22]

To expect artists and critics to "restore the objective process," to make of them "heroes" in the corny stories of "rightness," downgrades other activities; it orders artists to synthesize a priori their ideas.

Indeed, Buchloh writes that important art works concern their own "historical" manifold and contradictions. This means that in the area of, say, sculpture, such works (today) embody a value when they are capable of posing for their audience the obsolescence of the category entitled "sculpture." That is, "critical sculptural practice" makes present the totality of its reality, the "historical value" that sculpture is not sculpture — recent "antisculpture" tries to "prove that sculpture as a category has lost its material and historical legitimacy."[23] There is nothing to expect from sculpture when considered as an effective medium of cultural criticism. Artists who are aware of precedence, domination, and who have the ability to master enough of the materials to make this relation, "obtain a more operative, functional dimension of use-value" when they combine the constructive and the allegorical. The latter is, of course, the correct narrative formation (in Hayden White's terms). For example, Rodchenko's "introduction of the monochrome" and his "abandonment of conventional attributions of the "meaning" of color in favor of the pure *materiality* of color" are said to have been motivated by

> the demystification of aesthetic production . . . the elimination of art's
> esoteric nature, the rationalistic transparence of its conception and
> construction supposedly inviting wider and different audiences.
> Rodchenko aims to lay the foundations for a new culture of the collective
> rather than continuing one for the specialized, bourgeois elite.[24]

Consciousness of this "new culture" equals the self-same "historical consciousness" of the "impossibility" of a "new culture" within bourgeois norms; indeed, the "repetitive neo-avant-garde" of the 1950s and after is defined by its "subservience" to the commodity form: "where the primary process maintained its supremacy — this realm was now in the process of being converted into an area of specialization for the production of luxurious perceptual fetishes for privileged audiences."[25] The painter Yves Klein manifests the "disavowal of the historical legacy of modernism itself." All this negative freight is presenced by the "historical attitude," and pivots on what the "neo-avant-garde" refuses to do with and to the past:

> The primary function of the neo-avant-garde was not to reexamine this
> historical body of aesthetic knowledge [e.g., the aesthetico-political
> reduction of color to monochromatism] but to provide models of cultural
> identity and legitimation for the reconstructed liberal bourgeois audience
> of the postwar period.[26]

The only "real" critical function for art-making is a "historical attitude" that positions the present so as to study the past. Art as criticism is one with "historical" recoding.

Buchloh's arguments suppose something like the following chain, ordered by the cultural "logic" of negativity: as commodity fetishism alienates us from ourselves (the contrary of a "new culture"), progressive art is "alienated from conventions" and ought to generate its identity in criticism; the latter state is brought into being through the negation of the present (commodity fetishism as it settles on us). The argument is circular, and supposes that use value resides in remaining conscious of the negative subject-of-history, commodity fetishism, and using this consciousness to preserve a sense of a better world. This succeeds in making the present just about null and void in terms of energy and excess, its space of action or performance subsumed by the obligation of establishing straight lines, no matter what: this "historical consciousness" dominates the present. "History" is thus preserved as the subject of references. And arguments are returned to their model in Lukács, who set forth a very explicit valuation of what is involved:

> Literature and art history is a mass graveyard where many artists of talent rest in deserved oblivion because they neither sought nor found any association to the problems of advancing humanity and did not set themselves on the right side in the vital struggle between health and decay.[27]

"History" retains the conceptual value of what Merleau-Ponty once called the "theological idea of a rational basis of the world," what, in another context, Arthur Danto called melodramatic staples such as "fatal," "destined," "doom," which dramatize what is an essential fact about the historical organization of the past."[28] "Men are responsible for the histories they are involved in. . . . Men have to be accountable for the incommensurability of intention and outcome."[29] Someone has to answer for.

For the most part, the American left — I am referring to its academic incarnation — makes sense when it critiques the conditions of production, particularly rates of profit, work conditions, bias in the media, and so on. But as is now clear from Baudrillard's critique of the left's "identity" with the overvaluation of labor as the self-defining human event, the left has virtually nothing to say by way of affirmation that is not utopian. Immediate value, not use value, is a form of life threatened with extinction in every discussion of criticism. Demands, like that of Jay's for the maintenance of a "liberating totalization," are hollow, that is, they are incapable of realizing value. One could say that the infinitive form itself has been appropriated and put to its own integrating menu by the left, as in this statement from Habermas:

> The project of modernity has not yet been fulfilled. . . . the project aims
> at a differentiated relinking of modern culture with an everyday praxis
> that still depends on vital heritages . . . the reappropriation of the expert's
> culture from the standpoint of the life-world.[30]

Coming from the "past," as it were, are "consensus," the "project," and "vital heritages," which wash over the present, which is flooded by the goal of "relinking," the most concrete instance of which here is "re-appropriation," one of those "noun-verbs" about which Greimas has something to say. Greimas reminds us that "appropriation" is a highly specific form of *acquisition*.[31] The doing of "reappropriation" as set forth by Habermas supposes that a subject has satisfied the *tests* required of a "reflexive realization of an object," in this case, the right to "relink" selves and institutions, powers, rights, justices, fairnesses. Just how this occurs and in what manner this "right" is gained is nowhere argued for by Habermas. How can anyone claim a right to "guide" and "lead" others to continuities that have been obscured and unrecognized by the "bad" side of modernity? It bases itself upon an act that says "We have studied and therefore this is what must be done." The left is incapable, like the right — and every other hyperpolitical faction — of the self-perception that it is in a muddle of cultural "logic" (because one has a command code at one's disposal, one can educe reality, the real, the should). Deleuze: yes, negation is opposed to affirmation, but affirmation *differs* from negation when ideas are irreducible to use-value.

The left, because of its valorization of playing now for the "long run," is hardly timid in demanding narrations that recode these commands. Perry Anderson, in *In the Tracks of Historical Materialism*, writes that historical materialism has no "competing story" for the "integration of successive epochs of historical evolution."[32] Presumably, concepts such as class conflict, hegemony, domination, and so on, perform the integrating of human experience, and language and signs thereof. But the terms drawn from any inventory of modernizing Capital are invariably painful and negative: oppression, exploitation, dispersion are intrinsic to modernity. How is the negative connected with Anderson's "integration"? Anderson writes approvingly of Alec Nove's "seductive model" of a "historical outcome" that would combine "realism" and "radicalism":

> [In] Nove's "feasible socialism" . . . all private ownership of the principal
> means of production is abolished in an economy where income
> differentials are held within a range of 1:2 or 1:3, a much more drastic
> compression than in even the most egalitarian of existing societies in the
> East.[33]

Anderson, whose notion of East European egalitarianism is bizarre in the extreme, no doubt believes that a narrative of work differentials is what a political culture requires in order to come into being. Merleau-Ponty: "equilibrium is more probable than chaos" gives us a historicism of avoidance and disavowal of conflict with Capital.

The art left has joined with the academic left in becoming bureaucratic players of essentially the same game. It continuously asserts that "the sense of history, of the referent, eroded [are] symptoms of the same 'schizophrenic' collapse of the subject and historical narrativity — signs of the same process of reification and fragmentation under late capitalism"[34] This mania to "historicize" — here the reduction of "history" to the "referent," the confusion of the "referent" with the "real," the re-iteration of a demand for the Same — does away with critique, with art-making as well: this is performed by equating the sensible world with the "power" of "late capitalism" that only asks how "late" is it? Whose clock is ticking?

Consensus among academic leftists has resulted in the fact that the concept of an avant-garde today rests solely with academic practices; "reading" and "interpreting" and "plotting" maintain their critical exchange value, no matter what permutations Capital brings about. One critic has said that Haacke's negation of the museum shows that artists "have to take into account the institutional limitations of [one's] role. Without consideration of the political character of the institutional framework within which a work is presented, the work is in danger of being neutralized, absorbed and turned into an insignia of power."[35] As Brood-thaers emphasized, the constancy of the transformation of object into merchandise justifies this "historical judgment" to, in effect, politicize everything. But this "critical" academic left automatically becomes the institution that studies this "constancy" of reification, commodification, hence as activists in the successful reduction of cognition (an oxymoronic bliss?) to a counterpolitics.

The argument comes down to the belief that experimentation is "finished" as a "historical reality," where, as I said earlier, in place of such emphases as Dada "shock" or Russian Constructivism, progressives ought to use art/critique so as to *rival* appropriating institutions (for example, with countergalleries, alternative "spaces"), to build alternatives, to keep going the sense of an "open" future. Huyssens says all this better than any other writer: "having gone through the modernist purgatory" (e.g., autonomization, formal analysis), progressive artists and writers ought to spend their time in the "recuperation of buried and mutilated traditions . . . exploring forms of gender and race based subjectivity in aesthetic productions and experiences . . . [in a] refusal to be limited to standard canonizations."[36] Such is the limpid agenda; its focal term is "recuperation," which makes cultural "work" part of the "recovery" of the self and the body from the bad powers that have thus far dominated "history." This omits consideration of how it is possible that "recuperation" combines with "critical" in the first place: is more subjectivity, however different, not another repetition of what gets co-opted in the first place — subjects who want more identity? What does one expect from a cultural "exploration" of "gender and race"? Isn't this another *product* of a larger research myth, and isn't there a question here as to the status of the concept of product, given the actual ambiguity of the form-thing? What Huyssens wants to see is the closing of the "gap" between "high and low" culture, where awareness of this "divide" is a condition for resolving it. But isn't this another element of Hegelianism, although subdued: consciousness ought to serve a continuous past-future, rather than connect with texts and objects that challenge these alignments? Huyssens believes that progressives ought not simply to resist extensions of pop and camp into political categories (e.g., the "imagification" of politics, the desubstantialization of the body one sees in the selling of chemicalized foodstuffs) but actively take up and refurbish for the present such cultural models as John Heartfield's use of photography to counter the snapshot, the gallery, the museum, fine art, appropriationist forms, audiences; the favored term is to "salvage" the spirit or heritage of the avant-garde.[37]

But this amounts to projecting that the new technologies invented for military or business purposes could be used to subvert the status quo. Since the earlier technologies gave rise to collage, assemblage, montage, and photomontage, the argument is that current ones (e.g., video) should be deployed to initiate a "revolutionary culture, an art of life." But this is also the essence of reactivity: the Hegelian moment is reactivated in the desire to wrest "freedom" and "creativity" out of a technology immediately destructive of alternative rhythms of labor — the word-processing eye-hand coordination, which accelerates their coupling, may be destructive in and of itself. Huyssens acknowledges the successes of the "culture industry" (e.g., the mass spectacles of Disneyland), but does not allow this to make the schematization of temporal succession more difficult: the false "liberation" of pornography is still something to overcome; the future belongs to groups like the Mothers of Medusa who critique galleries for the underrepresentation of women. In short, against all of the forms of an aestheticization of everyday life, it is the consciousness of a "search for tradition" that informs progressive art-making and criticism. As modernism has become an institution and so linked to neoconservatism, and as postmodernism revels in its lack of "history," it is the job of a reconstituted "avant-garde" (which is virtually identical with academia) to persist in "the utopian hopes of the historical avant-garde . . . to address those human experiences which either have not yet been subsumed under capital, or which are stimulated but not fulfilled by it."[38] Ecce Academia!

Two Instances of Theorizing a Cultural Event: Lyotard and Baudrillard

Works of art and criticism can hardly have — in such terms as the left enables to have an impact — any sort of important role to play. As left criticism becomes institutionalized, it embraces the larger indifference of having an impact, what can be called the "event status" of action. The issue is the peculiarity of treating art texts as events, not as representations. Now I trace two "models" of cultural events, the term "model" restricted to the sense of designating a "thought experiment," a process Deleuze has described as

> epistrata and parastrata . . . moving, sliding, shifting and changing on the
> Ecumenon or unity of composition of a stratum . . . shaken by
> phenomena of cracking and rupture . . . accelerations and blockages,
> comparative speeds, differences in deterritorialization creating relative
> fields of reterritorialization.[39]

Lyotard's Model of the Postmodern

The term "postmodern" is so far advanced today in cultural criticism that it is identical with one or more senses of "after." Jameson employs the term to suggest a "dialectical" third stage of capitalism, the near completion of a universal and global formation, while neoconservatives like Hilton Kramer have used the term to designate the return of avant-garde practices. Yet the most interesting aspect of the term "postmodern," at least in Lyotard's usage, is its postponement of a clear "historical register." Indeed, the term is barely temporalized at all in one of its chief articulations:

> The postmodern would be that which, in the modern, puts forward the
> unpresentable in presentation itself; that which denies itself the solace of
> good forms . . . to share collectively the nostalgia for the unattainable;
> that which searches for new presentations, not in order to enjoy them, but
> in order to impart a stronger sense of the unpresentable. . . . A
> postmodern artist or writer . . . cannot be judged according to a

determining judgment. . . . Those rules are what the work of art itself is looking for. . . . work and text have the characters of an *event* . . . too late for their author . . . their realization . . . too soon.[40]

Meaghan Morris writes that this notion is "banal because it restores us to the paradox of a history driven by the sole, and traditional imperative to break with tradition."[41] What she does not allow is that the term has already been removed from the sense of "breaking" with time, and proposes a different frame in the consideration of temporality and some functions of the symbolic.

In two essays from the early 1970s, "Freud according to Cézanne" and "Adorno as the Devil," Lyotard focused on the "position of desire" within Western modernism. The concept of desire is linked to the concept of exchange since in both cases one is dealing with symbols that transport subjects to the meaning of events, where there is supposedly an

anonymous desire that supports the institution in general and makes it acceptable . . . exchanges that imposed a *symbolic* value on the object, just as the neurotic's unconscious produces and relates representatives of the repressed . . . Oedipal origin.[42]

The symbolic provides for an exteriorization of meanings. The psychoanalytic "discovery" of neurotic interiority supposes that events can only become exterior (to the analyst, to the scientist, to the artist), and that interiority is already exchangeable the instant it is symbolized. In this view, what is modern is less a "break" than it is a ratcheting upward in the demand for symbolization: what does not exchange does not warrant the categorical status of the symbol that represents.

When artists and writers undergo their own acceleration of dispersion, when in a particular system there comes to be no dominant formula for doing something one way rather than another, then one is bereft of what could be called criteria that operate as rules of symbolizing. The term "postmodern" summarizes the experience(s) of not being dependent upon the rules — or their failure — for symbolizing events and acts; instead of a "history" created out of a dialectic between the coming into existence of the new on the ashes of the passing out of existence of forms, modernity is itself suspended as something symbolizable insofar as effects are not suitable for immediate determinations of sense:

All formulae are failures and successes, they do not *follow one another* except in a superficial history; they are *contemporary with one another* in the underground where Cézanne's immobile desire generates disjointed figures, fragmented spaces, incompatible points of view.[43]

What Lyotard considers to be a structural determinant of Western culture is the simultaneous disappearance of meanings related to a nondomesticated unconscious and their reinvention as official modes of culture. The category entitled symbol is problematical in and of itself. Symbols, whether expressive or representative, always fulfill some desire or fate — they are in some manner "on time," that is, appropriate to a situation's understandability. But this conjunction of temporality and symbol has also been absorbed by the larger failure of interpretation, where narrative authority based on universal ideas of society and culture has been invalidated, where "it is therefore tempting to lend credence to the great narrative of decadence."[44] (Many interpretations support "postmodernism" with the satisfactions of imaging decline.) This deficiency of the symbolic suspends interpretation, placing its self-symbolization up for contention. (In this it is like speculative knowledge that "names itself," where "statements are treated as their own autonyms" [self-referential], which subtend a temporality of identity, of the "life span" of particular peoples or classes.)[45] Symbolic theories, however, continue to promise an art of "giving back," of "enabling" an "incitement premium," an energy that produces figures beyond the "barriers of repression,"[46] a displaying of the figurative apparatus (e.g., making real the unreal). There is Freud, dumbstruck before Michelangelo's *David*, introspecting on the release of a sense of awe which has affected his unconscious, this awe becomes the speech that attends the satisfaction of recognizing his desire in Michelangelo in David in Freud . . . There is Adorno, who, as is well known, championed Schoenberg's "new music," and for whom such music "delights in recognizing its wretchedness and finds all its beauty in forbidding itself the appearance of the beautiful."[47] Such "denunciatory art" in fact relies upon an imaginary speculation: that the nonfulfillment of beauty is nonetheless satisfied, realized, or, to be somewhat perverse about it, "fulfilled" by an indefinite projection of "hope" in the future, negative "hope" being the symbol of a last meaning. This is the symbolism of "passage," of enduring the barely endurable, of putting up with the agonizing martyrdom of alienation.

Lyotard's arguments about the concept of the "postmodern" are not married to notions of symbolic binding, whether or not they are denunciatory; the concept is not, as it were, "cut" for the "hand or foot" of thought in a cognitive "climb." As the argument is suggested in *The Differend*, every attempt to resurrect temporality to serve functions of periodization also erects something universal, necessary, binding, an obligation, a symbolic (integrating) metanarrative regardless of its illocution form (as story, as essay, as image, as theatre, as declarative assertion). If "postmodern" is reduced to the cultural competition over whose narrative model or symbolic construct is the most cosmopolitan, then the term is "boxed in" at the start within a myth of opposition and stories that are projections of interpretations, "a begging of the question."[48] Periodization deploys, across an abyss of language games, the single game of "linking" "moments and their ends," anchored in the desirability of speculation, the satisfaction of bringing to an end. Periodization makes desirable certain ideas of participation, of belonging, of being part of a collective group: it makes possible the symbolization of ends as things which do not end, which continue as a transcendence of any specific end.

The term "postmodern" does not designate "after modernism" but a spacing for alternatives to the sterility of "outcomes" given in the speculative discourse of ethics and cognition. Such speculation is a principle of last resort, where the use value of cultural works emerges as a device in negating the now. In art-making this can effect "hatred for art, the work of art [which] approaches knowledge [of the Devil, Capital]."[49] A nonsymbolic art and criticism does not mean withdrawal or defeat or other terrorisms perpetuated by the politicians of thought, the police of pedagogic systems everywhere. Manfred Frank detects, he believes, in some of the writings of "postmodernists," a "certain return to the vitalism of desire," a "Nietzscheist retrogression."[50] But there is nothing remotely "vitalist" about a sense of desire in which it is accepted becoming "active in the order of energies"; if references to "energy" and similar terms somehow restore vitalism, how is an energetics reducible to a right-wing activism? Nor is the concept of "postmodern" a generational reaction to the "lack of response [of the father, or representatives] . . . and the forbidden."[51] What governs Lyotard's construction is the decision that within an overall modernism dominated by the exchange principle there can be various "mutations" of "considerable significance." This sets aside "revolutionary" concepts that promise a "rupture" in the future for a "reconstructed society," for the suspension of symbolicity enables the present to achieve an *indifference* toward "the transferential function," to

> the rule of castration and the difference of the sexes . . . ; this requires a setting-aside of one's having to take up
> the site of masochistic and sadistic manipulations, that in it both desire and the fascinated gaze are spurned . . . , and which does not mourn the annihilation of objects as symbolic values coincident with desire and culture and their conversion into indifferent terms of a system that no longer has outside itself any instance to which these objects circulating in its heart can be grounded.[52]

This exteriorization cannot be contained by resubjectification. As it is put in *Just Gaming*, the appropriate temporality for such descriptions is that of a speech act in which the content is incessantly forgotten "for a nonforgetting of time as a beat in place. . . . what does not get forgotten is the temporal beat that does not stop sending narratives to oblivion."[53] Or, as it is put in relation to object making in general, its "dispossession" of what an audience supposedly "knows," the privileged representation of tragedy (oedipalization) can only be frustrated by works that upend "a space of donation or exchange."[54] As Rey Chow has noticed, some of Lyotard's terms for displaying "postmodern" can be connected to a "trampoline effect" of "classical Chinese aesthetics," "whereby the tightening of a spring means that its sudden release will launch infinite, vaster spaces of the unseen."[55] Being elated to others through speaking (or making) does not entail the promulgation of "historical time," as the repetition of chronos and periodizations; if something can be said that is not a repetition, a reversion to preexisting stories, then the "is happening" has not yet happened, that is, something *is happening* that is not reduced to our political "tribulations."[56]

Again, these notions propose a radical desubjectification—a "looseness" in the links between sender and receiver such that there is no language system, certainly not speculative *patience* and its insistence upon conceptual reductionisms, that commands what one can say in any situation.[57] Victor Burgin suggests, by way of comparison, that one can link "postmodern" with the "condition" offered by "feminism, Marxism, psychoanalysis and semiotics"—their "common" ingredient being their status within academic work, where "critical work" should be attached to "projects . . . *held in common* by a constituency which may be, or may not be, large." Such a "post-Romantic aesthetics" will now transcend "creating" and "making," which belong to a failed Romanticism.[58] End of art = fulfillment of a "historical" mission. What is "held in common" is *essentially* the *test* of one's "rightness." The "held in common" is thereby a figure of symbolic representation—the will is saved, aesthetics passes into ethicocognitive safety.

If we take up this rush to seize the present as equal to a confirmation of what one "knows," and if we think about images, there are arguments to be made for treating the event in a nonhistorical manner. Lyotard's *Driftworks* suggests three types of images that make historicist recoding difficult. Certain early-twentieth-century drawings of Picasso's do away, he claims, with both a cognitive and an ontological "reading" of the nude: it is impossible to read some nudes as "exclusive forces," so that the cultural perception is set aside by the figure's capacity to evoke a consideration of acts of perception; the visible "nude" is not necessarily related to the oneirics of interpretation (to an erotics of the binarism male/female). Such first-level image-figures dissolve "visible outlines" but do not prevent the figuration of nudity from being appropriated for a number of purposes. On a second level, that of "form-figures," the "linear invariable" of a figure can become unrecognizable and, in certain Pollock paintings, there is an active "disinvestment" of form. This disruption of form-figure is conceivable as the invention of texts whose genre rules are, as in Lyotard's arguments concerning the work of Daniel Buren, suspended; the object itself forestalls psychic or emotional "investment" "in" images. What is at stake here is an invention of ambiguities of form and an expansion of illusions, both of which pass onto delight in constructing. The principle here is entirely radical:

> Desire does not wish to see but to lose itself through a discharge upon and within the object. . . . no loss can be envisaged because there is no objectivist or gestaltist exit. . . . it attempts . . . to break up . . . the spring of the eye.[59]

Questions of image and form suppose a third dimension of images, that of matrix-figures; here, such presentations concern the spacing or the distinctiveness between sensible images and concepts. Matrix-figures belong to what is "outside what is recognizable," what could, by a Structuralist, be called the surplus of the signified — something(s) never really captured by language or art, politics, or the social. In *The Postmodern Condition* and other places, this dimension evokes the "unpresentable," the "sublime," and similar concepts in an overall project of "dememorization." Indeed, on the level of sound, the matrix-figure, like that of Cézanne's attempt to "stop misleading the eye," moves away from the couple of symbol and analysis and toward

> no resolution in the vanishing point, where the multiple gathers itself together, [so that] there will be no history, no salutary epiphany . . . language without intention that requires not religion but faith. Schoenberg criticises music . . . to turn it into a discourse . . . a space of Lutheran, Hebrew, auditory, sober domination. . . . What is needed is a practice . . . [to] liquidate, liquify . . . the element that selects what is musical . . . [to] establish all noise as sound, body noise, the unheard-of noises of the social body.[60]

It ought to be obvious that even at the level of the image Lyotard leaves no room for an opening to an autonomous "historical" treatment of the materials; practices of the figural are neither on the way to being rhetorics nor oppositions to the ruling jargons and codes. Instead, such "ephemeral traces" manifest the "maximum of anxiety," and no resolution at all of social problems; they are analogous to any piece of writing that has proposed one version or another of an "open work." Again, where oppositional works are modeled on the production of use values against an odious exchange value, "indifferent" works are *pagus*, "a place of ceaseless negotiations and ruses."[61]

The existing cultural players have something precise at stake in a full-fledged discussion of Lyotard's terms. I am referring to the implications of symbolic "indifference" toward every type of *official culture*, institutionalized in the forms of university presses, curatorial texts, the reviewing processes, grants from the National Endowment for the Arts, and so on. Considered socially, an official culture appears as the social bond that is reasserted in the face of the difficulty of communication: the "people" are asserted as "passing judgments"; others need to be "listened to." Judgments and evaluations from the most various groups "conform to the relevant criteria . . . accepted in the social circle of the knower's interlocutors."[62] Its "opinion" sets forth and defines a "competent" cultural life and so must be able to present criteria by which to mediate cultural conflict or strife. As Lyotard has pointed out in many places, the metanarratives (emancipation of humanity, liberation of science, freedoms of the self) of modernity served this function; they are today incredible in terms of contemporary social structures — inoperative when considered in a blunt analysis of actual social conflict. What is at stake are the representative functions as such.

An unofficial "postmodern" could mean surplus, not "after." A surplus of affects, of sounds, of ideations, not their control, their management, their articulation by groups whose interest lies in the integration of dispersive signs. Social bonds are not "historical" but argumentative; for Lyotard, the "mourning process" concerning the various "shatterings of reality" that recompose and decompose modernism does not mean that one has to "start all over again." "Most people have lost the nostalgia for the lost narrative. It in no way follows that they are reduced to barbarity. . . . That is what the postmodern world is all about."[63] So to insist once more: "postmodern" is not a category by which our thoughts pass onto the "next" phase or stage or moment of a "history"; it designates where one is "posting" oneself to, how one is "posted" to language and institution, culture, and active object-making. "History" is not something that anyone speaks, that anyone plays. Most of all, the concept of a symbol ceases to be something that comes "at" one from an "elsewhere" and without which desire is somehow unfulfilled, lacking proper interpretations.

Baudrillardian Demonics That Shatter History

The vanity and narcissism of the Los Angeles and New York art worlds have transformed Baudrillard's writings into citations in the making of objects for sale, while the obtuseness of many on the left depicts Baudrillard's arguments as defeatist, pessimist, and cynical.[64] In what follows I try to establish an argumentative thread showing that Baudrillard's writings give us a full-blown suggestion of something other than what Jameson has designated as a negative "postmodernism." Jameson has called the latter a "shift of position" where past/present/future become locked in a "perpetual present . . . perpetual change," determined by the "internal and superstructural expression of a whole new wave of American military and economic domination throughout the world."[65] Baudrillard's texts offer a "fall into a view of present history as sheer heterogeneity, random difference, a co-existence of a host of distinct forces whose effectivity is undecidable." Jameson expresses the fear that the passions of class relations will not have an *objective reference*. "Historical knowledge" helps, enables us to "reflect . . . on the most effective forms of any radical cultural politics today."[66] In reading Baudrillard, one comes to perceive just how sentimental the left actually is, how its adherence to a conjunction of subject/object amounts to an inability to devise strategies that challenge its own "classicism."

A Baudrillardian fact: the Western "history" incarnated at the fourteen-thousand-year-old Lascaux caves in France, with their prehistoric animal drawings, is harmed by the carbon dioxide of human breathing; government officials have decided that only "scholars" and the state can have access to these "documents." An "exact replica" is constructed some five hundred yards away in which, according to Baudrillard, "the duplication is sufficient to render both artificial."[67] This "fact" of Western ethnology, this "fourth dimension of ethnology" where everything becomes museumified in becoming saved — or can only be saved in becoming museumified — implies the success of a series of processes that have no single culminating symbol or mark, but which is suggested in "an irreparable violence towards all secrets, the violence of a civilization without secrets. The hatred by an entire civilization for its own foundations."[68] Instead of Lyotard's notion of objects that displace symbolicity by maintaining an exteriority that frustrates control, Baudrillard's "posthistoricism" reminds us that the attempts to "possess" the past at Lascaux may be connected to the "triumph" of a demonic narrative, of the becoming normal of ex-terminations and which appear in resurrections of sign-value.

Among the most important topics in Baudrillard's writings are his construction of processes that are "more than historical" and the particular effects that can be ascribed to art and critical events in this "surplus historical" world. Functionally, Baudrillard suggests that official culture should be treated as it rationalizes the implosion of its own norms.

The quotable and, to some, rash and excessive statements by Baudrillard refer to writings in which the present is described in what can be called the terminology of a "scorched culture": the brain has triumphed over the body; the physical landscape is mostly one or another desert; time is blown apart from the inside, by a "desire" which does not so much become silent in its workings as it is attached to a death instinct far more ordinary than the one Freud gave us. In front of the Berlin Wall after the "fall" of the East, "here, at the pinnacle of history self-exposed by its violence, everything is eerily quiet. . . . history is being antiquated as vague terrain. . . . the signs . . . are the true conductors of lethal energy, the electrodes of electrocution . . . the Hertzian relays of our memories that crackle."[69] More: the invasion of intimacy by information (talk shows), this generalized verbal confessionalism, marks Nietzsche's gregarious man come home; the evil demon of "communication," which does anything but what its proper name signifies (dissignification?), ushers in a "diabolical conformity" of images set within an overintegrated social order: "I pick up the telephone receiver and it's all there: the whole marginal network catches and harasses me with the insupportable good faith of everything that wants and claims to communicate."[70] Such a-eventualities designate "history" as a concept utterly displaced by reality. Objectivity cannot prove "history."

The texts of Baudrillard leave no doubt that such a context — hyperrealism, simulation, the triumph of the death instinct, the normalcy of distortion, the impossibility of old-fashioned bohemian alienation — has been brought about ("caused," as it would be put in classical terms) by real structures that are not reducible to the social names we usually apply to the events and occurrences of "history." Academic language is in "midair" if its support, the Real, disappears. "Class conflict" does not synthesize what occurs in relations between working and owning classes but refers to a language of social scientists, which has tried to tame and domesticate conflicts that are irreducible to social classes.

We can get a handle on this by recalling the essay "The Concept of History," in which Hannah Arendt pointed out the intellectual destruction of perceptual difference — events — which occurred when historians of the modern period, basing their sense of objectivity on the scientific myths of noninterference and nondiscrimination with the facts, set up the *ideals* of an *autonomous* "historical process" and constructed "objectivity" as the mirroring of this "process," giving themselves simulacra of "scientificity." Freed from the charges of subjectivity, they brought about the separation of "history" from everyday life and embedded it in a "knowledge" of "life." "History" became a stable discourse, which it never was in the ancient world. Through the nineteenth and twentieth centuries, the profession's erudition allowed narration to be seen as itself a kind of science, one of the forms of articulation, as Foucault put it. Knowledge was presented to its readers as autonomous, distant/proximate, past yet causal, and something irreversible. For Arendt, as for Baudrillard, this "history" as language was constituted in descriptions of "life processes." It was released from anyone's sensuality/experience and so could become a pure procession in the liquidation of things, events, and specific causes, all of which begin to disappear from the understanding of particular social actors. The language of objectivity succeeded not in being objective but in restraining the presentation of nonsubjective processes. Arendt is quite clear on this: so many processes from the past are going off that a kind of entropy of will parallels historicism. With religion shattered in its capacity to provide controlling interpretations of disruptive events, and with the social becoming entirely indifferent toward any sense of "immortality," only the simulacra of Vico's "cycles" or Fichte's "plans" or Marx's "class conflict" temporarily postponed what Arendt called the "melancholy haphazardness" of a modernity unrestrained vis-à-vis tradition and stability, especially the cycles of gift giving and exchange that characterized so-called nonhistorical peoples of the West. The main statistical category of society, the "silent majority," began to understand that there could be no "historical reconciliation" given our acceptance of, and even desire for, the destruction of ourselves by processes we consider irreversible.[71] Here too is the basis for Habermas's charge of an identity between antimodernism and young conservatives.[72] Accumulation that never accumulates (almost everyone dies without "estate"), long life with numbing boredom, pedagogic activities in which more and more people become positively inept (which means more dependent on what remains of the social): such are events hemmed in by structures that are *simultaneously integrative and terrorist*, where one is not allowed not to be "educated" by the media or one is not allowed not to be too skeptical toward the projects of one's academic "colleagues." There is virtually no time outside the timings established by the going players.

The past is not past when it goes off in random ways in futures no one intended.

Baudrillard's consideration of this "reversion of history," this ricochet effect, is in keeping with the concept of "history" becoming absorbed and ultimately nullified by processes that are autonomous and inhuman, an inversion, if you will, of the felicity projected onto classical theories of "history." "History" is more like an "Evil Demon driven by a silent strategy," an idea more out of Burroughs and company than Marx and Engels, artists whose skills have often been turned toward a critique of language (and abhorred by more normal social science), particularly their naiveté toward authority and language, which is endemic to Americans.[73] Since there is no question of anyone knowing the "face" of "history," its supposed effects are annulled, released to become virtual objects in their own right: the ambivalence of "fatal strategies" makes it undecidable in advance whether one should pursue a strategy of subjective liberation or one of becoming objectively impossible to the further socializations to come.

Considered on the level of signification, of the distinctiveness of signs, we can posit three specific eras of this becoming social, this "culmination" of the present as simulacra, this drowning of the event in sign-value. Taking the early modern era as a conventional starting point, Baudrillard argues that in it iconic signs prevailed over indexical ones. In the concern with maintaining an analogical connection between signs, this era was dominated by *obliged* signs (what Louis Marin, in his *Portrait of the King*, designates as the conjunction of power and representation) whose "grid" was composed of the categories of reciprocity and difference. It was a society of a "ferocious hierarchy, since transparency and cruelty for signs go together. . . . signs are limited in number . . . not widely diffused. . . . each one functions with its full value as interdiction. . . . signs therefore are anything but arbitrary."[74]

This "natural theatre of life" gave way to the modern era of industrialization and the machinic operations that pervaded every sphere of life; its human pole, its subjective referent, is manifested in *indices*, here devices of a prosthetic order (e.g., eyeglasses), arithmetized and patterned. The first order simulacra of iconic signs were increasingly absorbed by this "second power," what Marx called the triumph of dead labor; appearances were subjected to regimes of reproduction structured by equivalence and indifference between the various series. For Baudrillard the second mode was already "a time of lesser scope" by comparison to the Renaissance's enjoyment of doubles, mirrors, masks, theatres, and even Jesuits with their elaborate games.[75] This second era is also that of the integrative ideologies (nationalism, etc.) and media (newspapers, modern film), and manifests the largest number of subjects who are made equivalent, particularly by reference to monetary forms and their attending "cultural logics" (accumulation, conspicuous consumption).

The languages and discourses of value are dissolved in the third era, where "production no longer has any sense," where "the simulacra win out over history," where combinations between different series (e.g., work, family) are controlled by

> models from which proceed all forms according to the modulation of their differences. Only affiliation to the model makes sense, and nothing flows any longer according to its end, but proceeds from the model, the "signifier of reference," which is a kind of anterior finality and the only resemblance there is. . . . Not quantitative equivalences, but distinctive oppositions. No longer the law of capital, but the structural law of value.[76]

This is an era that is structurally oxymoronic given its (dis)structuration of experience: the triumph of debt forms which, we were told, are destructive but which no one can do anything about without virtual self-destruction; the triumph of liberations, of every sort, which have spawned, in every domain, phenomena of runaway *productivism*:

> Production everywhere and always seeks to exterminate seduction in order to establish itself over the single economy governing force relations; we must also keep in mind that sex or its production seeks everywhere to exterminate seduction in order to establish itself over the single economy governing relations of desire.[77]

Baudrillard presents "phrases" (in Lyotard's terms), cognitive and speculative statements, which are brutally nonmythic; one is not dealing with a "philosophy of history" whose readers are directed onto "ends" and "finalities" of an ascent toward the future, but rather with events of the here and now that are already a kind of shock treatment; there must be no question of a preposterous "taking over" of the existing apparatus, of "coming to power." The "takeover" is precisely a mythology insofar as it supposes that criticism itself remains militarized — enlightened.

In another sense, Baudrillard's texts are quite explicit about thinking to a present/future where objectivity has assumed new forms, most of which leave our conceptual grids flailing and groping, laughable, in many cases, for their pretentiousness, among other things. Instead of "history," with its attendant belief that all events are comparable to that which drives them (a small-scale revolt here makes "sense" because it is attached to the large form of class struggle, which is thought to give sense), we are embedded in a "cycle" (*pace* Vico) that has obliterated the sense of terms like "opposition," "resistance," and so on. If "cycle" evokes too strongly the myths of the "new," and thus of "beginning" and "breakthrough," even if a return, there is something which nonetheless thwarts even this desire. Capital allows one to think about the success of an *objective* atemporality:

We have already seen signs of the first order, complex signs and rich in illusion, change, with the machines, into crude signs, dull, industrial, repetitive, echoless, operational and efficacious. What a mutation, even more radical still, with signals of the code, illegible, with no gloss possible, buried like programmatic matrices light years away in the depths of the "biologica" body. . . . End of the theatre of representation, the space of signs, their conflict, their silence; only the black box of the code, the molecular emitter of signals from which we have been irradiated, crossed by answers/questions like signifying radiations, tested continuously . . . by the search for the smallest indivisible element . . . the code.[78]

Third-order sign: it is reported that the distinction between nature and sport (but what do these terms actually mean?) has fallen to enthusiasts in Malibu, California, who want to build an underwater reef to ensure the persistence of "surf," to protect waves in danger of disappearing.[79]

What is human sociality? One might suggest what perspective this gives to our usual thoughts about change. Consider again claims that a university culture "stands for" pedagogic benevolence, which ranges from its offering of (free) concerts and films to its regimen of laboratory research, and which extends to public lectures of all sorts. This academic culture, whether it wants to or not, enacts rules which enable it to constitute a "culture" that is perceived as socializing; its "end" is that of a perpetual socialization of the present. For Baudrillard, on the other hand, all such "ends" — functions of the university — are in fact only a "fate," that is, only socializing already socialized "fatalities." Baudrillard argues that an "invested" opposition makes an objective deception: Capital does not "hold" power through rational means in the first place; corporations are not a "center" to which and around which one is to mobilize an opposition, a resistance, a future, deploying the phrase-regimens of cognition and speculation (truth and should). For Baudrillard, Foucault managed to talk himself into the myth that "power . . . is the last term, the irreducible web, the last tale that can be told . . . what structures the indeterminate equation of the word."[80] Baudrillard is saying that we have, individually and institutionally, convinced ourselves into believing that there is no seduction or reversibility of power: adherence and resistance to power require that power be thought of as "hegemonic," "centered," and the like because such thinking satisfies an *imaginary catastrophe*; but nothing occurs according to the way it is imagined, which dislocates subjective and objective polarities, even if this goes unrecorded.

We remove ourselves from "history" — rather than extending it — if we move beyond the negative forms of civilization (substitution?) and acknowledge that "history" is not a Hegelian subject but our installation of a number of irreversibles (accumulation, the substitution of signs for realities). Indeed, for a writer constantly assaulted for defeatism and similar sins by progressives of all sorts, Baudrillard is quite explicit in a counterproposal to history:

> Accumulation, progress, growth, production, value, power and desire itself are all irreversible processes — inject the slightest dose of reversibility into our economical, political, institutional, or sexual machinery (dispositif) and everything collapses at once.[81]

The Mirror of Production (1975) argues that the modern era dissolved by its fantastic *overvaluation* of economic production, the reduction of all other series to the deformations of industrial reproduction; once it consumed itself in its own techniques — feeding on its earlier incarnations — "economism" of both the liberal and left varieties gave way not to a "culturalism" that is more "real" than production, but rather to codes and simulacra that no longer require the brakes and throttles of consciousness: digality and DNA, modulation, feedback, and tests — these are a "more radical mutation" than anything dreamed of in critical economic or cultural categories. Such terms suggest a social apriorism built into political and cultural events: what happens is captured a priori in its presentification, by the requirement of reproducing more sign-values.

Is the idea of a differentiating, affirmative "outside" possible in this metacontext? The idea of "history" served as a cultural measure in what was the political control of economic practices. Industrial politics based this control on linguistically based cultural extractions; the self-legitimation of "history" meant embedding in "the masses" those "wants" which they themselves could not articulate but which progressive intellectuals could "read." The past, present, and future were combined so that "thoughtful nostalgia" merged with the right sort of "safe" speculation for the future (e.g., we have a "duty" to an anthro-ontologic reconstruction of ourselves); intellectuals were assigned to refurbish and supply figures of arrival, finality, end, closure, negation of distance, the fulfillment of desire, and the "realization of history," as Bohrer put it. Baudrillard: the implosion of that order evokes

> the effacement of terms and of distinct oppositions, and thus that of the medium and the real. Hence the impossibility of any mediation, of any dialectical intervention between the two or from one to the other. . . .
> Hence the impossibility of a sense (meaning), in the literal sense of a unilateral vector which leads from one pole to another. This critical — but original — situation must be thought through to the very end; it is the only one we are left with.[82]

In a situation where "we can no longer fix the way things are going,"[83] of a global "catastrophe in slow motion,"[84] where "human rights, dissidence, antiracism, the antinuclear movement, and the environment are gentle ideologies," the context is one of "*post coitum historicum*, after the orgy . . . ," which implies that "in dealing with the epidemic of visibility menacing our entire culture today, we must, as Nietzsche quite correctly said, cultivate mendacious and deceptive clear-sightedness."[85] Now these aphorisms concerning the West's "posthistoricity" and strategies of dealing with it are nothing if not a challenge to the roles which intellectuals have taken up toward Capital and its sociality.

Baudrillard telescopes all these matters into a question that allows for nonrepetition of modernist critical strategies: "Does the ironic art of disappearance succeed the art of survival?"[86] Rephrased, how does this enigmatic question suggest an event status for critical activity?

Where Nietzsche, in opening and closing the *Genealogy of Morals*, said that "mankind" would rather "will nothingness" than abandon the will, Baudrillard's refrain is that in the midst of the "semiorrhage" of values and norms (in the Weberian sense), the rupture between meaning and sense decontextualizes critical interventions that voice meanings that objectivity depends upon in order to be understood and which also fulfill subjectively based interests. The invariance of subjective/objective copresence no longer protects the intelligentsia — within and without the university — from a problematical social status. There is something beyond the signification-manipulations of a critical intellectual, which is to say that in Baudrillard's "counterinterpretation," it makes more sense today to "let us for one time hypothesize that there is a fatal and enigmatic bias in the order of things."[87] With this, we would do better to imagine "a sovereign object which recreates within us . . . original disturbance and seeks to surprise us." Instead of a repetitive cycle of rationalist attempts to create the category of aesthetics, or the self, or the reconciliation of subject/object as mediations in the "fulfillment" of social problematics, we might abandon and jettison such cultural ideals and move toward the practice of objects: "to leave the field open for objective irony is also a challenge."[88]

This becoming-objective, this "art of disappearance," takes place in relation to the catastrophe of socialized expectations. A mode of this disappearance is embodied in the preference of the "silent majorities" for soccer rather than voting, in the choice *for* spectacle rather than for an "enlightened" terrorism.[89] The "immemorial" task of the masses — their fascination with strategies that do not "maximize" image and word or encourage the superproductivity of meaning — and strategies from the second era of signification (the Book) govern the divide between intellectuals and society. For intellectuals it is suggested that our texts and objects now fail to connect with everything but *our own simulacra, image power, formation of exchange*. In doubting and negating everything, in affirming and consecrating everything, in describing and rewriting everything, intellectuals remain prisoners of the futile role of the subject-in-consciousness, and enforce the pretense that our efforts *translate and represent* for the truth of others, the reality of the world.

Works of art and writings have no possible way of being "normally" used in this Baudrillardian scenodrama; of course, a more "aware" text is more interesting than one that is not. But the issue is that the term "criticism" refers to something already an epiphenomenon and restricted to the context of narrow cultural distinctions. Even the mass-consumed academic text, rare indeed, has only sign-value of an effective difference. In addition, the mode of an "indefinite reproduction," one of the extended forms of this third sign-era, carries away every modern projection onto works of art: since it is not possible to now separate or autonomize the category of art in terms of its absolute distinctiveness, it is not possible to hold art to signify,

> as art, the value of a finality without purpose. Art and industry can then exchange their signs. Art can become a reproducing machine (Warhol), without ceasing to be art, since the machine is only a sign. . . . And so art is everywhere, since artifice is at the very heart of reality. And so art is dead, not only because its critical transcendence is gone, but because reality itself, entirely impregnated by an aesthetic which is inseparable from its own structure, has been confused with its own image.[90]

Simulacra *escalate* amidst critical interventions: in a tumbling together of categories, in an overlapping of oxymorons. Here the "health-management" physician does not have enough time to examine patients without loss of income; the academic does not have enough time to instruct; and the "defense" industry obliterates the sense of "defense" since it cannot fire multimillion-dollar missiles on account of faulty $16 switches. What gains is the objective irony of the world, and we intellectuals should have the nerve to say so.[91]

Intellectual "work" cannot, in such constructions, take on the role of Lyotard's "saving the honor of the name" or other critical perspectives, whether "radical" or "revolutionary." Baudrillard places all such functions in the past. Yet Baudrillard leaves room for writing to invoke its own disappearance, for a kind of overthrow of the make-believe, which determines that, as intellectuals, we should pretend to be naive in relation to the audience of students. The dyads through which negation might realize utopia, the moralizing which would "be more rational" than existing statements, or a psychology which would "found" a "theory of need" are not an intellectual's responsibility. Events of theorization, in the face of the objective dissuasion of culture and the social, where "forgetfulness" of "extermination is part of the extermination itself,"[92] would have to release themselves from a never-satisfied "reflection" and "negation" (and affirmation) and approach or find thoughts that make the future *strange*:

> Theory is . . . destined to be diverted, deviated and manipulated. It would be better for theory to divert itself. . . . theory can . . . defy the world to be more: more objective, more ironic, more seductive, more real or more unreal. . . . It has meaning only in terms of this exorcism.[93]

What would this look like? What could it appear as? Could an event — without culturalist prejudices as to appearance — by seduction challenge thought in such a way that it passes from metaphor (sign-value) to *metamorphosis*, that is, a transformation of substance and function?

Concluding Remarks

It is absurd to summarize here two authors, many texts, and a number of interesting ideas. Reading Lyotard, who shifts the art event to the domain of dispossession and enunciation, and confronting Baudrillard, whose writings evoke the history of metaphysics and cultural theory, enables one to suggest that writing can offer devices by which one can challenge thought systems that hyperpoliticize or reduce life. Such writings enable one to think, perhaps, some "last thoughts" on "history," thoughts that take their cue from Lévi-Strauss and the death of events in the triumph of modernization. Reading Lyotard, that amplifier of concepts, and Baudrillard, whose sentences constantly provoke a challenge to subjectivity, one can glimpse a thinking that is no longer "historical" and an art no longer representational.

Notes

Introduction

1. E. Said, *Orientalism* (New York: Vintage, 1979), pp. 15, 328.
2. G. Vattimo, *The End of Modernity* (Baltimore: Johns Hopkins University Press, 1988), pp. 20ff.
3. I. Kant, *Philosophical Writings*, ed. E. Behler (New York: Continuum, 1986), pp. 251–55.
4. G. Deleuze, "Plato and the Simulacrum," *October* 27 (Winter 1983), p. 55.
5. J.-F. Lyotard, *Des dispositifs pulsionnels* (Paris: Union Générale d'Editions, 10/18, 1973), pp. 80–83.
6. See J.-J. Lecercle, *Philosophy Through the Looking Glass* (La Salle, Ill.: Open Court, 1985), p. 191.
7. G. Spivak, *In Other Worlds* (New York: Routledge, 1988), pp. 90–91.
8. J.-F. Lyotard, *The Differend: Phrases in Dispute*, trans. G. Van Den Abbeele (Minneapolis: University of Minnesota Press, 1988), p. 13.
9. P. de Man, *The Resistance to Theory* (Minneapolis: University of Minnesota Press, 1986), p. 48.
10. M. Phillipson, *Painting, Language and Modernity* (London: Routledge and Kegan Paul, 1985), p. 28.
11. C. Levin, "Art and the Sociological Ego," in *Life After Postmodernism*, ed. John Fekete (New York: St. Martin's Press, 1987), p. 57.
12. F. Jameson, *Postmodernism* (Durham, N.C.: Duke University Press, 1990), p. 62. Jameson's italics.
13. G. Deleuze and F. Guattari, *A Thousand Plateaus* (Minneapolis: University of Minnesota Press, 1987), p. 109.
14. D. Harvey, *The Condition of Postmodernity* (London: Blackwell, 1989), p. 18.
15. S. Aronowitz, *The Crisis in Historical Materialism* (New York: Praeger, 1981), pp. 305, 319.
16. F. Nietzsche, *Beyond Good and Evil* (New York: Modern Library, 1927), p. 552.
17. K. Lowith, *From Hegel to Nietzsche* (New York: Holt, Rinehart and Winston, 1964), p. 192.
18. Ibid., p. 286.

19. Cf. Hannah Arendt, *Between Past and Future* (New York: Meridian, 1961), pp. 223ff.; M. Calinescu, *Faces of Modernity* (Bloomington: Indiana University Press, 1977), pp. 247ff.

20. Lowith, *From Hegel to Nietzsche*, p. 193.

21. See, in particular, G. Deleuze, *Nietzsche and Philosophy* (New York: Columbia University Press, 1983), pp. 145ff.

22. These remarks are based on J.-F. Lyotard, "Memorandum on Legitimation," in *The Postmodern Explained* (Minneapolis, University of Minnesota Press, 1993), pp. 58–59. See also Eric Alliez and Michel Feher, "The Luster of Capital," *Zone* 1 & 2 (1987), pp. 315–59. Alliez and Feher analyze the capitalistic process of "valorization," which, by defining information (including "knowledge") as both a source of value and a form of merchandise (i.e., as labor power), subsumes the totality of time under its own law of unequal exchange. They also analyze the transformation of the "free subject" of spatial subjection into the "human capital" of temporal enslavement. For a lucid account of "machinic enslavement" (*agencement machinique*) in which human beings are incorporated as a piece of the machine of time and capital, see "7000 B.C.: The Apparatus of Capture," in Deleuze and Guattari's *A Thousand Plateaus*, pp. 424–73. Deleuze and Guattari distinguish "machinic enslavement" (temporal) from "social subjection": in the latter the human being is not a component of the machine but is subjected to exterior (spatial) conditions that allow for agency. I am grateful to Biodun Iginla of the University of Minnesota Press for the last two references.

23. G. Deleuze and F. Guattari, *Anti-Oedipus* (Minneapolis: University of Minnesota Press, 1983), p. 230.

24. Lowith, *From Hegel to Nietzsche*, p. 300.

25. A. DePalma, "Research Files at Columbia Are Destroyed While Federal Audit Is Pending," *New York Times*, May 23, 1992, p. 9.

26. J.-F. Lyotard, *The Postmodern Condition* (Minneapolis: University of Minnesota Press, 1984), p. 48.

27. J. Baudrillard, "The Anorexic Ruins," in *Looking Back on the End of the World*, eds. D. Kamper and C. Wulf (New York: Semiotext[e], 1989), p. 31.

28. In the struggles over knowledge, today one reads that academic officers recruit new faculty by embracing such practices as "to not honor contracts with people whom we had given temporary appointments to." Cf. the chilling interview with Provost R. Orbach, now chancellor of UC Riverside: E. Ahn, "Provost Explains Letters and Science Overhiring," *UCLA Daily Bruin*, vol. CXXX, no. 108, April 23, 1990, p. 14.

1.   What Is Criticism For?

1. R. Barthes, *Writing Degree Zero* (New York: Hill and Wang, 1968), p. 31.

2. L. Mulvey, *Visual and Other Pleasures* (Bloomington: Indiana University Press, 1989), pp. 128ff.

3. P. Anderson, *In the Tracks of Historical Materialism* (Chicago: University of Chicago Press, 1984), p. 105.

4. Suggested by Baudrillard in *In the Shadow of the Silent Majorities* (New York: Semiotext[e], 1983).

5. Cf. J.-F. Lyotard, "Adorno as the Devil," *Telos* 19 (Spring 1974), and the important essay "Freud according to Cézanne," in *Des dispositifs pulsionnels* (Paris: Union Générale d'Editions, 10/18, 1973).

6. G. Deleuze, *Nietzsche and Philosophy* (New York: Columbia University Press, 1983), p. 110.

7. See Ann Wordsworth's perceptive comments on the dispute between Foucault and Derrida in "Derrida and Foucault: Writing the History of Historicity," in *Post-Structuralism and the Question of History* (Cambridge: Cambridge University Press, 1987), p. 124.

8. R. Krauss, "The Cultural Logic of the Late Capitalist Museum," *October* 54 (Fall 1990), p. 10.

9. Ibid.

10. G. Deleuze, "Plato and the Simulacrum," *October* 27 (Winter 1983), pp. 52–53.

11. See John Tagg, *Grounds of Dispute* (Minneapolis: University of Minnesota Press, 1992), preface.

12. At the "high" university, one has to rank among contestants for a post in the top five or ten candidates considered on a national scale. Résumés are circulated within departments by heads of search committees who make "their candidate" look like the only rational selection, accomplished at times by cutting and pasting from all one's letters of recommendations and then circulating this as a straight recommendation.

13. Cf. J. Baudrillard, *Le système des objets* (Paris: Gallimard, 1968).

14. Cf. the remarks by G. Deleuze in *Foucault* (Minneapolis: University of Minnesota Press, 1988), p. 15, and A. J. Greimas, *On Meaning* (Minneapolis: University of Minnesota Press, 1987), p. 49.

15. J. Weiner, "The Red and the Black," *The Nation* (June 24, 1991), p. 854.

16. Cf. Nietzsche's remarks in *The Use and Abuse of History* (Indianapolis: Bobbs-Merrill, 1949), pp. 35ff.

17. Prof. John Toews, quoted in the *Chronicle of Higher Education* (January 11, 1989), p. A7.

18. Cf. the remarks by H. Foster in *Vision and Visuality* (Seattle: Bay Press, 1988), p. ix.

19. Cf. N. Bryson's use of Lacanian categories in "The Gaze in the Expanded Field," in *Vision and Visuality*, ed. H. Foster (Seattle: Bay Press, 1988), p. 92.

20. Cf. Deleuze, *Foucault*, p. 118.

21. A. Huyssens, *After the Great Divide* (Bloomington: Indiana University Press, 1987), p. 198.

22. Cf. T. Veblen, "The Higher Learning," in *The Portable Veblen* (New York: Viking, 1948), p. 520.

23. E. Said, *The World, the Text, and the Critic* (Cambridge: Harvard University Press, 1983), p. 520. p. 49.

24. G. Bataille, *Inner Experience*, trans. L. A. Boldt (Albany: State University of New York Press, 1988), p. 181.

25. R. Barthes, *S/Z* (New York: Farrar, Straus and Giroux, 1974), p. 5.

26. J. Smith, "The Transcendence of the Individual," *Diacritics* (Summer 1989), p. 87.

27. For the extreme implications of this, see J. Baudrillard's *Fatal Strategies* (New York: Semiotext[e], 1990), p. 71, in particular "the tautological and grotesque perfection of the truth processes."

28. J. Baudrillard, *Simulations* (New York: Semiotext[e], 1983), pp. 149, 152. I am indebted to Jeremy Gilbert-Rolfe for reminding me of the force of this Baudrillardian description.

29. J. Baudrillard, *The Mirror of Production* (St. Louis: Telos, 1975), pp. 19–20.

30. See the remarks of G. Bataille, *The Accursed Share: An Essay on General Economy* (New York: Zone Books, 1988), p. 33.

31. J. Riddel, "Neo-Nietzschean Clatter—Speculation and the Modernist Poetic

Image," in *Boundary 2: Why Nietzsche Now?*, vol. 9, nos. 3 and 10 (Spring/Fall 1981), p. 213.

32. Cf. M. de Certeau, *Heterologies* (Minneapolis: University of Minnesota Press, 1986), p. 217. See the closing remarks by Carlo Ginzburg in discussing the historiography of A. Momigliano and his inability to break from idealism ("Momigliano and De Martino," *History and Theory*, vol. 30, no. 4 [1991], pp. 46–48).

33. Cf. G. Deleuze, *Cinema One: The Movement Image* (Minneapolis: University of Minnesota Press, 1986), pp. 82–84.

34. Baudrillard, *In the Shadow of the Silent Majorities*, pp. 46–47. I am referring to chemical laboratories that are now perfecting fake sensations of fat-consumption (as in ice cream) and to the more obvious behavior of the glamour and attraction of cultural work.

35. V. Descombes, *Modern French Philosophy* (Cambridge: Cambridge University Press, 1980), p. 154.

36. G. Deleuze and F. Guattari, *Kafka: Toward a Minor Literature* (Minneapolis: University of Minnesota Press, 1986), p. 82.

37. H. Arendt, "The Concept of History," in *Between Past and Future* (New York: Meridian, 1961), pp. 86–89.

38. F. Jameson, "Postmodernism or the Cultural Logic of Late Capitalism," *New Left Review* 146 (July–August 1984), p. 86.

39. T. Adorno, *Negative Dialectics* (New York: Seabury Press, 1972), pp. 247–48.

40. Cf. T. Adorno and M. Horkheimer, *Dialectic of Enlightenment* (New York: Herder and Herder, 1972), pp. 166–67, 219.

41. Cf. Lyotard, "Adorno as the Devil," *Telos* 19 (Spring 1974).

42. The phrase is from P. Anderson, "postscript," *In the Tracks of Historical Materialism* (Chicago: University of Chicago Press, 1984), p. 105.

43. J.-F. Lyotard, *The Differend: Phrases in Dispute*, trans. G. Van Den Abbeele (Minneapolis: University of Minnesota Press, 1988), p. 90.

44. See A. Danto, "Art Evolution and History," *Journal of Aesthetics and Art Criticism* (1986), p. 233.

45. G. Deleuze, "Plato and the Simulacrum," *October* 27 (Winter 1983), p. 55.

46. Cf. *Zone* 5 (1989).

47. Deleuze and Guattari, *A Thousand Plateaus* (Minneapolis: University of Minnesota Press, 1987), p. 79.

48. A. Ross, "Introduction," in *Universal Abandon* (Minneapolis: University of Minnesota Press, 1988), pp. vii-viii.

49. Cf. such a list in *Zone* 5 (1989), presented by B. Dudens.

50. Cf. the remarks by Deleuze and Guattari, *A Thousand Plateaus*, pp. 369ff.

51. I am indebted to Mario Biagioli for this term.

52. See F. Jameson, "On Negt and Kluge," *October* 46 (1988), pp. 176–77. I hope that I am not valorizing a small fetish in the history of logic or criticism; my point here is that Jameson *omits* any comparison, driving us, his readers, into agreement with terms and implications that have not been stated.

53. See the extraordinary opening of J. Baudrillard in *Simulations*, pp. 2–3.

54. Baudrillard, *Simulations*, p. 11.

55. See S. Wolin, "Revolutionary Action Today," in *Post-Analytic Philosophy*, ed. J. Rajchman and C. West (New York: Columbia University Press, 1985), p. 256.

56. Cf. Deleuze and Guattari, *A Thousand Plateaus*, pp. 492ff.

57. P. Sloterdijk, "Cynicism—The Twilight of False Consciousness," *New German Critique* 33 (Fall 1984), p. 192.

58. Deleuze and Guattari, *A Thousand Plateaus*, p. 293.

59. C. Ginzburg, "Checking the Evidence: The Judge and the Historian," *Critical Inquiry*, vol. 18, no. 1 (Autumn 1991), p. 82.

60. Cf. G. Bataille, *Inner Experience*, pp. 16, 118.

61. J. Kristeva, *Tales of Love*, trans. Leon Roudiez (New York: Columbia University Press, 1987), p. 381.

62. Deleuze and Guattari, *A Thousand Plateaus*, p. 294.

63. J. Baudrillard, *The Ecstasy of Communication* (New York: Semiotext[e], 1988), p. 86.

64. U. Eco, *Travels in Hyperreality* (New York: Harcourt Brace Jovanovich, 1986), pp. 83ff.

65. J.-F. Lyotard, *The Postmodern Condition* (Minneapolis: University of Minnesota Press, 1984), p. 4.

66. Cf. J.-F. Lyotard, "Freud according to Cézanne."

67. Cf. P. Sloterdijk, "Cynicism," p. 206.

68. G. Bataille, *Visions of Excess*, ed. Allan Stoekl (Minneapolis: University of Minnesota Press, 1985), pp. 38, 43.

69. Suggested by the critic J. Gilbert-Rolfe.

70. R. Krauss, *The Originality of the Avant-Garde and Other Modernist Myths* (Cambridge: MIT Press, 1987), p. 5. This vanity is expressed in the following solemn and corny gnosticism: "Method is what criticism is, seriously, read for." Freshmen composition students could devour the pomposity here. On Nietzsche and scholars, see the remarks by Foucault, "Nietzsche, Genealogy, History," in his *Language, Counter-Memory, Practice* (Ithaca: Cornell University Press, 1977), pp. 142–43.

71. See J. Tagg, *The Grounds of Dispute* (Minneapolis: University of Minnesota Press, 1992).

72. G. Deleuze and F. Guattari, *Anti-Oedipus* (Minneapolis: University of Minnesota Press, 1983), p. 208.

2. The Academic Thing

1. G. Deleuze, *Nietzsche and Philosophy* (New York: Columbia University Press, 1983), p. 147. The phrase "unlocated knowledge" is from John Tagg, *The Grounds of Dispute* (Minneapolis: University of Minnesota Press, 1992).

2. F. Jameson, *The Political Unconscious* (Ithaca: Cornell University Press, 1981), p. 291.

3. G. Spivak, *In Other Worlds* (New York: Routledge, 1988), p. 249.

4. F. Nietzsche, "On the Truth and Lies in a Nonmoral Sense," in *Philosophy and Truth*, ed. and trans. D. Breazeale (New Jersey: Humanities Press International, 1979), p. 80.

5. M. Carpenter, "Eco, Oedipus and the 'View' of the University," *Diacritics* (Spring 1990), pp. 77ff.

6. Cf. J.-F. Lyotard and J.-P. Thébaud, *Just Gaming* (Minneapolis: University of Minnesota Press, 1985), p. 76.

7. J.-F. Lyotard, *The Differend: Phrases in Dispute*, trans. G. Van Den Abbeele (Minneapolis: University of Minnesota Press, 1988), p. 13.

8. Summary of Consent Decree Provisions, _____ University (September 1976).

9. G. Spivak, *In Other Worlds*, p. 116.

10. These remarks are based upon Foucault's essay "Nietzsche, Genealogy, History" in *Language, Counter-Memory, Practice* (Ithaca: Cornell University Press, 1977), p. 154.

11. G. Deleuze, "Active and Reactive," in *The New Nietzsche*, ed. David Allison (Cambridge: MIT Press, 1985), pp. 82, 86.

12. I employ the term as used by J.-J. Goux in *Symbolic Economies: After Marx and Freud* (Ithaca: Cornell University Press, 1990).

13. J. Baudrillard, "The Structural Law of Value and the Order of Simulacra," in *The Structural Allegory*, ed. J. Fekete (Minneapolis: University of Minnesota Press, 1984), p. 72. One might also reread Nietzsche's *Advantage and Disadvantage of History* for a parallel criticism.

14. Minutes, Search Committee in European Intellectual History, history department, _____ University, April 26, 1977.

15. Memorandum from Professor R. to history department faculty, December 30, 1977.

16. Letter from Professor James _____, history chair, to President _____, January 18, 1978.

17. Memorandum from the Search Committee to the history department, March 20, 1978.

18. C. Levin, "Carnal Knowledge of Aesthetic States: The Infantile Body, the Sign, and the Postmortemist Condition," *Canadian Journal of Political and Social Theory*, vol. 11, nos. 1–2 (1987), p. 91.

19. G. Deleuze and F. Guattari, *A Thousand Plateaus* (Minneapolis: University of Minnesota Press, 1987), p. 135.

20. Memorandum, May 4, 1978, to the history department from the Search Committee in European Intellectual History.

21. P. Virilio, *Popular Defense and Ecological Struggles* (New York: Semiotext[e], 1990), pp. 17, 20.

22. J.-F. Lyotard, *The Postmodern Condition* (Minneapolis: University of Minnesota Press, 1984), p. 63.

23. Ibid., pp. 54–55.

24. Letter from history chair _____ to Sande Cohen, June 2, 1978.

25. At the University of California, Los Angeles.

26. Letter from G. to Academic Council, October 21, 1985.

27. Ibid.

28. Lyotard, *The Differend*, p. 142.

29. A. Danto, "The Artworld," in *Philosophy Looks at the Arts*, ed. J. Margolis (Philadelphia: Temple University Press, 1987), p. 166.

30. E. McDowell, "Publishers Are Uneasy at Booksellers' Meeting," *New York Times*, June 5, 1989, p. D14.

31. G. Deleuze, "Plato and the Simulacrum," *October* 27 (1983), p. 55.

32. Paper given by Félix Guattari at the California Institute of the Arts, February 12, 1991.

33. H. Arendt, *The Human Condition* (New York: Anchor, 1959), p. 295.

34. Letter from Academic Council to President R. _____, November 8, 1985.

35. Some students had complained of sexual harassment; one filed documents in the school and with the provost, and bitterly left the school complaining of administrative neglect. In her reply to the student, Dean C. noted that she would not bring charges because, among other things, "The actions . . . could constitute . . . the mildest and the most difficult to prove form of sexual harassment, i.e. unwelcome sexual advances. . . . However, the # of specific instances you cite [4] . . . would make a marginal case" (Memorandum to _____, from Dean C., October 31, 1983). Strange that a

dean of an art school would "know" what was marginal or not within the law and that it was unthinkable to pursue feminist principles before the law.

36. Deleuze and Guattari, *A Thousand Plateaus*, p. 214.

37. Cf. A. Stoekl, *Politics, Writing, Mutilation* (Minneapolis: University of Minnesota Press, 1985), pp. 63ff.

38. Dean _____, letter to Appeal Commission, December 9, 1985. How do legal affirmation and denial differ from affirmation and denial considered as semantic categories? What is the mixture that gives the term "legal" "force and consequence"? Legal commands result in orders—confiscation, attachment, punishments of all sorts, penalties, fines, and so on.

39. Deleuze and Guattari, *A Thousand Plateaus*, p. 177.

40. G., letter of November 13, 1985, to President _____, document A, Appeals Commission.

41. Dean C., letter to Appeals Commission, December 9, 1985.

42. F. G. Bailey, *Morality and Expediency* (London: Blackwell, 1977), p. 95.

43. G. Deleuze and F. Guattari, *Kafka: Toward a Minor Literature* (Minneapolis: University of Minnesota Press, 1986), p. 44.

44. Ibid., p. 72.

45. Aside from authoring a "request" of December 11 that I "confess" to bias, on December 20 Dean C. wrote a memorandum requesting, among other things, "that [she] be informed in a timely manner of who the commission has interviewed." This accelerated the *exclusions* that then came into existence, effectively blocking the interviewing of *students*, since the Appeal Commission could not "protect" them from faculty retribution.

46. On this theme, see J. Kristeva, *Tales of Love*, trans. Leon Roudiez (New York: Columbia University Press, 1987), pp. 310ff.

47. G. Bataille, *Visions of Excess*, ed. Allan Stoekl (Minneapolis: University of Minnesota Press, 1985), pp. 59–60.

48. Dean C. to Appeal Commission, December 17, 1985.

49. J. Baudrillard, *Selected Writings*, ed. M. Poster (Stanford: Stanford University Press, 1988), pp. 187–88.

50. R. Barthes, "The Wisdom of Art," in *Calligram: Essays in New Art History from France*, ed. N. Bryson (New York: Cambridge University Press, 1988), pp. 166–80.

51. T. J. Clark, "Arguments about Modernism: A Reply to Michael Fried," in *Pollock and After: The Critical Debate*, ed. F. Frascina (New York: Harper and Row, 1985), p. 83.

52. Statement to Appeal Commission by a famous California conceptual artist, December 26, 1985.

53. Letter to Sande Cohen from _____, December 19, 1985.

54. G. Deleuze and C. Parnet, *Dialogues* (New York: Columbia University Press, 1987), p. 41.

55. As reported by the secretary to the Appeal Commission, Dean C. contacted, on her own, G.'s former employers; this famous critic and G. had an extensive and troublesome "history," including disputes over editorial policies at a magazine they had cofounded. I could only react; my colleagues on the commission were able to insert the past directly into issues at the school—mythical "history" as pure weapon.

56. Dean C., letter to Appeal Commission, January 8, 1986. Program Director _____, letter of January 6, 1986.

57. Notes of Appeal Commission, January 14, 1986.

58. G., letter to Appeal Commission, January 14, 1986.

59. *Majority Recommendation*, to President _____, January 22, 1986.

60. *Majority Recommendation*, p. 2.

61. G. Spivak, *In Other Worlds*, p. 101.

62. J. Baudrillard, *The Mirror of Production* (St. Louis: Telos, 1975), p. 131.

63. University of _____, document entitled "The Call: _____ Summary of Policy and Procedure, Lecturer Series, 1987–88," April 26, 1988, p. 6.

64. As stated by J. Baudrillard in *La Société de consommation* (Paris: Gallimard, 1970), pp. 99ff. I am not saying that analysis of, for example, cell structure is *ever equivalent* to the ceaseless *rewriting* of, say, the "American Revolution." They are not, and in that *nonequality* there are lots of nonnarcissistic texts.

65. Lyotard, *The Postmodern Condition*, p. 5.

66. Baudrillard, *Selected Writings*, p. 189.

67. This is taken from University of _____, document entitled "The Allocation and Use of Faculty Resources in the College of Letters and Science," December 16, 1987, p. 6.

68. Ibid., p. 6.

3. Habermas's Bureaucratization of the Final Solution

1. J.-F. Lyotard, *Peregrinations: Law, Form, Event* (New York: Columbia University Press, 1988), p. 23.

2. These remarks are drawn from J.-F. Lyotard's *The Differend: Phrases in Dispute*, trans. G. Van Den Abbeele (Minnesota: University of Minnesota Press, 1988), p. 169.

3. M. Broszat/S. Friedlander, "A Controversy about the Historicization of National Socialism," *New German Critique* 44 (Spring/Summer 1988), p. 124.

4. J. Habermas, *The New Conservatism: Cultural Criticism and the Historians' Debate*, ed. and trans. Shierry Nicholsen (Cambridge: MIT Press, 1989), pp. 229–30. My italics.

5. As Derrida remarks in "White Mythology," the semantic effect of Habermas's phrase "burned into our national history" supposes *the acceptable repression* of the metaphorical sense of that "unloading ramp." One is dealing with significations where "language is to be filled, achieved, actualized, to the point of erasing itself, without any possible play, before the (thought) thing which is properly manifested in the truth."

6. Habermas, *The New Conservatism*, p. 252. My italics.

7. Ibid., p. 233.

8. P. Sloterdijk, "Cynicism—The Twilight of False Consciousness," *New German Critique* 33 (Fall 1984), p. 191.

9. Habermas, *The New Conservatism*, p. 235.

10. Cf. the remarks in Habermas's "Modernity—An Incomplete Project," in *The Anti-Aesthetic*, ed. H. Foster (Port Townsend, Wash.: Bay Press, 1983), p. 11.

11. Cf. G. Deleuze, *Nietzsche and Philosophy* (New York: Columbia University Press, 1983), p. 73.

12. Habermas, *The New Conservatism*, p. 235.

13. Cf. the remarks by J. Habermas, *Communication and the Evolution of Society* (Boston: Beacon Press, 1979), p. 166, and *The Theory of Communicative Action*, vol. 1, trans. T. McCarthy (Boston: Beacon Press, 1984), pp. 307–308.

14. Habermas, *The New Conservatism*, p. 236.

15. Ibid., p. 237.

16. Ibid., p. 164.

17. Ibid., pp. 43, 69, 201.

18. Ibid., p. 193.

19. Ibid., p. 54.

20. Ibid., pp. 58–59.

21. Cf. Julia Kristeva, *La révolution du langage poétique* (Paris: Seuil, 1974), "Prolegomenon."

22. Habermas, *The New Conservatism*, p. 62.

23. Ibid., p. 225.

24. Ibid., pp. 64, 69.

25. These remarks are based upon some suggestions by Deleuze and Guattari in *A Thousand Plateaus* (Minneapolis: University of Minnesota Press, 1987), pp. 229–32.

26. G. Bennington and R. Young, "Introduction: Posing the Question," in *Post-Structuralism and the Question of History*, ed. D. Attridge, G. Bennington, and R. Young (Cambridge: Cambridge University Press, 1987), p. 9.

27. Habermas, *The Theory of Communicative Action*, p. 136.

28. J.-F. Lyotard, "The Sublime and the Avant-Garde," *Artforum* (April 1984), p. 37. One might compare this sense of the sublime with Deleuze and Guattari's notion of a "line of flight," in particular the latter's statements that such lines are "deterritoralizing," that they are becomings which can "cross the wall" in "getting out of the black holes," but which are also the potential "microfascism" of "turning to destruction, abolition pure and simple, the passion of abolition" (*A Thousand Plateaus* [Minneapolis: University of Minnesota Press, 1987]), pp. 229ff.

29. An example of which is R. Krauss's rewriting art history according to an uncritical reception of Lacanian psychoanalysis. In asserting that the historicism of Gombrich relied upon the optical and geometrical model of an "essentially mimetic account of art's ambitions, of the artist's enduring struggle to replicate for others the optically registered panorama of what he sees," Krauss invokes the Lacanian "counter-schema" of modern painting being about the metaphysical "desiring subject [who] has a horror of seriality, of replication, of substitution, of the copy." It is as if one goes from the smoothing/integration of a mythic realism in Gombrich to the equally mythic "negative" of the "seriality of the object," a replacement that does away with painting generating an object's capacity to elicit an effect in a viewer that is not "historical." An "is it happening?" is crushed by the elimination of what Lyotard calls the possible "discrepancy between thought and the real world." Cf. R. Krauss, "The Future of an Illusion," in R. Cohen (ed.), *The Future of Literary Theory* (New York: Routledge, Chapman and Hall, 1989), pp. 288–89, and Lyotard, "The Sublime and the Avant-Garde," p. 38.

30. Lyotard, "The Sublime and the Avant-Garde," p. 40.

31. J.-F. Lyotard, "Presenting the Unpresentable: The Sublime," *Artforum* (April 1982), p. 67.

32. J.-F. Lyotard, *Des dispositifs pulsionnels* (Paris: Union Générale d'Editions, 10/18, 1973), p. 90.

33. For a brilliant analysis of this concept, see the essay by Charles Levin, "Art and the Sociological Ego," in *Life After Postmodernism*, ed. John Fekete (New York: St. Martin's Press, 1987).

34. J. Tagg, *Grounds of Dispute* (Minneapolis: University of Minnesota Press, 1992).

35. J.-F. Lyotard, *The Differend: Phrases in Dispute*, trans. G. Van Den Abbeele (Minneapolis: University of Minnesota Press, 1988), p. 13.

36. Ibid., p. xii. See, in this context, the scenario of Baudrillard, particularly the idea that this nonexistence of affirmative or positive cultural universals has been inverted to the benefit of the negative: "we are in a state of excess . . . which incessantly

develops without being measured against its own objectives . . . impacts multiplying as the causes disintegrate" ("The Anorexic Ruins," in *Looking Back on the End of the World* [New York: Semiotext(e), 1989], p. 29.)

37. See S. Friedlander, *Probing the Limits of Representation: Nazism and the "Final Solution"* (Cambridge: Harvard University Press, 1992), introduction. Friedlander re-iterates the oldest myth about the so-called linguistic relativism of Hayden White's tropological method, namely, that it promotes "anything goes," extreme skepticism toward "history," including nihilism. Friedlander refuses to read exactly what was argued in *Metahistory* and elsewhere. When Friedlander asserts that Final Solutions must be connected to morality, described as "one senses when some interpretation or representation is wrong," then the linguistic form—double subjectivism and gnomicism of "one senses"—calls forth a question about language, about the enunciation of its form, and so on. There's nothing relativistic at all in White's position, in calling the question about what "one senses" might mean.

38. Lyotard, *The Differend*, p. 89.

39. Ibid., p. 97; Habermas, *The New Conservatism*, p. 193.

40. Lyotard, *The Differend*, p. 98.

41. K. Bohrer, "The Three Cultures," in *Observations on "The Spiritual Situation of the Age,"* ed. J. Habermas (Cambridge: MIT Press, 1985), p. 154.

42. Lyotard, *The Differend*, p. 100.

43. Ibid., p. 101.

44. J. P. Faye's *Langages totalitaires* (Paris: Hermann, 1972) is exemplary on all this.

45. J.-F. Lyotard, *Driftworks* (New York: Semiotext[e], 1984), p. 36.

46. Lyotard, *The Differend*, p. 101.

47. Ibid., p. 101.

48. Such judgments continue the practice of inoculation, as Barthes persuasively argued in *Mythologies*, which here amounts to evading what is not reducible to law.

4. The Disappearance of History

1. A. Funkenstein, "History, Counterhistory, and Narrative," paper delivered at UCLA conference on the "Final Solution: Probing the Limits of Representation," April 28, 1990. In *Nazism and the Final Solution*, ed. S. Friedlander (Cambridge: Harvard University Press, 1992), pp. 66–67.

2. A. Negri, *The Savage Anomaly: The Power of Spinoza's Metaphysics and Politics*, trans. M. Hardt (Minneapolis: University of Minnesota Press, 1991), p. 225. My thanks to Michael Hardt for this reference.

3. J. Baudrillard, *Simulations* (New York: Semiotext[e], 1983), pp. 72–73.

4. G. Deleuze and F. Guattari, *Anti-Oedipus* (Minneapolis: University of Minnesota Press, 1983), p. 126.

5. G. Deleuze and F. Guattari, *A Thousand Plateaus* (Minneapolis: University of Minnesota Press, 1987), pp. 94, 97.

6. See the balanced remarks of Stephen Bann, *The Clothing of Clio* (Cambridge: Cambridge University Press, 1984), p. 177.

7. F. Nietzsche, *The Use and Abuse of History* (Indianapolis: Bobbs-Merrill, 1957), pp. 22–23.

8. See the remarks by Deleuze in G. Deleuze and C. Parnet, *Dialogues* (New York: Columbia University Press, 1987), pp. 144–45.

9. Nietzsche, *The Use and Abuse of History*, p. 38.

10. R. G. Collingwood, *An Essay on Philosophical Method* (Oxford: Clarendon, 1933), pp. 210–11.

11. G. Bataille, *Visions of Excess*, ed. Allan Stoekl (Minneapolis: University of Minnesota Press, 1985), p. 222.

12. C. Levin, "Carnal Knowledge of Aesthetic States: The Infantile Body, the Sign, and the Postmortemist Condition," *Canadian Journal of Political and Social Theory*, vol. 11, nos. 1–2 (1987), p. 93.

13. G. Deleuze, *Foucault* (Minneapolis: University of Minnesota Press, 1988), p. 22.

14. M. Phillipson, *Painting, Language and Modernity* (London: Routledge and Kegan Paul, 1985), p. 67.

15. R. Koselleck, *Futures Past* (Cambridge: MIT Press, 1985), pp. 14–17ff.

16. Ibid., p. 29.

17. Ibid., p. 115.

18. Deleuze and Guattari, *Anti-Oedipus*, pp. 128ff. Thanks to my class at Cal-Arts, spring 1992, for this reference.

19. J.-F. Lyotard and J.-P. Thébaud, *Just Gaming* (Minneapolis: University of Minnesota Press, 1985), p. 76.

20. See F. Jameson, *The Political Unconscious* (Ithaca: Cornell University Press, 1981), p. 261.

21. G. Deleuze, *Cinema One: The Movement Image* (Minneapolis: University of Minnesota Press, 1986), p. 68.

22. J.-F. Lyotard, *The Differend: Phrases in Dispute*, trans. G. Van Den Abbeele (Minneapolis: University of Minnesota Press, 1988), p. 148. Lyotard's italics.

23. G. Deleuze and C. Parnet, *Dialogues* (New York: Columbia University Press, 1987), p. 65.

24. S. Friedlander, *Probing the Limits of Representation: Nazism and the "Final Solution"* (Cambridge: Harvard University Press, 1992), p. 90. Ginzburg writes hysterically in this essay, going so far at one point as to order into thought the associational chain that Gentile's use of the term "practice" was always tied to fascism, and this connects with skepticism in historiography (pp. 90, 93–94).

25. M. de Certeau, *Heterologies* (Minneapolis: University of Minnesota Press, 1986), p. 205.

26. C. Ginzburg, "Just One Witness," in *Probing the Limits*, p. 95. Ginzburg's discourse has all the effects of neurotic sadomasochism, this celebration of being a "slave" to reality "in itself."

27. K. Bohrer, "The Three Cultures," in *Observations on "The Spiritual Situation of the Age,"* ed. J. Habermas (Cambridge: MIT Press, 1985), p. 154.

28. R. Barthes, *S/Z* (New York: Farrar, Straus and Giroux, 1974), p. 5.

29. Cf. R. Krauss, "The Future of an Illusion," in R. Cohen (ed.), *The Future of Literary Theory* (New York: Routledge, Chapman and Hall, 1989), pp. 284ff.

30. S. Aronowitz, *The Crisis in Historical Materialism*, (New York: Praeger, 1981), p. 135.

31. J. Habermas, *The Theory of Communicative Action*, vol. 1 (Boston: Beacon Press, 1984), p. 287.

32. Deleuze and Guattari, *A Thousand Plateaus*, p. 77. Cf. S. Cohen, *Historical Culture: On the Recoding of an Academic Discipline* (Berkeley: University of California Press, 1986), chapter 2.

33. In the February 1991 issue of the *New Art Examiner*, Catherine Lord, the chair of studio art at UC Irvine, approvingly cites a colleague who has composed a "list" and

has made an "index" of books in contemporary art theory that do not "index the name Lesbian." This left version of an old-right formation is disturbing precisely on account of its tactics, which reinvent the Catholic Church.

34. J. Baudrillard, *Forget Foucault* (New York: Semiotext[e], 1987), p. 21.

35. Ibid., pp. 40–41.

36. Ibid., p. 48.

37. Ibid., pp. 22ff.

38. J. Baudrillard, *Selected Writings*, ed. M. Poster (Stanford: Stanford University Press, 1988), pp. 187–88.

39. Baudrillard, *Simulations*, pp. 44–55.

40. Cf. the important remarks by Lyotard on Kant's distinctions in *The Differend*, pp. 161ff.

41. Baudrillard, *Simulations*, p. 101.

42. Baudrillard, *Forget Foucault*, pp. 70–71.

43. As both Jameson and Habermas argue.

44. Cf. Hayden White, "The Politics of Historical Interpretation," *Critical Inquiry*, vol. 9, no. 1 (September 1982), pp. 130–37.

45. H. Arendt, *Between Past and Future* (New York: Meridian, 1961), p. 89.

46. Lyotard, *The Differend*, p. 70.

47. See the comments by Deleuze in *Nietzsche and Philosophy* (New York: Columbia University Press, 1983), p. 137.

48. J. Tagg, *Grounds of Dispute* (Minneapolis: University of Minnesota Press, 1992).

49. Deleuze, *Foucault*, p. 119.

50. Deleuze and Parnet, *Dialogues*, p. 93.

51. As quoted in the *Chronicle of Higher Education*, October 4, 1989, p. A4.

52. Lyotard and Thébaud, *Just Gaming*, p. 34.

53. W. Benjamin, *Illuminations* (New York: Schocken Books, 1969), p. 254.

54. Bataille, *Visions of Excess*, p. 128.

55. T. J. Clark, *The Painting of Modern Life* (Princeton: Princeton University Press, 1985), p. 15, conclusion.

56. J. Gilbert-Rolfe, *Immanence and Contradiction* (London: Out of London Press, 1984), p. 51. This view is that of a "neoclassicism" *within* visual experimentation; it "sees" in successful "modern masterpieces" a "contextualizing [of] the historical itself within the artistic device," which would make artworks both *literal presentations of their own interpretations* and *historical* mediums where the past still "lived."

57. I take this to be the gist of Lyotard's work on narrative and modern culture. His *Postmodern Condition*, with the important "Answering the Question: What Is Postmodernism?", *Just Gaming*, *Driftworks*, and articles in *Artforum* are an excellent starting place for an English-reading audience.

58. J.-F. Lyotard, *The Postmodern Condition* (Minneapolis: University of Minnesota Press, 1984), p. 81.

59. Deleuze and Guattari, *A Thousand Plateaus*, p. 142.

60. Ibid., p. 84.

61. Lucretius, *On the Nature of the Universe*, trans. R. E. Latham (Baltimore: Penguin, 1971), p. 68.

62. Deleuze and Guattari, *A Thousand Plateaus*, pp. 109–10.

63. These remarks are a paraphrase of Paul de Man, *The Resistance to Theory* (Minneapolis: University of Minnesota Press, 1986), pp. 69–70.

64. Ibid., p. 15.

65. Deleuze and Guattari, *A Thousand Plateaus*, p. 228.

66. Lyotard, *Peregrinations: Law, Form, Event* (New York: Columbia University Press, 1988), p. 25.

67. Ibid., p. 27.

68. G. Graff, "The Teaching of Literature," in R. Cohen, (ed.), *The Future of Literary Theory*, p. 256.

69. C. Levin, "Art and the Sociological Ego," in *Life After Postmodernism*, ed. John Fekete (New York: St. Martin's Press, 1987), p. 41.

70. F. Nietzsche, *The Use and Abuse of History*, p. 40.

71. Deleuze, *Nietzsche and Philosophy*, p. 192.

72. Deleuze and Guattari, *Anti-Oedipus* (Minneapolis: University of Minnesota Press, 1983), p. 151.

73. M. Jay, *Marxism and Totality* (Berkeley: University of California Press, 1984), pp. 517ff.

74. Deleuze and Guattari, *A Thousand Plateaus*, p. 337.

75. Deleuze and Parnet, *Dialogues*, p. 122.

76. Deleuze, "Plato and the Simulacrum," *October* 27 (Winter 1983), p. 53.

77. Lyotard, *The Differend*, p. 155.

78. L. Stone, "Dry Heat, Cool Reason," *Times Literary Supplement*, January 31, 1992, p. 3.

79. W. and M. Kneale, *The Development of Logic* (London: Oxford University Press, 1962), p. 155.

80. Deleuze and Guattari, *A Thousand Plateaus*, p. 170.

81. See Deleuze's "Plato and the Simulacrum," p. 47.

82. G. Deleuze and F. Guattari, *On the Line* (New York: Semiotext[e], 1983), pp. 12–13.

83. G. Deleuze, "The Schizophrenic in Language: Surface and Depth in L. Carroll and A. Antonin," in V. W. Gras (ed.), *European Literary Theory and Practice* (New York: Delta, 1973), pp. 282, 284–85.

84. G. Deleuze and F. Guattari, *Kafka: Toward a Minor Literature* (Minneapolis: University of Minnesota Press, 1986), p. 22.

85. Ibid., p. 26.

86. Ibid., p. 83. See also the complementary remarks in G. Deleuze, *Proust and Signs* (New York: Braziller, 1972), p. 143.

87. K. Bohrer, "The Three Cultures," in *Observations on "The Spiritual Situation of the Age,"* ed. J. Habermas (Cambridge: MIT Press, 1985), p. 154.

88. Deleuze, *Nietzsche and Philosophy*, pp. 170ff.

89. Deleuze, "Plato and the Simulacrum," p. 46. My italics.

90. Deleuze and Guattari, *On the Line*, p. 108.

5. Criticism and Art Events: Reading with Lyotard and Baudrillard

1. L. Berkowitz, quoted in the *Chronicle of Higher Education*, April 12, 1989, p. B5.

2. B. Buchloh, "Parody and Appropriation in F. Picabia, Pop and Sigmar Polke," *Artforum* (March 1982), p. 34.

3. Cf. G. Deleuze *Cinema One: The Movement Image* (Minneapolis: University of Minnesota Press, 1986), pp. 206ff.

4. F. Jameson, *Fables of Aggression: Wyndham Lewis, the Modernist as Fascist* (Berkeley: University of California Press, 1979), p. 20. By this conflation of modernism and Stalinist Hegelianism, Jameson helps to disclose the identity between the American

professoriat and Hegelianism *tout court*, which remains—left, right, and center at any time—a power in the creation of "serious" myths.

5. B. Buchloh, "The Primary Colors for the Second Time: A Paradigm Repetition of the Neo-Avant-Garde," *October* 37 (Summer 1986), p. 51.

6. Cf. G. Deleuze and F. Guattari, *A Thousand Plateaus* (Minneapolis: University of Minnesota Press, 1987), pp. 332–33. Cf. also Evelyne Keitel, *Reading Psychosis* (London: Blackwell, 1989), pp. 96–97.

7. K. Bohrer, "The Three Cultures," in *Observations on "The Spiritual Situation of the Age*," ed. J. Habermas (Cambridge: MIT Press, 1985), pp. 125–56. This essay is very important in considering arguments that do not write off romanticism.

8. P. Burger, "Literary Criticism in Germany Today," in Habermas (ed.), *Observations*, p. 217.

9. Ibid., p. 218.

10. J. Habermas, (ed.), *Observations*, p. 7. Cf. Habermas, "Modernity—An Incomplete Project," in *The Anti-Aesthetic*, ed. H. Foster (Port Townsend, Wash.: Bay Press, 1983), pp. 3–15.

11. Bohrer, "The Three Cultures," p. 131.

12. J.-F. Lyotard, *Peregrinations: Law, Form, Event* (New York: Columbia University Press, 1988), p. 42.

13. J.-F. Lyotard, "Acinema," in *The Lyotard Reader*, ed. A. Benjamin (London: Blackwell, 1989), p. 174.

14. See the comments by A. Plotnitsky, "Interpretation, Interminability, Evaluation: From Nietzsche Toward a General Economy," in *Life After Postmodernism*, ed. J. Fekete (New York: St. Martin's Press, 1987), pp. 120–41.

15. Bohrer, "The Three Cultures," p. 133.

16. Ibid., p. 152.

17. Ibid., p. 154.

18. Deleuze, *Cinema One*, p. 206.

19. Buchloh, "Parody and Appropriation," p. 28.

20. Cf. A. Sekula, "Dismantling Modernism," in *Theories of Contemporary Art*, eds. N. Klein and R. Hertz (New York: Prentice-Hall, 1985), pp. 163–66.

21. J. Baudrillard, *The Mirror of Production* (St. Louis: Telos, 1975), p. 66.

22. J. Baudrillard, *Selected Writings*, ed. M. Poster (Stanford: Stanford University Press, 1988), p. 182.

23. Cf. B. Buchloh, "Michael Asher and the Conclusion of Modernist Sculpture," in *Theories of Contemporary Art*, p. 225–42.

24. Cf. B. Buchloh, "The Primary Colors for the Second Time: A Paradigm Repetition of the Neo-Avant-Garde," p. 44.

25. Ibid., p. 50.

26. Ibid., p. 51

27. G. Lukács, *Writer and Critic and Other Essays* (New York: Grosset and Dunlap, 1970), p. 109.

28. A. Danto, *Analytic Philosophy of History* (Cambridge: Cambridge University Press, 1968), p. 168.

29. R. Koselleck, *Futures Past* (Cambridge: MIT Press, 1985), p. 211.

30. Habermas, "Modernity—An Incomplete Project," p. 13.

31. A. J. Greimas and J. Courtes, *Semiotics and Language: An Analytic Dictionary* (Bloomington: Indiana University Press, 1982).

32. P. Anderson, *In the Tracks of Historical Materialism* (Chicago: University of Chicago Press, 1984), pp. 86–87.

33. Ibid., p. 101.

34. H. Foster, "(Post)modern polemics," *New German Critique* 33 (Fall 1984), p. 76.

35. S. Germer, "Haacke, Broodthaers, Beuys," *October* 45 (Summer 1988), p. 65.

36. A. Huyssens, *After the Great Divide* (Bloomington: Indiana University Press, 1986), p. 198.

37. Ibid., p. 8.

38. Ibid., p. 15.

39. Deleuze and Guattari, *A Thousand Plateaus*, p. 55.

40. J.-F. Lyotard, *The Postmodern Condition* (Minneapolis: University of Minnesota Press, 1984), p. 81.

41. M. Morris, "Postmodernity and Lyotard's Sublime," *Art and Text* 16 (Summer 1984), p. 63.

42. J.-F. Lyotard, "Freud according to Cézanne," in *Des dispositifs pulsionnels* (Paris: Union Générale d'Editions, 10/18, 1973), pp. 76–77.

43. Ibid., p. 80.

44. Lyotard, "Universal History and Cultural Differences," in *The Lyotard Reader*, p. 318.

45. Cf. Lyotard, *The Postmodern Condition*, pp. 34–35.

46. Lyotard, "Freud according to Cézanne," p. 77.

47. J.-F. Lyotard, "Adorno as the Devil," *Telos* 19 (Spring 1974), p. 128.

48. J.-F. Lyotard, *The Differend: Phrases in Dispute*, trans. G. Van Den Abbeele (Minneapolis: University of Minnesota Press, 1988), section 223.

49. Lyotard, "Adorno as the Devil," pp. 127ff.

50. M. Frank, *What Is Neostructuralism?* (Minneapolis: University of Minnesota Press, 1989), p. 86.

51. Lyotard, "Adorno as the Devil," p. 16.

52. Lyotard, "Freud according to Cézanne," p. 88.

53. J.-F. Lyotard and J.-P. Thébaud, *Just Gaming* (Minneapolis: University of Minnesota Press, 1985), p. 34.

54. Cf. J.-F. Lyotard, *Driftworks* (New York: Semiotext[e], 1984), especially the essay "Jewish Oedipus," from which these remarks are drawn. I am grateful to John Johnston for referring me to this text.

55. R. Chow, "Rereading Mandarin Ducks and Butterflies: A Response to the 'Postmodern Condition,' " *Cultural Criticism* 5 (1986–87), p. 87.

56. Lyotard, *The Differend*, sections 130ff.

57. See Lyotard, *The Lyotard Reader*, pp. 273–74.

58. Cf. V. Burgin, "Some Thoughts on Outsiderism and Postmodernism," *Block* (1986).

59. Lyotard, *Driftworks*, pp. 67–68.

60. Ibid., pp. 107–8.

61. Lyotard and Thébaud, *Just Gaming*, p. 43.

62. Lyotard, *The Postmodern Condition*, p. 19.

63. Ibid., p. 41.

64. See, for example, the scattered remarks by Huyssens in *After the Great Divide*, especially p. 208 where, by implication, Baudrillard's writings are associated with aestheticism on account of their preoccupation with matters of form and sign.

65. F. Jameson, "Postmodernism or the Cultural Logic of Late Capitalism," *New Left Review* 146 (July-August 1984), pp. 56–57.

66. Ibid., p. 57.

67. J. Baudrillard, *Simulations* (New York: Semiotext[e], 1983), p. 18.

68. Ibid., p. 21.

69. J. Baudrillard, "The Anorexic Ruins," in *Looking Back on the End of the World*, eds. D. Kamper and C. Wulf (New York: Semiotext[e], 1989), p. 35.

70. J. Baudrillard, *The Ecstasy of Communication* (New York: Semiotext[e], 1988).

71. Cf. H. Arendt, "The Concept of History," in *Between Past and Future* (New York: Meridian, 1961), pp. 63, 87.

72. J. Habermas, *The New Conservatism: Cultural Criticism and the Historians' Debate*, ed. and trans. Shierry Nicholsen (Cambridge: MIT Press, 1989), pp. 176–77.

73. Baudrillard, *The Ecstasy of Communication*, p. 83.

74. J. Baudrillard, *Simulations* (New York: Semiotext[e], 1983), p. 84.

75. Ibid., p. 95.

76. Ibid., p. 101. See also Baudrillard, *The Mirror of Production*.

77. J. Baudrillard, *Forget Foucault* (New York: Semiotext[e], 1987), p. 48.

78. Baudrillard, *Simulations*, pp. 104–5.

79. *New York Times*, July 21, 1989, p. A7.

80. Baudrillard, *Forget Foucault*, p. 40.

81. Ibid., p. 47.

82. J. Baudrillard, *In the Shadow of the Silent Majorities* (New York: Semiotext[e], 1983), pp. 102–3.

83. Baudrillard, *Forget Foucault*, p. 127.

84. Baudrillard, "The Anorexic Ruins," p. 33.

85. Ibid., pp. 43, 45.

86. Baudrillard, *Selected Writings*, p. 203.

87. Ibid., p. 205.

88. Ibid., p. 205.

89. Baudrillard, *In the Shadow of the Silent Majorities*, pp. 10–11.

90. Baudrillard, *Simulations*, pp. 151–52.

91. J. Baudrillard, *The Ecstasy of Communication* (New York: Semiotext[e], 1988), pp. 81–82.

92. J. Baudrillard, *The Evil Demon of Images* (Sydney: Power Institute, 1988), p. 23.

93. Baudrillard, *The Ecstasy of Communication*, p. 100.

Bibliography

Adorno, T. *Negative Dialectics*. New York: Seabury Press, 1972.

Adorno, T. and M. Horkheimer. *Dialectic of Enlightenment*. New York: Herder and Herder, 1972.

Ahn, E. "Provost Explains Letters and Science Overhiring." *UCLA Daily Bruin*, vol. CXXX, no. 108 (April 23, 1990).

Alliez, E. and M. Feher. "The Luster of Capital." in *Zone* 1 and 2 (1987).

Anderson, P. *In the Tracks of Historical Materialism*. Chicago: University of Chicago Press, 1984.

Arendt, H. *Between Past and Future*. New York: Meridian, 1961.

———. *The Human Condition*. New York: Anchor, 1959.

Aronowitz, S. *The Crisis in Historical Materialism*. New York: Praeger, 1981.

Bailey, F. G. *Morality and Experience*. London: Blackwell, 1977.

Bann, S. *The Clothing of Clio*. Cambridge: Cambridge University Press, 1984.

Barthes, R. *S/Z*. New York: Farrar, Straus and Giroux, 1974.

———. "The Wisdom of Art." In *Calligram: Essays in New Art History from France*, edited by N. Bryson. New York: Cambridge University Press, 1988.

———. *Writing Degree Zero*. New York: Hill and Wang, 1968.

Bataille, G. *The Accursed Share: An Essay on General Economy*. New York: Zone Books, 1988.

———. *Inner Experience*, translated with an introduction by L. A. Boldt. Albany: State University of New York Press, 1988.

———. *Visions of Excess*, edited by A. Stoekl. Minneapolis: University of Minnesota Press, 1985.

J. Baudrillard. "The Anorexic Ruins." In *Looking Back on the End of the World*, edited by D. Kamper and C. Wulf. New York: Semiotext(e), 1989.

———. *The Ecstasy of Communication*. New York: Semiotext(e), 1988.

———. *The Evil Demon of Images*. Sydney: Power Institute, 1988.

———. *Fatal Strategies*. New York: Semiotext(e), 1990.

———. *Forget Foucault*. New York: Semiotext(e), 1987.

———. *In the Shadow of the Silent Majorities*. New York: Semiotext(e), 1983.

———. *La Société de consommation*. Paris: Gallimard, 1970.

———. *Le système des objets*. Paris: Gallimard, 1968.

————. *The Mirror of Production*. St. Louis: Telos, 1975.

————. *Selected Writings*, edited by M. Poster. Stanford: Stanford University Press, 1989.

————. *Simulations*. New York: Semiotext(e), 1983.

————. "The Structural Law of Value and the Order of Simulacra." In *The Structural Allegory*, edited by J. Fekete. Minneapolis: University of Minnesota Press, 1984.

Benjamin, W. *Illuminations*. New York: Schocken Books, 1969.

Bennington, G. and R. Young. "Introduction: Posing the Question." In *Post-Structuralism and the Question of History*, edited by D. Attridge, G. Bennington, and R. Young. Cambridge: Cambridge University Press, 1987.

Bohrer, K. "The Three Cultures." In *Observations on "The Spiritual Situation of the Age,"* edited by J. Habermas. Cambridge: MIT Press, 1985.

Broszat, M. and S. Friedlander. "A Controversy about the Historicization of National Socialism." *New German Critique*, 44 (Spring/Summer 1988).

Bryson, N. (ed.). *Calligram: Essays in New Art History from France*. Cambridge: Cambridge University Press, 1988.

————. "The Gaze in the Expanded Field." In *Vision and Visuality*, edited by H. Foster. Seattle: Bay Press, 1988.

Buchloh, B. "Michael Asher and the Conclusion of Modernist Sculpture." In *Theories of Contemporary Art*, edited by N. Klein and R. Hertz. New York: Prentice-Hall, 1985.

————. "Parody and Appropriation in F. Picabia, Pop and Sigmar Polke." *Artforum* (March 1982).

————. "The Primary Colors for the Second Time: A Paradigm Repetition of the Neo-Avant-Garde." *October* 37 (Summer 1986).

Burger, P. "Literary Criticism in Germany Today." In *Observations on "The Spiritual Situation of the Age,"* edited by J. Habermas. Cambridge: MIT Press, 1985.

————. *The Theory of the Avant-Garde*, translated by M. Shaw. Minneapolis: University of Minnesota Press, 1984.

Burgin, V. "Some Thoughts on Outsiderism and Postmodernism." *Block* (1986).

Calinescu, M. *Faces of Modernity*. Bloomington: Indiana University Press, 1977.

Carpenter, M. "Eco, Oedipus and the 'View' of the University." *Diacritics* (Spring 1990).

Castoriadis, C. *Crossroads in the Labyrinth*. Cambridge: MIT Press, 1984.

de Certeau, M. *Heterologies*. Minneapolis: University of Minnesota Press, 1986.

Chow, R. "Rereading Mandarin Ducks and Butterflies: A Response to the 'Postmodern Condition.'" *Cultural Criticism* 5 (1986–87).

Clark, T. J. "Arguments about Modernism: A Reply to Michael Fried." In *Pollack and After: The Critical Debate*, edited by F. Frascina. New York: Harper and Row, 1985.

————. *The Painting of Modern Life*. Princeton: Princeton University Press, 1985.

Coates, W. H. and H. V. White. *The Ordeal of Liberal Humanism*. New York: McGraw-Hill, 1970.

Cohen, S. *Historical Culture: On the Recoding of an Academic Discipline*. Berkeley: University of California Press, 1986.

Collingwood, R. G. *An Essay on Philosophical Method*. Oxford: Clarendon, 1933.

Danto, A. *Analytic Philosophy of History*. Cambridge: Cambridge University Press, 1968.

————. "Art Evolution and History." In *Journal of Aesthetics and Art Criticism* (1986).

————. "The Artworld." In *Philosophy Looks at the Arts*, edited by J. Margolis. Philadelphia: Temple University Press, 1987.

Deleuze, G. "Active and Reactive." In *The New Nietzsche*, edited by D. Allison. Cambridge: MIT Press, 1985.

———. *Bergsonism*. New York: Zone Books, 1988.

———. *Cinema One: The Movement Image*. Minneapolis: University of Minnesota Press, 1986.

———. *Foucault*. Minneapolis: University of Minnesota Press, 1989.

———. *Nietzsche and Philosophy*. New York: Columbia University Press, 1983.

———. "Plato and the Simulacrum." *October* 27 (Winter 1983).

———. *Proust and Signs*. New York: Braziller, 1972.

———. "The Schizophrenic in Language: Surface and Depth in L. Carroll and A. Artaud." In *European Literary Theory and Practice*, edited by V. W. Gras. New York: Delta, 1973.

Deleuze, G. and F. Guattari. *Anti-Oedipus*. Minneapolis: University of Minnesota Press, 1983.

———. *Kafka: Toward a Minor Literature*. Minneapolis: University of Minnesota Press, 1986.

———. *Mille Plateaux*. Paris: Minuit, 1980. English translation *A Thousand Plateaus*. Minneapolis: University of Minnesota Press, 1987.

———. *On the Line*. New York: Semiotext(e), 1983.

Deleuze, G. and C. Parnet. *Dialogues*. New York: Columbia University Press, 1987.

DePalma, A. "Research Files at Columbia Are Destroyed While Federal Audit is Pending." *New York Times* (May 23, 1992).

Derrida, J. "White Mythologies." *New Literary History*, vol. 1, no. 6 (1974).

Descombes, V. *Modern French Philosophy*. Cambridge: Cambridge University Press, 1980.

Eagleton, T. "Two Approaches in the Sociology of Literature." *Critical Inquiry*, vol. 14, no. 3 (Spring 1988).

Eco, U. *Travels in Hyperreality*. New York: Harcourt, Brace Jovanovich, 1986.

Ewen, S. *All Consuming Images*. New York: Basic Books, 1988.

Faye, J. P. *Langages totalitaires*. Paris: Hermann, 1972.

Foster, H. "(Post)modern polemics." *New German Critique* 33 (Fall 1984).

———. (ed.). *Vision and Visuality*. Seattle: Bay Press, 1988.

Foucault, M. *Language, Counter-Memory, Practice*. Ithaca: Cornell University Press, 1977.

Fowler, R. and G. Kress. "Critical Linguistics." In R. Fowler et al., *Language and Control*. London: Routledge, 1979.

Frank, M. *What Is Neostructuralism?* Minneapolis: University of Minnesota Press, 1989.

Friedlander, S. (ed.). *Probing the Limits of Representation: Nazism and the "Final Solution."* Cambridge: Harvard University Press, 1992.

Funkenstein, A. "History, Counterhistory, and Narrative." In *Nazism and the Final Solution*, edited by S. Friedlander. Cambridge: Harvard University Press, 1992.

Gardner, H. "The Academic Community Must Not Shun the Debate Over How to Set National Educational Goals." *Chronicle of Higher Education* (November 8, 1989).

Gates, H. L. "Whose Canon Is It, Anyway?" *New York Times Book Review* (February 26, 1989).

Germer, S. "Haacke, Broodthaers, Beuys." *October* 45 (Summer 1988).

Gilbert-Rolfe, J. *Immanence and Contradiction*. London: Out of London Press, 1984.

Ginzburg, C. "Checking the Evidence: The Judge and the Historian." *Critical Inquiry*, vol. 18, no. 1 (Autumn 1991).

———. "Just One Witness." In *Probing the Limits: Nazism and the "Final Solution,"* edited by S. Friedlander. Cambridge: Harvard University Press, 1992.

———. "Momigliano and De Martino," *History and Theory*, vol. 30, no. 4 (1991).

Goux, J.-J. *Symbolic Economies: After Marx and Freud.* Ithaca: Cornell University Press, 1990.

Graff, G. "The Teaching of Literature." In *The Future of Literary Theory*, edited by R. Cohen. New York: Routledge, Chapman and Hall, 1989.

Gray, J. "Fashion, fantasy or fiasco?" *Times Literary Supplement* (February 24–March 2, 1989).

Greenberg, C. "Avant-Garde and Kitsch." *Partisan Review* 5 (Fall 1939).

Greimas, A. J. *On Meaning.* Minneapolis: University of Minnesota Press, 1987.

Greimas, A. J. and J. Courtes. *Semiotics and Language: An Analytic Dictionary.* Bloomington: Indiana University Press, 1982.

Habermas, J. *Communication and the Evolution of Society.* Boston: Beacon Press, 1984.

———. "Introduction." In *Observations on "The Spiritual Situation of the Age."* Cambridge: MIT Press, 1985.

———. "Modernity—An Incomplete Project." In *The Anti-Aesthetic*, edited by H. Foster. Port Townsend: Bay Press, 1983.

———. *The New Conservatism: Cultural Criticism and the Historians' Debate*, edited and translated by S. Nicholsen. Cambridge: MIT Press, 1989.

———. *The Theory of Communicative Action*, vol. 1, translated by T. McCarthy. Boston: Beacon Press, 1984.

Hall, S. "On Postmodernism and Articulation." *Communication Inquiry*, vol. 10, no. 2 (Summer 1986).

Harvey, D. *The Condition of Postmodernity.* London: Blackwell, 1989.

Huyssens, A. *After the Great Divide.* Bloomington: Indiana University Press, 1986.

Irigaray, L. *Speculum of the Other Woman.* Ithaca: Cornell University Press, 1987.

Jameson, F. *Fables of Aggression: Wyndham Lewis, the Modernist as Fascist.* Berkeley: University of California Press, 1979.

———. "On Negt and Kluge." *October* 46 (1988).

———. *The Political Unconscious.* Ithaca: Cornell University Press, 1981.

———. "The Politics of Theory: Ideological Positions in the Postmodern Debate." *New German Critique* (Fall 1984).

———. *Postmodernism.* Durham, N.C.: Duke University Press, 1990.

———. "Postmodernism or the Cultural Logic of Late Capitalism." *New Left Review* 146 (July–August 1984).

Jay, M. *Marxism and Totality.* Berkeley: University of California Press, 1984.

Johnston, J. "Ideology, Representation, Schizophrenia: Toward a Theory of the Postmodern Subject." In *After the Future*, edited by G. Shapiro. Albany: State University of New York Press, 1990.

Kant, I. *Observations on the Feeling of the Beautiful and Sublime*, translated by J. Goldthwait. Berkeley: University of California Press, 1965.

———. *Philosophical Writings*, edited by E. Behler. New York: Continuum, 1986.

Keitel, E. *Reading Psychosis.* London: Blackwell, 1989.

Kneale, W. and M. *The Development of Logic.* London: Oxford University Press, 1962.

Koselleck, R. *Futures Past.* Cambridge: MIT Press, 1985.

Krauss, R. "The Cultural Logic of the Late Capitalist Museum." *October* 54 (Fall 1990).

———. "The Future of an Illusion." In *The Future of Literary Theory*, edited by R. Cohen. London: Routledge, Chapman and Hall, 1989.

————. *The Originality of the Avant-Garde and Other Modernist Myths*. Cambridge: MIT Press, 1987.

Kristeva, J. *La révolution du langage poétique*. Paris: Seuil, 1974.

————. *Tales of Love*, translated by L. Roudiez. New York: Columbia University Press, 1987.

Labov, W. "The Study of Language in its Social Context." In *Language and Social Context*, edited by P. Giglioli. New York: Penguin, 1972.

Lecercle, J.-J. *Philosophy Through the Looking Glass*. La Salle, Ill.: Open Court, 1985.

Levin, C. "Art and the Sociological Ego." In *Life After Postmodernism*, edited by J. Fekete. New York: St. Martin's Press, 1987.

————. "Carnal Knowledge of Aesthetic States: The Infantile Body, the Sign, and the Postmortemist Condition." *Canadian Journal of Political and Social Theory*, vol. 11, nos. 1–2 (1987).

Lotman, J. et al. "Theses on the Semiotic Study of Culture." In *The Tell-Tale Sign*, edited by T. Sebeok. Lisse/Netherlands: de Ridder, 1975.

Lowith, K. *From Hegel to Nietzsche*. New York: Holt, Rinehart and Winston, 1964.

Lucretius, *On the Nature of the Universe*, translated by R. E. Latham. Baltimore: Penguin, 1971.

Lukács, G. *Writer and Critic and other Essays*. New York: Grosset and Dunlap, 1970.

Lyotard, J.-F. "Adorno as the Devil." *Telos* 19 (Spring 1974).

————. *Des dispositifs pulsionnels*. Paris: Union Générale d'Editions, 10/18, 1973.

————. *The Differend: Phrases in Dispute*, translated by G. Van Den Abbeele. Minneapolis: University of Minnesota Press, 1988.

————. *Driftworks*. New York: Semiotext(e), 1984.

————. *The Lyotard Reader*, edited by A. Benjamin. London: Blackwell, 1989.

————. "Notes on Legitimation." In *The Public Realm*, edited by R. Schurmann. Albany: State University of New York Press, 1983.

————. *Peregrinations: Law, Form, Event*. New York: Columbia University Press, 1988.

————. *The Postmodern Condition*. Minneapolis: University of Minnesota Press, 1984.

————. "Presenting the Unpresentable: The Sublime." *Artforum* (April 1982).

————. "The Sublime and the Avant-Garde." *Artforum* (April 1984).

Lyotard, J.-F. and J.-P. Thébaud. *Just Gaming*. Minneapolis: University of Minnesota Press, 1985.

de Man, P. *The Resistance to Theory*. Minneapolis: University of Minnesota Press, 1986.

McDowell, E. "Publishers Are Uneasy at Booksellers' Meeting." *New York Times* (June 5, 1989).

Morris, M. "Postmodernity and Lyotard's Sublime." *Art and Text* 16 (Summer 1984).

Mulvey, L. *Visual and Other Pleasures*. Bloomington: Indiana University Press, 1989.

Negri, A. *The Savage Anomaly: The Power of Spinoza's Metaphysics and Politics*, translated by M. Hardt. Minneapolis: University of Minnesota Press, 1991.

Nietzsche, F. *Beyond Good and Evil*. New York: Modern Library, 1927.

————. "On the Truth and Lies in a Nonmoral Sense." In *Philosophy and Truth*, edited and translated by D. Breazeale. New Jersey: Humanities Press International, 1979.

————. *The Use and Abuse of History*. Indianapolis: Bobbs-Merrill, 1957.

Phillipson, M. *Painting, Language and Modernity*. London: Routledge and Kegan Paul, 1985.

Plotnitsky, A. "Interpretation, Interminability, Evaluation: From Nietzsche toward a General Economy." In *Life After Postmodernism*, edited by J. Fekete. New York: St. Martin's Press, 1987.

Riddel, J. "Neo–Nietzschean Clatter—Speculation and the Modernist Poetic Image." In *Boundary 2: Why Nietzsche Now?*, vol. 9, nos. 3 and 10 (Spring/Fall 1981).

Rose, M. "What's Right with Remedy: A College Try." *Los Angeles Times* (April 23, 1989).

Ross, A. "Introduction," *Universal Abandon*. Minneapolis: University of Minnesota Press, 1988.

Rousseau, J.-J. *A Discourse on Inequality*, translated and with an introduction by M. Cranston. Suffolk: Viking, 1984.

Said, E. *Orientalism*. New York: Vintage, 1973.

———. "Response." *Critical Inquiry*, vol. 15, no. 3 (Spring 1989).

———. *The World, the Text, and the Critic*. Cambridge: Harvard University Press, 1983.

Sekula, A. "Dismantling Modernism." In *Theories of Contemporary Art*, edited by N. Klein and R. Hertz. New York: Prentice-Hall, 1985.

Sloterdijk, P. "Cynicism—The Twilight of False Consciousness." *New German Critique* 33 (Fall 1984).

Smith, J. "The Transcendence of the Individual," *Diacritics* (Summer 1989).

Spivak, G. *In Other Worlds*. New York: Routledge, 1988.

Stoekl, A. *Politics, Writing, Mutilation*. Minneapolis: University of Minnesota Press, 1985.

Stone, L. "Dry Heat, Cool Reason." *Times Literary Supplement* (January 31, 1992).

Tagg, J. *The Burden of Representation*. New York: Macmillan, 1988.

———. *Grounds of Dispute*. Minneapolis: University of Minnesota Press, 1992.

Todorov, T. *Theory of the Symbol*. Ithaca: Cornell University Press, 1982.

Vattimo, G. *The End of Modernity*. Baltimore: Johns Hopkins University Press, 1988.

Veblen, T. "The Higher Learning." In *The Portable Veblen*. New York: Viking, 1948.

Virilio, P. *Popular Defense and Ecological Struggles*. New York: Semiotext(e), 1990.

Wehler, H. U. "Historiography in Germany Today." In *Observations on "The Spiritual Situation of the Age,"* edited by J. Habermas. Cambridge: MIT Press, 1985.

Weiner, J. "The Red and the Black," *The Nation* (June 24, 1991).

West, C. "Ethics and Action in F. Jameson's Marxist Hermeneutics." In *Postmodernism and Politics*, edited by J. Arac. Minneapolis: University of Minnesota Press, 1986.

White, H. "The Politics of Historical Interpretation." *Critical Inquiry*. vol. 9, no. 1 (September 1982).

Wolin, S. "Revolutionary Action Today." In *Post-Analytic Philosophy*, edited by J. Rajchman and C. West. New York: Columbia University Press, 1985.

Wordsworth, A. "Derrida and Foucault: Writing the History of Historicity." In *Post-Structuralism and the Question of History*. Cambridge: Cambridge University Press, 1987.

Index

academia: and autonomy, ix; and bureaucracy of writing, 57; and constancy, 14–15; and culture, 1–2; as culture, 151; and discursive integration, 8; exile from, 11; and general form of enunciation, 16; and Good Object, 4; and historicization, xxi; and narcissistic production, 62; and repression of immediacy, 30. *See also* language; order-words

academic thing, and impersonal force, 51

academic writing: and avant-garde, 36; and tenure, 36

achrony, and nonpsychologism, 112

active memory, and writing, 20

Adorno, Theodor, 2, 13, 62, 73, 141

aestheticization of opposition, 4

affirmation: and time sense, 86; and writing, 23

affirmative action: and autonomy, 38; and intellectual perplexity, 33–34; and political inoculation, 31–32

ahistoricity: and priorities, xiii; and problematic future, 113–14; and the unhistorical, 118–19

Althusserians, 92

Anderson, Perry, 2, 136

apocalypse, and capital, xxii

appropriation, and historicism, 136

arationalism, xiii

areferentiality, and impossibility of history, 22–23

Arendt, Hannah, xviii, 12, 19, 23, 94, 105, 113, 114, 147

argumentation, and nonacademic form, 31

Aristotle, 17–18

Aronowitz, Stanley, xv, 19, 99

art: and discursivity, 47, 53; and elision, 53; and historical recoding, 134; and historicism, 133; and the left, 137; and *posthistoire*, 103; proliferation of the category, 53; and suspension of use, 154

Artaud, Antonin, 103

asociality, and capital, 48

autopsy, as cultural form, 27

avant-garde, and historicity, 129

Aztecs, 91

Bailey, George, 51

Bakke case, 38

Bann, Stephen, 80

Barthes, Roland, 1, 3, 9, 36, 53, 82, 101, 114

Bataille, Georges, 9, 20, 30, 87, 108, 127

Baudrillard, Jean, x, xvi, xxi, xxiii, 5, 10, 13, 17–18, 21, 37, 53, 58, 62, 83, 102–03, 107, 114, 133, 135, 144, 146–55

Bauer, Bruno, xix

Bauman, Zygmund, 95

Baumgarten, Lothar, 108

Beckett, Samuel, 108

Ben-Gurion, David, 101
Benjamin, Walter, 25, 85
Bennington, Geoff, xxiii, 72
Berger, Peter, 128
Berkowitz, Leslie, 124
"between," and historicity, 105
Beuys, Joseph, 129
Bohrer, Karl, xxiii, 75, 127–28, 130–31
Bond, Edward, 131
book: and aggressive reaction, 20; and
    memory, 20; and mythic purposes, 3
Booth, John Wilkes, 94
Bourdieu, Pierre, 15
Braudel, Fernand, 91
Broodthaers, Marcel, 137
Buchloh, Benjamin, 124, 127, 133, 135
bureaucracy, transpolitical, 56
Burroughs, William, 149
Bush, George, 96

Calinescu, Matei, xviii, 80, 128
Capital: and art, 53; and asociality, 48;
    and desocialization, xviii; and ecstatic
    unnecessariness, xxii; and Final
    Solution, 70; and intellectual
    perspectives, xix; and the irrational,
    79; and liquidation of culture, 24; and
    modernity, xviii, 70; and Nazism, 80;
    and non-Marxist critique, xvii; and
    oxymoronic setup, xviii; and
    philosophy of history, 91–92; and
    tenure, 37; and terrorism, 74
Capitalism: and academic reduction, xvii;
    and intellectuals, xii; and Nietzsche,
    xv–xvi
Carpenter, Mary, 30
Carroll, Lewis, 119
Castro, Fidel, 96
Certeau, Michel de, 20, 37, 95, 100
Cézanne, Paul, xi, 144
Chandra, Sheila, 19–20
choice, and history, 86
Chow, Rey, 143
chronicity, and historical consciousness,
    91
Clark, Tim, 74, 109–10
Cohen, Sande, 43
Collingwood, R. G., 86
conformism, and historicism, 65

constancy, as effect of language, 15–17
criticism: and ahistoricity, 14; and
    commodification, 3; Hegelian-
    Marxian tradition of, xv–xvii; and
    identity, x; and left mythology, 137–
    38; as myth, 4; and nonhistorical
    materialism, 26; and power, 8; and
    reductionism, 68; and structural limit,
    28; and use value, 47
crisis of the subject, and indifference, 98–
    99
Cubism, xi, 131, 133
cultural imperialism, xv
culture: and capitalism, xvii–xviii; and
    demand structures, 126–27; and
    economic fusion, 22; and high and
    low arrangement, 138; and hot/cold
    distinction, 101; as machine of
    rehabilitation, 68; and management,
    101; and nihilism, 120–21; and
    officiality, 145; and Platonism, 121;
    and state vs. war-machine conflict,
    54–55; and tautologic setup, 128
cynicism, 2, 19

Dada, 108, 129, 137
Danto, Arthur, 14, 97, 135
Darwinism, 14, 50
decoding, and academia, 46
decolonization, xi
deconstruction: and events, 10–11; and
    Nietzsche, 10–11
deidentification, and capital, 91
Deleuze, Gilles, x, xv, xix, 3, 5, 14, 15,
    22, 36, 28, 48, 51, 55, 88, 91–92, 94–
    95, 107, 115–18, 120–21, 132, 136,
    139
Deleuze and Guattari, 7, 10, 20, 34, 42
delinearization, and order-words, 112–13
deMan, Paul, xiii, 16, 112
dememorization, and the sublime, 144
demythologization, 53–55
derealization, and superhistory, 101
Derrida, Jacques, 17, 79, 11
Descombes, Vincent, 11
desubjectification, and order-words, 143
dialectics, and repression of semantics, 29
difference, conceptual, 12
Differend, and academia, 31

Humboldt, Wilhelm von, 96
Huyssens, Andreas, 8, 127, 137–38
hyperfunctionalism, and *posthistoire*, 104

images: and nonhistorical thought, 143–
44; and oversaturation, 77
immediate value, and use value, 135
indifference, and alienation of language,
10
intellectuals: new possibilities, 153–54;
and self-reduction, 39; and suspension
of goals, xi; and values, xiii
irreversibility, and culture, 102

Jackson, Jesse, 83
Jakobson, Roman, xv, 55
Jameson, Fredric, xiv, xv, xxii, 5–6, 13,
17, 29, 92, 98, 126–27, 136, 146
Jay, Martin, 115, 135
Joyce, James, 133

Kafka, Franz, 51, 108, 119
Kant, Immanuel, ix, xi, 72
Kissinger, Henry, 97
Klein, Yves, 134
Koselleck, Reinhart, 89
Kramer, Hilton, 139
Krauss, Rosalind, 4, 24, 97–98
Kristeva, Julia, 5, 115

labor, and affirmative action, 32–33
Labov, William, 21
Lacan, Jacques, 110
Lang, Fritz, 126
language: and alienation, xi; and arguing,
xiii; and deculturalization, 120; and
desemanticization, 7; and
dispossession, 73–80; and elimination
of objects, 5; and identity, xii; and
myth, 8, 45; and Nazism, 78; and
negative rules, 54; and pass-words,
xv; and reduction to Capital, 6; and
scientization of humanities, 34; and
simulacra, 5
Lascaux caves, 146
law, and destruction, 51
Lecercle, J.-J., xii
left: and acceptance of capital, xvi–xviii;
and art criticism, 121–39

Leninism, xiii
Levin, Charles, xiv, 42, 47, 88
Lévinas, Emmanuel, xiv
Lévi-Strauss, Claude, 14, 23, 28, 101,
105, 108, 155
Lord, Catherine, 167–68 n. 33
Lotman group, 101
Lowith, Karl, xv
Lucretius, 111
Lukács, Georg, xvii, 53, 135
Lyotard, Jean-François, x–xi, xii, xx,
xxiii, 2, 22, 31, 33, 43–44, 47, 62–64,
71–81, 90, 93, 101, 105, 114, 117,
127–28, 130–31, 139–46, 150,
154–55

McCarthyism, 26
Mandarinism, Western, 35, 42
Mandelbaum, Maurice, 64
Manet, Edouard, 109
Mapplethorpe, Robert, 11
Marcuse, Herbert, 22
Marin, Louis, 149
Marx, Karl, xi, xvi, 6, 11, 13, 24, 34, 39,
58, 106, 148–49
Marxian psychoanalysis, xi, 38
Marxism, and retrospective finality, 133
maximization, and concentration, 59
Mellon Foundation, 32, 34
Megill, Allan, xii, 64
Melville, Herman, 125
memory: and mythic consensus, 123–24;
and order-words, 123–24
Merleau-Ponty, Maurice, 135
Michelangelo, 141
Minimalism, 4
modern, the, and existentialism, 87–88
modernism: and cultural insolubles, 111;
and dispossession, 76; and erosion of
history, 89; and Hegelianism, 125–26;
and indifference, 142; and
insubordination, 108; and lines, 126;
as maze, 87; and the *pagus*, 145; and
shattering of reality, 72; and the
superhistorical, 109
modernity: and academia, 26–27;
ambiguity of, 80; and ambiguity of
history, 131; and cultural insolubles,
111; and desocialization, 117; and
dispossession, 73; and fear of

future, 90; and the irreversible, 67; and suspension of symbols, 140
Morris, Meaghan, 140
Mothers of Medusa, 138
Mulvey, Laura, 1

narration: and alienation, 107; and historical, 97
Nazism: and depsychologization, 76; and impossibility of sense, 78
Negri, Antonio, 83
newcomers, and existing players, 26
Nietzsche, Friedrich, x–xi, xv–xviii, 6–7, 10–11, 17, 21, 25–26, 29, 31, 63, 71, 85–86, 92–93, 103, 114, 118, 123, 147, 153
nihilism: and acceptance of form, xii; and capital, xvi; and deconstruction, 10; displaced by speculative psychology, 71; and Final Solution, 75; and nonhistory, xiii
nonhistorical context: and criticism, 96; and the superhistorical, 111
Nove, Alec, 136

Oedipus, 73
Orbach, Raymond, 158 n. 28
order-words: and academic control, 50; and criticism, xv, 15–16, 28, 32; and indirect discourse, 100; and nullification of language, 40; and objective delirium, 107; and Platonism, 120
Orton, Joe, 131
Orwell, George, 95–96
overcoding, 48–49; and cultural determination, 118;
oxymoronic, the: and the ahistorical, 106; and Capital, xiv; and command language, xiv; and cultural forms, 21–23; and despotic academia, 42; and intellectuals, xiv; and rational myths, 121; and simulacra, 103; and the social, xiii; and strangeness, xiv

pass-words, and commands, xv
Peirce, Charles S., 41, 57
periodization, and postmodernism, 142–43
perversion, and history, 90

Phillipson, Michael, xiv, 88
phrasing, psychological, and historicism, 66
Picasso, Pablo, 143
Pink Floyd, 17
Pinter, Harold, 131
Plato, 120
Platonism, 2, 118–20
posthistoire: and the undecidable, 149; and the strange, 113–14
posthistoricism: and Baudrillard, 147–53; and demonic narrative, 146
postmodern, the, 125; uses, 139–45
precedence, and normative, 47
priorities, and history/nihilism, xiii
productivism, and Baudrillard's critique, 150
prognosis, and failure of "historical" learning, 90
Pudovkin, Vsevolod, 126

Rainer, Yvonne, 8
ranking, and perplexities of academic practice, 33
reaction: and academic writing, 1–2; and aggression, 20; and criticism, xxi–xxii; and historicization, xxii
reduction: and the Final Solution, 66–67; and language, 2–3, 6; and the social, xiii–xiv
rehistoricization, and cultural sign-value, 97–98
research: and meaning, 6–7; myths of, 57–60
reterritorialization: and bureaucracy, 56; and language, 5
reversibility, and *posthistoire*, 102–3
rhetorics of study, and academia, 38
Riddel, Joseph, 11
Rodchenko, Alexandr, 134
Rorty, Richard, xxii, 26
Ross, Andrew, 16
Rousseau, Jean-Jacques, 18
Rushdie, Salman, 18
Russian Constructivism, 137
Ryman, Robert, 108

Said, Edward, ix, xi, 9
Sarnoff, William, 48
Sartre, Jean-Paul, 22–23, 73

Sande Cohen teaches philosophy and critical theory in the department of critical studies at California Institute of the Arts and at Art Center College of Design, Pasadena. He is the author of *Historical Culture: On the Recoding of an Academic Discipline* (1986) and of numerous articles on cultural criticism and ideology.